Voting and Collective Decision-Making

Every day thousands of decisions are made by all kinds of committees, parliaments, councils and boards by a 'yes–no' voting process. Sometimes a committee can only accept or reject the proposals submitted to it for a decision. On other occasions, committee members have the possibility of modifying the proposal and bargaining an agreement prior to the vote. In either case, what rule should be used if each member acts on behalf of a different-sized group? It seems intuitively clear that if the groups are of different sizes then a symmetric rule (e.g. the simple majority or unanimity) is not suitable. The question then arises of what voting rule should be used. *Voting and Collective Decision-Making* addresses this and other issues through a study of the theory of bargaining and voting power, showing how it applies to real decision-making contexts.

ANNICK LARUELLE is Professor of Economics at the University of Caen, Lower Normandie.

FEDERICO VALENCIANO is Professor of Mathematics and Game Theory at the University of the Basque Country, Bilbao.

Voting and Collective Decision-Making

Bargaining and Power

ANNICK LARUELLE and FEDERICO VALENCIANO

CAMBRIDGE
UNIVERSITY PRESS

University Printing House, Cambridge CB2 8BS, United Kingdom

Cambridge University Press is part of the University of Cambridge.

It furthers the University's mission by disseminating knowledge in the pursuit of education, learning and research at the highest international levels of excellence.

www.cambridge.org
Information on this title: www.cambridge.org/9780521873871

© Federico Valenciano and Annick Laruelle 2008

This publication is in copyright. Subject to statutory exception and to the provisions of relevant collective licensing agreements, no reproduction of any part may take place without the written permission of Cambridge University Press.

First published 2008

A catalogue record for this publication is available from the British Library

Library of Congress Cataloguing in Publication data
Laruelle, Annick.
    Voting and collective decision-making : bargaining and power /
    Annick Laruelle and Federico Valenciano.
        p.   cm.
    Includes bibliographical references and index.
    ISBN 978-0-521-87387-1 (hardback)
    1. Decision making–European Union countries.   2. Voting–European Union
    countries.   3. Game theory.   I. Valenciano, Federico.   II. Title.
    HD30.23.L374 2008
    324.601–dc22   2008023552

ISBN 978-0-521-87387-1 Hardback

Cambridge University Press has no responsibility for the persistence or accuracy of URLs for external or third-party internet websites referred to in this publication, and does not guarantee that any content on such websites is, or will remain, accurate or appropriate.

To my parents
Annick

For loved ones gone and those still around
Federico

Contents

List of figures		*page* x
Preface		xi
1	**Preliminaries**	**1**
	1.1 Basic set-theoretic notation	1
	1.2 Some combinatorics	2
	1.2.1 Permutations and combinations	2
	1.2.2 Some useful approximations	3
	1.3 Voting rules	4
	1.3.1 Dichotomous voting rules	5
	1.3.2 Some particular voting rules	7
	1.4 Expected utility theory	10
	1.4.1 Players, games and game theory	10
	1.4.2 Preferences and utility	10
	1.4.3 Lotteries and expected utility	11
	1.4.4 Expected utility preferences	13
	1.5 Some basic game theory notions	18
	1.5.1 Equilibrium	19
	1.5.2 Cooperative and non-cooperative game theory	20
	1.5.3 Subgame perfect equilibrium	21
	1.5.4 Basic cooperative models	24
	1.6 Exercises	26
2	**Seminal papers, seminal ambiguities**	**30**
	2.1 Seminal papers and seminal ambiguities	30
	2.1.1 Nash (1950): The bargaining problem	30
	2.1.2 Shapley (1953): The value of a TU game	34
	2.1.3 Shapley–Shubik (1954): A power index	37
	2.1.4 Banzhaf (1965): Power as decisiveness	39
	2.1.5 Penrose (1946), Rae (1969) and Coleman (1971)	41

viii   *Contents*

| | | 2.1.6 | Through the axiomatic glasses: Dubey (1975), Dubey–Shapley (1979) | 41 |

2.1.6 Through the axiomatic glasses: Dubey
       (1975), Dubey–Shapley (1979)   41
2.2   Clear-cut models to dissipate ambiguity   44
2.3   Further reading   46
       2.3.1 Axiomatic approach   47
       2.3.2 Probabilistic approach   48
2.4   Exercises   48

3 'Take-it-or-leave-it' committees   52
3.1   The take-it-or-leave-it scenario   52
3.2   Success and decisiveness in a vote   54
3.3   Preferences, behaviour and probabilities   55
3.4   Success and decisiveness ex ante   57
3.5   A priori assessments based on the voting rule   60
       3.5.1 Rae index   62
       3.5.2 Banzhaf(–Penrose) index   62
       3.5.3 Coleman indices   63
       3.5.4 König and Bräuninger's inclusiveness index   65
       3.5.5 Summary and remarks   65
3.6   Success versus decisiveness   67
       3.6.1 Success is the issue in a take-it-or-leave-it
              scenario   67
       3.6.2 Conditional success   69
       3.6.3 Summary   70
3.7   The choice of voting rule: egalitarianism
       and utilitarianism   71
       3.7.1 Egalitarianism   74
       3.7.2 Utilitarianism   74
3.8   The choice of voting rule in a committee
       of representatives   77
       3.8.1 An ideal two-stage decision procedure   78
       3.8.2 Egalitarianism in a committee of
              representatives   81
       3.8.3 Utilitarianism in a committee of
              representatives   87
3.9   Exercises   97
3.10   Appendix   99

Contents

			ix

4 Bargaining committees — 105
4.1 The bargaining scenario — 106
4.2 A model of a bargaining committee: voting rule and voters' preferences — 107
4.3 Cooperative game-theoretic approach — 109
    4.3.1 Rationality conditions — 110
    4.3.2 Axiomatic characterizations — 112
    4.3.3 Discussion — 116
4.4 A non-cooperative model of a bargaining committee — 117
    4.4.1 Probabilistic protocols — 119
    4.4.2 Bargaining protocols under a voting rule — 123
    4.4.3 Discussion — 127
4.5 Egalitarianism and utilitarianism in a bargaining committee — 128
4.6 The neutral voting rule in a committee of representatives — 130
4.7 Exercises — 134

5 Application to the European Union — 136
5.1 Voting rules in the European Council — 136
5.2 The Council as a take-it-or-leave-it committee — 142
    5.2.1 Criteria based on probabilities — 143
    5.2.2 Criteria based on utilities — 156
5.3 The Council as a bargaining committee — 163
5.4 Exercises — 170

Conclusions — 172
References — 176
Index — 182

Figures

1.1	Battle of the sexes in sequential form	*page* 22
2.1	A bargaining problem: (a) Classical à la Nash model (b) Assuming 'free disposal'	32
2.2	The Nash bargaining solution	33
2.3	A three-person bargaining problem	34
4.1	Continuation payoffs after the choice of proposer in a three-person problem	122

Preface

The important changes that have taken place in the European Union as a result of the latest enlargements have made it necessary to redesign decision-making procedures again and again. This has contributed to a renewal of interest in issues related to the choice and design of dichotomous voting procedures in recent years, to a conspicuous increase in the number of academic papers, both theoretical and applied, related in one way or another to these issues and to heated debates within the scientific community. As a result of this 'fever' there have been various movements within this community that have gone beyond the academic realm, including press articles and explicit attempts to influence politicians or their advisers on the choice of voting rule for the EU Council of Ministers. At the basis of some of these recommendations is what is called, perhaps a little ostentatiously, 'a priori voting power theory'. The main purpose of this book is to provide a critical revision of the foundations of this theory and of the recommendations that stem from it, based on more than ten years of joint research on the subject.

Prior to this collaboration, the first author of this book was preparing her Ph.D. One of the chapters of her thesis sets out the application to the EU Council of the two-stage model of the decision-making process in committees of representatives[1]. This model assumes that each representative follows the will of the majority in his/her constituency on every issue. Then, assuming that each citizen votes 'yes' or 'no' independently with probability 1/2, one can calculate the probability of a citizen being crucial or decisive for a given voting rule in the committee. This (usually very small) probability is interpreted as the 'a priori voting power' of the citizen and is known as the citizen's 'Banzhaf index'. If this interpretation is accepted, egalitarianism recommends choosing a voting rule that gives equal Banzhaf indices to all citizens whatever their constituency. This recommendation is known as the (first) 'square

---

[1] Joint work with Mika Widgrén [52].

xi

xii

Preface

root rule' because it entails choosing the rule for which each representative in the committee has a Banzhaf index proportional to the square root of the population that he/she represents.

This model was also the starting point of our joint research. Since then our views have changed considerably, to the extent that we refused to sign a letter addressed to the EU Governments and supported by a group of scientists endorsing the square root rule as the choice of voting rule for the EU Council[2]. Ten years of work lie behind this shift of views.

As shown in [52], citizens of different countries had different Banzhaf indices for the qualified majority rule in the fifteen-member EU. Our first endeavour was to seek a measure of inequality in this context [41, 43], but we soon turned our attention to the foundations. Why the Banzhaf index? Why not the Shapley–Shubik index, apparently preferred by game theorists, or any other 'power index'? We first addressed the question of the axiomatic foundations of power indices in the framework of simple games [39, 40, 42] only to honestly conclude that there were no conclusive arguments for the superiority of any of them on these grounds alone. We then turned our attention to the probabilistic approach [37, 44, 45, 46]. In this approach voters' behaviour is described by a probability distribution over vote configurations, and power indices are interpreted as probabilities either of being decisive or of obtaining one's preferred outcome. This point of view led us to adhere for a while to the Banzhaf index as the best-founded index, but we soon grew increasingly dubious about its consistency. One of the factors that contributed to these doubts was our critical examination of the so-called 'postulates and paradoxes' so popular in the literature on power indices, their inconsistencies and their lack of real discriminating capacity [47]. To our surprise, the notion of success or satisfaction, i.e. the likelihood of obtaining one's preferred outcome, which is inextricably intermingled with decisiveness in any pre-conceptual notion of voting power, behaved even better than decisiveness with respect to some postulates. This sparked doubts concerning the soundness of the notion of voting power as the likelihood of being decisive, and led us to consider the notion of success or satisfaction as the relevant issue in certain voting situations [38]. On the other hand, a most inspiring interview in 2002 with David Galloway, who had twenty years

---

[2] Available at www.esi2.us.es/~mbilbao/pdffiles.letter.pdf

Preface xiii

of experience working for the Council of Ministers of the European Union, made it clear to us that bargaining was a (if not 'the') crucial ingredient in the workings of the Council. Bargaining is a genuine game situation that calls for a game-theoretic approach. We thus considered an alternative model, one of whose primitives was the preference profile over the feasible agreements [48, 51]. It thus seemed clear that the analysis of voting situations required a preliminary description of the voting environment: a small committee does not make the same use of a voting rule as a Parliament. The model cannot include the voting rule as the unique ingredient, it must be enriched to describe the specificity of the voting environment.

In this way, a gradual process of accumulative reflection drove us finally to a radical change in our way of looking at several basic issues. This book presents our proposal for new foundations along with a systematic presentation of the changes that this entails in the whole theoretic edifice.

To begin with, a clear distinction must be drawn at the level of the environment between two extreme types of collective decision-making bodies or committees: committees with the capacity solely to accept or reject proposals submitted to it, and committees with the capacity to bargain among feasible agreements. This at first sight obvious distinction proves rich in conceptual consequences. First, it clarifies what one is talking about, something which has been established only vaguely from the outset in the voting power tradition, where the voting rule is the only clearly specified ingredient. Second, each type of situation requires a different model and a separate analysis. This neat distinction also clarifies the different issues posed by each type of decision-making environment. It is worth remarking here that the question of power is *not* the primary or basic issue in either case. Moreover, in the first type of committee (which we call 'take-it-or-leave-it committees'), where behaviour immediately follows preferences, the notion of voting power does not even make sense. In contradistinction, in a 'bargaining committee' the notion of bargaining power in a genuinely game-theoretic sense emerges as related to the likelihood of being decisive.

The normative recommendations that stem from this approach differ conspicuously from those based on the traditional approach, particularly for the choice of voting rule in a committee of representatives whose members act on behalf of groups of different sizes. The square root rule recommendation alluded to above appears in this light as correct but distorting and ill-founded if the goal is to obtain the preferred outcome. It can be re-founded in expected utility terms, but its possible validity (as well as that of the so-called 'second square root rule') is restricted to 'take-it-or-leave-it committees', where the very notion of voting power is irrelevant. By contrast, in the case of bargaining committees of representatives, the model yields completely different recommendations. But this is not the place to anticipate our conclusions in detail (impatient readers may skip to the Conclusions section at the end of the book).

We hope that by this point the readers will have a clear idea of what this book is about, and will perhaps understand how hard it was for us to find a title that was clear and concise enough. We were reluctant to include the words 'voting power' in the title, in spite of the fact that it is precisely those interested in voting power issues who will probably be most interested in the book. We believe that the 'sex-appeal' of these words is responsible to some extent for the obscurities that have survived for so long at the root of the topic. The feeling of importance that comes with the use of the word 'power' only makes a humble, rigorous and detached analysis more difficult (just the opposite of 'game theory', a frivolous name for an ambitious research programme).

The monograph most closely related to this book is *The Measurement of Voting Power: Theory and Practice, Problems and Paradoxes* by Felsenthal and Machover [22], published in 1998. It was a valuable attempt to conduct a critical revision of the foundations of traditional voting power theory, a tradition in which inertia, disregard of its inconsistencies and obscurities and the mechanical application of different indices on no clear grounds were the rule. These authors stress a distinction between two notions of voting power: 'I-power', or power to influence the outcome, and 'P-power', the expected share in a fixed prize. They hold that there are several points which support this distinction. For instance, I-power is a probabilistic notion related to 'policy seeking', while P-power is a game-theoretic notion related to 'office seeking'. The Banzhaf index is considered as the right measure of a priori I-power, and other candidates are rejected on the basis that they violate some I-power 'postulates' (i.e. supposedly desirable properties whose violations are referred to as 'paradoxes'). As to the second type of power, the Shapley–Shubik is presented with reserves as the most serious known candidate for a measure, but doubts are explicitly cast on the coherence of the very notion of P-power.

Preface xv

When their book appeared, we agreed with their critical views and found the intuition behind their I/P-power distinction to be basically correct. However, we felt that the distinction was too vague and insufficient. Moreover, as time passed, we felt that accepting it as a satisfactory remedy for the obscurities at the level of the foundations was only a conformist way of hindering a real progress in resolving the lack of clarity at a deeper level. We also found the foundations of the P-power notion unconvincing, to the extent that, as stated above, we adhered for a while the notion of voting power as influence as the only coherent notion of voting power, and discarded the Shapley–Shubik index. Interested readers will find a brief account of the different implications of the their approach and ours in the Conclusions section.

Another related book is Morriss' *Power: A Philosophical Analysis* [58, 59]. This author is also critical with the frequently unjustified applications of power indices. He conducts a careful discussion about the semantics of the word 'power', distinguishing between 'power-as-ability,' and 'power-as-ableness'. Indeed the book is intended to be more philosophical and less formal than ours. It may provide interesting additional reading (especially Part IV).

Our purpose is not to survey all the huge amount of material on the topic published over more than fifty years, though we do, of course, pay attention to what we consider the most significant contributions in the field. A few seminal contributions are presented in some detail.

As is clear from its title, in this book we consider only *dichotomous* voting rules that specify collective acceptance or collective rejection for each possible yes–no vote profile. We do not consider the possibilities of abstention or not showing up. These conditions preclude the difficulties evidenced by Arrow's [2] impossibility theorem when more than two alternatives are involved, and the possibility of 'strategic' voting [27]. Consequently, the copious social choice literature on these issues is orthogonal to this book.

We hope the book may be of interest and of use to students and researchers alike in political and social science, as well as in game theory and economics, especially the public economics, public choice, and social choice families. We try to present results and, especially, normative recommendations in an honest, humble, precise '*if . . . then*' form, in which the '*if*' part is explicit and transparent. This requires a formal formulation. However, to make the book accessible to as wide an audience as possible, we have tried to keep the level of formalization low enough not to discourage readers with less mathematical backgrounds but at the same time high enough to be precise. The meaning of formal statements is always expressed in plain words. Some proofs, especially in the case of technically complex published results, have been omitted. Chapter 4 may perhaps be the most difficult for those readers not familiar with game theory. Nevertheless, it is our hope that readers with less mathematical backgrounds can get a grasp of the main ideas presented in the book by skipping the mathematical details and just reading the rest.

The book is organized as follows. Chapter 1 presents the basic set-theoretic notation and some combinatorics, along with the notation and terminology on dichotomous (acceptance/rejection) voting rules used throughout the book. This chapter also contains two brief sections devoted to the basics of expected utility theory and a summary overview of a few basic concepts of game theory. In Chapter 2 a few seminal papers are briefly and critically reviewed, and the basic distinction in this book between 'take-it-or-leave-it' and 'bargaining' committees is introduced. Chapter 3 is devoted to 'take-it-or-leave-it' committees, a probabilistic model of which allows us: (i) to address the question of the conceptual and analytical distinction between the notions of success and decisiveness; (ii) to provide a common perspective in which several 'power indices' from the literature can be seen as variations of two basic ideas; and (iii) to address the question of the optimal voting rule in a take-it-or-leave-it committee from two points of view: egalitarianism and utilitarianism. Chapter 4 deals with bargaining committees. A game-theoretic model is proposed, and the question of the players' expectations is addressed first from a cooperative-axiomatic point of view, and then from a non-cooperative point of view. This chapter concludes with a recommendation for bargaining committees of representatives. Finally, in Chapter 5 the different rules used in the EU Council and some more recent proposals are examined from the point of view of the models presented in Chapters 3 and 4. A section with exercises at the end of each chapter is intended to provide readers with a means to check how well they have understood the chapters.

We would like to end this preface by expressing our gratitude to some people and institutions. We would like to thank people of various fields such as Fuad Aleskerov, Steve Brams, Nimrod Megiddo, Hans Peters, and Stef Tijs, who independently suggested to us the stimulating

Preface   xvii

notion of writing a book on this subject before the idea had crossed our minds.

We also thank Dan Felsenthal and Moshé Machover, our main scientific opponents in the last years. In spite of our sometimes overheated scientific arguments (particularly in their interesting and controversial 'petit comité' '*VPP*'s' meetings, to which they have never failed to invite us every year since the first meeting in 2001), our disagreements have always been stimulating and inspiring.

We also thank Jon Benito, Arri Chamorro, Elena Iñarra, Jean Lainé, Vincent Merlin, Maria Montero, Stefan Napel and Norma Olaizola who read some chapters and made valuable suggestions on how to improve them. Thanks also go to William Thomson, who taught the second author to make drawings, and to Chris Pellow who did his best to make our English sound better. It goes without saying that all mistakes and defects are entirely our responsibility.

Finally, we thank Chris Harrison and Philip Good, of Cambridge University Press. Chris encouraged us to present our project to Cambridge, and Philip has been in charge of in the latter stages.

We are also grateful for the financial support received since we committed ourselves to this project, from the Spanish Ministerio de Educación y Ciencia under projects BEC2003-08182 and SEJ2006-05455, the latter co-funded by the ERDF, from Acción Integrada HF-2006-0021, and from the French Government under the EGIDE-Picasso project. The first author also acknowledges financial support from the Spanish M.E.C. under the Ramón y Cajal Program at the earliest stages of this project.

Though less apparent, support from colleagues, friends and families was also important and is warmly acknowledged.

March 2008   Annick Laruelle
                                                              Federico Valenciano

1 | Preliminaries

This chapter provides some basic background data. Basic set-theoretic notation is introduced in Section 1.1, and some combinatorics in Section 1.2. Formal descriptions of voting rules and related notation and terminology to be used throughout the book are given in Section 1.3. In Section 1.4 the basics of decision facing risk and expected utility theory are provided. Section 1.5 contains a short overview of a few basic concepts from game theory.

1.1 Basic set-theoretic notation

In general, sets are denoted by capitals (e.g. N, S, M, etc.), and when they are finite the same small case letter $(n, s, m, \ldots)$ denotes their number of elements or cardinality (sometimes denoted by $\#N$, $\#S$, $\#M, \ldots$). We write $a \in S$ to express that an element a belongs to a set S, and $a \notin S$ otherwise. Given two sets A and B we write $A \subseteq B$ to express that all elements in A are also in B, and we write $A \subset B$ if $A \subseteq B$ and $A \neq B$. Symbols '$\cup$' and '$\cap$' denote the usual operations on sets of 'union' and 'intersection', while $A \setminus B$ denotes the set of those elements in A that do not belong to B. When B contains a single element i, i.e. $B = \{i\}$, we will often write $A \setminus i$ instead of $A \setminus \{i\}$ and $A \cup i$ instead of $A \cup \{i\}$. The set consisting of all subsets of a set N is denoted by 2^N (note that its cardinal is 2^n).

We write $f : A \to B$ to express that f is a map or a function from set A to set B, and, if $x \in A$, $x \mapsto f(x)$ to express that f maps x onto $f(x)$. If $C \subseteq A$, $f(C) = \{f(x) : x \in C\}$. A map $f : A \to B$ is said to be *injective* if whenever $x, y \in A$ and $x \neq y$, we have $f(x) \neq f(y)$; and is said to be *surjective* if for all $z \in B$, there exists an $x \in A$ such that $f(x) = z$. A map f is said to be *bijective* if it is both injective and surjective.

The set of real numbers is denoted by $\mathbb{R}$. The subset of $\mathbb{R}$ consisting of all non-negative (≥ 0) numbers is denoted by $\mathbb{R}_+$, while $\mathbb{R}_{++}$ denotes

1

the set of positive (>0) real numbers. For any pair of real numbers a, b, $[a, b]$ denotes the *segment* $[a, b] = \{x \in \mathbb{R} : a \leq x \leq b\}$. If $N = \{1, 2, \ldots, n\}$, $\mathbb{R}^N$ denotes the set of n-tuples $x = (x_1, \ldots, x_n)$, where $x_i \in \mathbb{R}$; or in other terms the set of maps x ($i \mapsto x_i$) from N to $\mathbb{R}$. We will write for any $x, y \in \mathbb{R}^N$, $x \leq y$ ($x < y$) if $x_i \leq y_i$ ($x_i < y_i$) for all $i = 1, \ldots, n$.

We write '$P \Rightarrow Q$' (or '$Q \Leftarrow P$') to express that 'P implies Q', and '$P \Leftrightarrow Q$' or 'P iff Q', to express that 'P is equivalent to Q'. The symbols '$\forall$' (for all), '$\exists$' (there exists), '$\nexists$' (there does not exist) are also used. We use the symbol '$x :=$' to mean that 'x is *by definition* equal to'.

1.2 Some combinatorics

1.2.1 Permutations and combinations

Let $A = \{a_1, a_2, \ldots, a_n\}$ a set of n elements. A *permutation* of A is an arrangement of its n elements in a certain order. For instance, if $A = \{1, 2, 3\}$, the possible permutations of A are 123, 132, 213, 231, 312, 321. Alternatively a permutation in A is often defined as a bijection $\pi : A \to A$, because there is a one-to-one correspondence between the set of ordered arrangements of its n elements and the set of bijections $A \to A$. For instance, in the above example, the permutation 213 can be associated with the bijection π:

$$1 \mapsto \pi(1) = 2$$

$$2 \mapsto \pi(2) = 1$$

$$3 \mapsto \pi(3) = 3.$$

Thus in the sequel we use the term 'permutation' in either sense without distinction.

The number of permutations of a set of n elements is given by

$$n! = n(n-1)\ldots 3 \cdot 2 \cdot 1.$$

A *combination* of (a set of) n elements of order r ($0 \leq r \leq n$) is a subset of r elements. The number of subsets of r elements of a set of n elements is denoted by C_n^r, and is given by

$$C_n^r = \frac{n!}{(n-r)! r!}, \tag{1}$$

Preliminaries 3

or with the usual notation

$$C_n^r = \binom{n}{r}.$$

Note that from (1) it follows immediately that for $0 \le r \le n$:

$$C_n^r = C_n^{n-r}, \tag{2}$$

and, as the total number of subsets of a set with n elements is given by 2^n, we have

$$C_n^0 + C_n^1 + \cdots + C_n^{n-1} + C_n^n = 2^n. \tag{3}$$

These two equalities enable us to derive others that will be useful later. If n is odd, i.e. $n = 2r + 1$ for some positive integer, by (2) and (3) we have

$$C_n^0 + \cdots + C_n^r = C_n^{r+1} + \cdots + C_n^n = 2^{n-1}. \tag{4}$$

If n is even, i.e $n = 2r$ for some integer r, by (2) we have

$$C_n^0 + C_n^1 + \cdots + C_n^r = C_n^r + C_n^{r+1} + \cdots + C_n^n,$$

and by (3) we have

$$C_n^r + C_n^{r+1} + \cdots + C_n^n = 2^{n-1} + \frac{1}{2} C_n^r, \tag{5}$$

and

$$C_n^{r+1} + \cdots + C_n^n = 2^{n-1} - \frac{1}{2} C_n^r. \tag{6}$$

1.2.2 Some useful approximations

It will sometimes be necessary to calculate expressions involving permutations or combinations. As the number of elements increases these calculations become increasingly laborious, and in some cases it will be useful to have well known formulae that provide sufficiently good

4 *Voting and Collective Decision-Making*

approximations. Some of them are based on *Stirling's formula*, which provides a good approximation of $n!$ for big enough n, given by[3]

$$n! \simeq n^n e^{-n} \sqrt{2\pi n}. \tag{7}$$

For instance, we will later need to calculate the number of subsets of size $n/2$ of a set of n elements for a given even number n, by (1), given by

$$C_n^{\frac{n}{2}} = \frac{n!}{(n - \frac{n}{2})!\frac{n}{2}!} = \frac{n!}{\frac{n}{2}!\frac{n}{2}!}.$$

If n is big enough this can be approximated by using (7), yielding

$$C_n^{\frac{n}{2}} \simeq 2^n \sqrt{\frac{2}{\pi n}}. \tag{8}$$

1.3 Voting rules

This book is mainly concerned with collective decision-making. This means situations in which a set of agents make decisions by means of a *decision procedure*. By a decision procedure we mean a well-defined rule for making collective choices based on individual choices. A decision procedure is thus a rather general notion that may include a wide variety of ways of mapping the profiles of individual actions to group decisions. By 'individual actions' we mean votes in a general sense, as specified by the decision procedure itself: for instance marking a candidate in a list, marking the approved alternatives within a set in the 'approval voting' system or assigning points to them according to certain constraints, or just voting 'yes' or 'no' on a proposal.

In this book we focus our attention on *dichotomous* voting rules that specify a collective 'yes' (acceptance) or a collective 'no' (rejection) for each possible profile of 'yes' or 'no' by individuals. We assume that voters are never indifferent between the two outcomes, and abstention

---

[3] It will be used for n ranging from the order of hundreds of thousands to the order of millions. But even for $n = 100$ the quotient $\frac{n! - n^n e^{-n}\sqrt{2\pi n}}{n!}$ is 0.00083.

Preliminaries 5

is not possible. In this section we introduce the notation and terminology related to such voting rules that will be used throughout the book.

1.3.1 Dichotomous voting rules

Throughout this book a voting rule is a well-specified procedure for making binary decisions (i.e. acceptance or rejection) by the vote of a committee of any kind with a certain number of members. That is, a voting rule associates a final outcome with any possible vote configuration (or result of a vote). If n is the number of seats in the committee, let us label them by $1, 2, \ldots, n$, and let $N = \{1, 2, \ldots, n\}$. The same labels are also used to represent the voters that occupy the corresponding seats. The precise result of a particular vote is specified by a *vote configuration*: a list indicating the vote cast by the voter occupying each seat. As we assume that voters are never indifferent between the two options and abstention is not possible, there are 2^n possible configurations of votes, and each configuration can be represented by the set of labels of the 'yes'-voters' seats. So, for each $S \subseteq N$, we refer to the result of a vote where the voters in S vote 'yes' while the voters in $N \setminus S$ vote 'no' as 'vote configuration S'. The number of 'yes'-voters in the configuration S is denoted by s.

In these conditions, an N-*voting rule* can be specified and represented by the set $\mathcal{W}_N$ of vote configurations that would lead to a final 'yes' (the others would lead to a final 'no'):

$$\mathcal{W}_N = \big\{ S : S \text{ leads to a final 'yes'} \big\}.$$

A vote configuration S is *winning* if $S \in \mathcal{W}_N$, and *losing* if $S \notin \mathcal{W}_N$. When N is obvious from the context we will omit the 'N' in 'N-voting rule' and write $\mathcal{W}$ instead of $\mathcal{W}_N$. In order to exclude unreasonable and inconsistent voting rules the following conditions are assumed for the set $\mathcal{W} \subseteq 2^N$:

1. The unanimous 'yes' leads to a final 'yes': $N \in \mathcal{W}$.
2. The unanimous 'no' leads to a final 'no': $\emptyset \notin \mathcal{W}$.
3. If a vote configuration is winning, then any other configuration with a larger set of 'yes'-voters is also winning: If $S \in \mathcal{W}$, then $T \in \mathcal{W}$ for any T containing S.

6 *Voting and Collective Decision-Making*

4. The possibility of a proposal and its negation both being accepted should be prevented. Namely, if a proposal is supported by S and its negation by $N \setminus S$, these two voting configurations cannot both be winning[4]. That is, if $S \in W$ then $N \setminus S \notin W$.

Definition 1 *A voting rule of n seats or an N-voting rule is a set $W \subseteq 2^N$ that satisfies the above four conditions.*

The set of all voting rules with set of seats N is denoted VR_N. We use the term *improper rule* to describe a set $W \subseteq 2^N$ that only satisfies the first three properties. A *minimal winning* vote configuration is a winning configuration that does not include any other winning configuration. An equivalent way to specify and represent a voting rule is by listing the minimal winning configurations, denoted $M(W)$.

Given an N-voting rule W, and a permutation $\pi : N \to N$, we denote by πW the voting rule $\pi W = \{\pi(S) : S \in W\}$.

Some special seats must be mentioned. A *veto seat* can prevent the passage of a proposal: if the vote from a veto seat is 'no' then the proposal is rejected. That is, i is a veto seat in W if

$$i \notin S \Rightarrow S \notin W$$

(or equivalently: $S \in W \Rightarrow i \in S$). In other words, i's support is necessary for a proposal to be accepted. The voter sitting in such a seat is referred to as a *vetoer*.

A *null seat* is a seat such that the vote cast by the voter occupying it never makes a difference. In other words the vote of the other voters determine the outcome irrespective of this voter's vote. That is, i is a null seat in W if

$$S \in W \Leftrightarrow S \setminus i \in W.$$

The voter sitting in such a seat is referred to as a *null voter*.

---

[4] In some cases no inconsistency arises from dropping the last condition. For instance, if the rule is used to include issues on the agenda and all proposals submitted to the vote have the form: 'shall we put A on the agenda?', and cannot be 'shall we not put A on the agenda?'.

Preliminaries 7

In voting rule W, seat j *weakly dominates* seat i (denoted $j \succeq_W i$) if for any vote configuration S such that $i, j \notin S$,

$$S \cup i \in W \Rightarrow S \cup j \in W.$$

If seat j weakly dominates seat i but seat i does not weakly dominate seat i, we say that seat j *dominates* seat i ($j \succ_W i$). Note that the domination relationship is not complete: seats cannot always be compared. Seats i and j are *symmetric* if $j \succeq_W i$ and $i \succeq_W j$. In other words, in the environment specified by the voting rule these seats are interchangeable. A voting rule is *symmetric* if any two seats are symmetric. Symmetric rules are also called *anonymous* rules because a voting rule W is symmetric if and only if (see Exercise 4) for any permutation $\pi : N \to N, \pi W = W$.

1.3.2 *Some particular voting rules*

A few special voting rules are specified in this section. In a *dictatorship*, the final outcome always coincides with the vote cast by one specific seat: the *dictator's seat*. Denoting seat i's dictatorship by W^i we have

$$W^i = \{ S \subseteq N : i \in S \}.$$

In a *T-oligarchy* or *T-unanimity* rule, only the votes from a set T of seats count: the final result is 'yes' if and only if all voters from the 'oligarchy' are in favour of the proposal. Denoting this rule by W^T, we can write

$$W^T = \{ S \subseteq N : S \supseteq T \}.$$

In the *unanimity rule* (denoted W^N) a proposal is accepted only with unanimous support, that is

$$W^N = \{N\}.$$

In the *simple majority*, a proposal is passed if the number of votes in favour of the proposal is strictly greater than half the total number of votes. That is, denoting the simple majority rule by W^{SM},

$$W^{SM} = \left\{ S : s > \frac{n}{2} \right\}.$$

8   *Voting and Collective Decision-Making*

Simple majority and unanimity are special cases of *q-majority rules*, where a proposal is passed if the proportion of votes in favour of the proposal is greater than q. That is, denoting the q-majority rule by $\mathcal{W}^{q\mathrm{M}}$,

$$\mathcal{W}^{q\mathrm{M}} = \left\{ S : \frac{s}{n} > q \right\}.$$

In order to prevent improper rules we require $\frac{1}{2} \leq q < 1$. Note that in all q-majority rules all seats are symmetric.

A *weighted majority rule* is specified by a system of positive *weights* $w = (w_1, \ldots, w_n)$, and a *quota* $Q > 0$, so that the final result is 'yes' if the sum of the weights in favour of the proposal is larger than the quota. Denoting this rule by $\mathcal{W}^{(w,Q)}$, we have

$$\mathcal{W}^{(w,Q)} = \left\{ S \subseteq N : \sum_{i \in S} w_i > Q \right\}.$$

Alternatively the quota can be expressed as a proportion of the total weight $q = \frac{Q}{\sum_{j \in N} w_j}$, and the rule denoted $\mathcal{W}^{(w,q)}$. That is,

$$\mathcal{W}^{(w,q)} = \left\{ S \subseteq N : \sum_{i \in S} \frac{w_i}{\sum_{j \in N} w_j} > q \right\}.$$

Again the condition $\frac{1}{2} \leq q < 1$ prevents improper rules. As the reader can easily check, all the above examples can be specified as weighted majority rules. Nevertheless, not all voting rules can be so represented[5] (see Exercises 5 and 6).

A *double weighted majority rule* is specified by a double system of positive weights $w = (w_1, \ldots, w_n)$ and $w' = (w'_1, \ldots, w'_n)$, and a double quota Q and Q', with each quota corresponding to a system of weights. The final result is 'yes' if each sum of the weights in favour of the proposal is larger than its corresponding quota. Denoting this rule

---

[5] Taylor and Zwicker [85, 86] give necessary and sufficient conditions for a voting rule to be representable as a weighted majority rule.

Preliminaries 9

by $\mathcal{W}^{((w,Q),(w',Q'))}$, we have

$$\mathcal{W}^{((w,Q),(w',Q'))} = \left\{ S \subseteq N : \sum_{i \in S} w_i > Q \text{ and } \sum_{i \in S} w_i' > Q' \right\}.$$

Note that

$$\mathcal{W}^{((w,Q),(w',Q'))} = \mathcal{W}^{(w,Q)} \cap \mathcal{W}^{(w',Q')}.$$

In fact two general ways of combining voting rules are *intersection* and *union* under certain conditions. Namely, if $\mathcal{W}$ and $\mathcal{W}'$ are voting rules their intersection $\mathcal{W} \cap \mathcal{W}'$ is also a proper voting rule, while their union $\mathcal{W} \cup \mathcal{W}'$ is sure to inherit conditions 1, 2, and 3 in 1.3.1, but not necessarily 4.

A different way of combining voting rules is by *composition*. Consider the following two-stage indirect voting procedure for a set M of m voters. Voters are not asked to vote directly but to elect representatives who report their preferences in the following way. The voters are divided into n disjoint groups (not necessarily of equal sizes): $M = M_1 \cup \cdots \cup M_n$. For each vote, the proposal is submitted to a vote within each group, and it is assumed that $\mathcal{W}_{M_1}$ is the voting rule used in group M_j to set the group's position. In a second stage, each representative reports his/her group's final decision ('yes' or 'no') as prescribed by the vote and the group's voting rule, and the decisions of the different groups are aggregated by means of $\mathcal{W}_N$, where $N = \{1, 2, \ldots, n\}$. The whole voting procedure is equivalent to an M-voting rule, denoted $\mathcal{W}_N[\mathcal{W}_{M_1}, \ldots, \mathcal{W}_{M_n}]$, which can be formally described as follows. For each $j \in N$, and each $S \subseteq M$, denote

$$S_j = S \cap M_j \quad \text{and} \quad C(S) := \{j \in N : S_j \in \mathcal{W}_{M_j}\}.$$

Therefore, S_j is the set of voters in S that belong to group M_j, that is, those in M_j that vote 'yes', and $C(S)$ is the set of representatives of groups in which the 'yes' won. Thus

$$\mathcal{W}_M = \mathcal{W}_N[\mathcal{W}_{M_1}, \ldots, \mathcal{W}_{M_n}] = \{S \subseteq M : C(S) \in \mathcal{W}_N\}.$$

1.4 Expected utility theory

1.4.1 Players, games and game theory

A game situation is one in which there exists interdependence between the decisions of two or more agents. That is, each agent has to choose an action or a sequence of actions, and whatever the level of information about the consequences of his/her acts or about the other agents, those consequences also depend on the other players' decisions. Game theory provides formal models, called *games*, for the analysis of such situations. There is a great variety of such models, depending on the amount of detail that is incorporated, the environment in which the *players* make decisions and the purpose of the model. In game-theoretic models in which players are rational agents[6], as is the case here, an important ingredient is the players' assessments or preferences concerning the possible outcomes of the game. This element should be factored into any analysis of what may be considered as the most advisable action for a player or what outcome can be expected as a result of rational interaction among the players.

This is formally incorporated into the model by means of the following assumption: each agent can express his/her preferences over the feasible outcomes by means of a binary relation (complete and transitive, see next paragraph), so that he/she acts accordingly trying to obtain the most preferred one of the feasible alternatives.

1.4.2 Preferences and utility

Let A denote a set of feasible alternatives. A binary relation, $\preceq$, over A is complete if for all $x, y \in A$, either $x \preceq y$ or $y \preceq x$; and it is said to be transitive if $x \preceq z$ whenever $x \preceq y$ and $y \preceq z$.

In a game, that is, in a game-theoretic model of a game situation, in which A represents the set of possible outcomes or results, a complete and transitive binary relation $\preceq$ over A associated with a player is interpreted as the expression of his/her *preferences* over A. If $x \preceq y$, we say that the player *weakly prefers* y to x. If $x \preceq y$ and $y \preceq x$, we say that the player is *indifferent* between x and y, and we write $x \sim y$; while

---

[6] Originally only rational interaction was considered as the object of game theory (in fact 'rational interaction' was the name suggested by R. Selten as a more adequate alternative to 'game theory', a term already consecrated by use). Nevertheless, some of the most successful applications of notions and results of game theory have been to 'irrational interaction', as is the case of the evolution of species.

Preliminaries 11

if $x \preceq y$ and $y \not\preceq x$ (where $y \not\preceq x$ means '*not* $y \preceq x$') we say that the player (*strictly*) *prefers* y to x, and write $x \prec y$. We write indistinctly $x \preceq y$ or $y \succeq x$, and $x \prec y$ or $y \succ x$.

In general it is more convenient to work with functions than with binary relations, and one way of doing so is by scoring alternatives by numbers according to their 'utility', so that more preferred alternatives are given more points. Formally, a *utility function* over a set of alternatives A is a map $u : A \longrightarrow \mathbb{R}$ which is interpreted as a representation of the preferences $\preceq_u$, given by (for all $x, y \in A$)

$$x \preceq_u y \quad \text{if and only if} \quad u(x) \le u(y).$$

We say that u represents $\preceq_u$.

Obviously any map from A to $\mathbb{R}$ can be interpreted as representing a preference relation on A, and it can immediately be checked that, whatever $u : A \longrightarrow \mathbb{R}$, the associated binary relation $\preceq_u$ is complete and transitive. If A is finite the converse is also true, that is to say, any complete binary relation over a finite set can be represented by a utility function. But this correspondence of preferences and utility functions is not one-to-one: if a binary relation is representable by a utility function then there are infinite utility functions representing it. For instance, if $\preceq=\preceq_u$ for some $u : A \to \mathbb{R}$, then $\preceq=\preceq_{\varphi \circ u}$ for all strictly increasing map $\varphi : \mathbb{R} \to \mathbb{R}$ (that is, s.t. $x \le y \Leftrightarrow \varphi(x) \le \varphi(y)$).

Example 1.1: Let $A = [0, M]$ be a continuum of quantities of a good (money, land, gold, etc.), and let $\preceq$ be the preference over quantities (assuming non-satiety) with 'the more the better'. This can be represented by the map $u_1(x) = x$. But, for instance, taking $u_2(x) = 2x + 100$, $u_3(x) = x^2$, or $u_4(x) = e^x$, we obtain alternative representations of the same preference relation.

As we consider utility functions as representation of preferences, that is, only the ranking provided by the utility function matters, we say that two utility functions $u_1, u_2 : A \to \mathbb{R}$ are *A-equivalent*, and we write $u_1 \approx_A u_2$, if they represent the same preferences on A. That is, if for all $x, y \in A$, $u_1(x) \le u_1(y) \Leftrightarrow u_2(x) \le u_2(y)$.

1.4.3 Lotteries and expected utility

Let A denote a set of alternatives. A *lottery* over A is a random mixture of a finite number of alternatives in A. A lottery is thus a random experiment whose possible outcomes are a finite number of alternatives in A, each of them occurring with a certain probability. As from a mathematical point of view the relevant information is encapsulated in these probabilities, a lottery will for all effects be identified with its associated probability measure. Any such probability measure can be represented by (and identified with) a map $l : A \longrightarrow \mathbb{R}_+$, such that its *support*, i.e. the set $\text{spt}(l) := \{x \in A : l(x) > 0\}$, is finite, and such that $\sum_{x \in \text{spt}(l)} l(x) = 1$, which associates with each alternative x its probability $l(x)$. The set of all such maps or lotteries is denoted by $\mathcal{L}(A)$. We identify each alternative x in A for all effects with the (degenerated) lottery in $\mathcal{L}(A)$ whose support is $\{x\}$, that is to say with the lottery that gives x with probability 1. Given $x, y \in A$ and μ ($0 \leq \mu \leq 1$) we denote indistinctly by $\mu x \oplus (1 - \mu)y$ or by $(1 - \mu)y \oplus \mu x$ the *binary lottery* such that $l(x) = \mu$ and $l(y) = 1 - \mu$.

Given a function $u : A \to \mathbb{R}$, the *expected utility function associated with* u, denoted $\bar{u}$, is the map $\bar{u} : \mathcal{L}(A) \to \mathbb{R}$, given by[7]

$$\bar{u}(l) := E[u(x)] = \sum_{x \in A} l(x)u(x).$$

Thus $\bar{u}$ associates the expected utility (as measured by u) of the outcome with each lottery.

It is important to remark that A-equivalent utility functions (in the sense specified in Section 1.4.2) may have non $\mathcal{L}(A)$-equivalent expected utility associated functions. In other words: $u_1 \approx_A u_2$ does *not* imply $\bar{u}_1 \approx_{\mathcal{L}(A)} \bar{u}_2$.

Example 1.2: Let $A = \{a, b, c\}$, and let $\preceq$ be the preference such that $a \succ b \succ c$. Among the infinite utility functions that represent this binary relation consider the following three:

$$u_1(a) = 10, \quad u_1(b) = 5, \quad u_1(c) = 0;$$
$$u_2(a) = 10, \quad u_2(b) = 8, \quad u_2(c) = 0;$$
$$u_3(a) = 10, \quad u_3(b) = 2, \quad u_3(c) = 0.$$

Obviously $\preceq = \preceq_{u_1} = \preceq_{u_2} = \preceq_{u_3}$. But lotteries in $\mathcal{L}(A)$ are ranked differently by their associated expected utility functions. For instance, let l be the lottery that gives each alternative with probability $1/3$. If we

---

[7] As the support of any lottery l is assumed to be finite, for the sake of brevity we write $\sum_{x \in A}$ instead of the more precise $\sum_{x \in \text{spt}(l)}$.

Preliminaries 13

compare l with alternative b according to each expected utility function we obtain

$$\bar{u}_1(b) = 5, \quad \bar{u}_1(l) = \tfrac{1}{3}(10 + 5 + 0) = 5,$$
$$\bar{u}_2(b) = 8, \quad \bar{u}_2(l) = \tfrac{1}{3}(10 + 8 + 0) = 6,$$
$$\bar{u}_3(b) = 2, \quad \bar{u}_3(l) = \tfrac{1}{3}(10 + 2 + 0) = 4.$$

Thus $b \sim_{\bar{u}_1} l$, $b \succ_{\bar{u}_2} l$, $b \prec_{\bar{u}_3} l$. Therefore $u_1 \approx_A u_2 \approx_A u_3$, but no two out of $\bar{u}_1, \bar{u}_2, \bar{u}_3$ are equivalent in $\mathcal{L}(A)$.

1.4.4 Expected utility preferences

In many game situations randomization is a natural ingredient. In some cases it is part of the objective description of the rules of the game (e.g., the initial shuffling in card games, the throw of a dice, etc.). In other cases there are 'mixed strategies' among the feasible actions of a player, that is, random choices of action, each of them with a certain probability. Also when the players' information is not complete, a probability distribution over the 'states of the world' may represent the (incomplete) information of a player about the environment. Thus the players' preferences should be extended to encompass and rank random outcomes.

Formally, if A denotes a set of deterministic alternatives, we have the following model of rational behaviour facing risk.

Definition 2 *A binary relation $\preceq$ on $\mathcal{L}(A)$ is a von Neumann–Morgenstern preference (or an expected utility preference) if there exists $u : A \to \mathbb{R}$, such that $\preceq_{\bar{u}} = \preceq$.*

Thus, the rational behaviour of a player with such preferences can be described as maximizing the expected utility $\bar{u}$ for a certain u. In view of Example 1.2, given a preference over a set of deterministic alternatives, this model does not prescribe a particular ranking of the lotteries over those alternatives. In other words, given a preference relation on A, there is an infinite number of different von Neumann–Morgenstern (vNM) preferences over $\mathcal{L}(A)$ consistent with that relation. In fact, Definition 2 only postulates some form of consistency in the way of ranking lotteries.

In order to see this more clearly we need to see explicitly *in terms of preferences* what Definition 2 amounts to assuming. This is what the following theorem does. In order to simplify the proof we assume that

14   *Voting and Collective Decision-Making*

in the set A there are most and least preferred alternatives. Thus we assume that there exist two alternatives $a, b \in A$, such that $b \preceq x \preceq a$ for all $x \in A$; and in order to avoid a trivial case we also assume that $a \succ b$. Then we have the following characterization:

Theorem 3 *A binary relation $\preceq$ on $\mathcal{L}(A)$ is a von Neumann–Morgenstern preference on $\mathcal{L}(A)$ if and only if the following conditions hold:*

(i) *$\preceq$ is complete and transitive.*

(ii) *For all $x \in A$ there exists $\mu_x \in [0, 1]$ such that*

    (ii-1) *$x \sim \mu_x a \oplus (1 - \mu_x)b$, and*
    (ii-2) *For all $l \in \mathcal{L}(A)$,*

$$l \sim \left(\sum_{x \in A} l(x)\mu_x \right) a \oplus \left(1 - \sum_{x \in A} l(x)\mu_x \right) b.$$

(iii) *For all $\mu, \mu' \in [0, 1]$,*

$$\mu a \oplus (1 - \mu)b \preceq \mu' a \oplus (1 - \mu')b \Leftrightarrow \left(\mu \leq \mu' \right).$$

Proof. (Necessity ($\Rightarrow$)): Let $\preceq$ be a von Neumann–Morgenstern preference relation on $\mathcal{L}(A)$. This means (Definition 2) that $\preceq = \preceq_{\bar{u}}$ for some $u : A \to \mathbb{R}$.

(i) Thus, as any binary relation representable by a utility function, $\bar{u}$ in this case, $\preceq$ is necessarily complete and transitive.

(ii) Let $x \in A$. As $b \preceq x \preceq a$, and $\preceq = \preceq_{\bar{u}}$, then $u(b) \leq u(x) \leq u(a)$.

Therefore there exists $\mu_x \in [0, 1]$ such that

$$u(x) = \mu_x u(a) + (1 - \mu_x)u(b).$$

Then we have

$$\bar{u}(\mu_x a \oplus (1 - \mu_x)b) = \mu_x u(a) + (1 - \mu_x)u(b) = u(x) = \bar{u}(x).$$

Thus $x \sim_{\bar{u}} \mu_x a \oplus (1 - \mu_x)b$, and we have (ii-1).
Now let $l \in \mathcal{L}(A)$, and let us denote by μ_x the number that satisfies (ii-1) whose existence has just been proved for each $x \in A$.

Preliminaries 15

Then

$$\bar{u}(l) = \sum_{x \in A} l(x)u(x) = \sum_{x \in A} l(x)(\mu_x u(a) + (1 - \mu_x)u(b))$$

$$= \left(\sum_{x \in A} l(x)\mu_x \right) u(a) + \left(1 - \sum_{x \in A} l(x)\mu_x \right) u(b)$$

$$= \bar{u} \left(\left(\sum_{x \in A} l(x)\mu_x \right) a \oplus \left(1 - \sum_{x \in A} l(x)\mu_x \right) b \right).$$

Then as $\preceq = \preceq_{\bar{u}}$, we have (ii-2).
(iii) Let $\mu, \mu' \in [0, 1]$:

$$\mu a \oplus (1 - \mu)b \preceq \mu' a \oplus (1 - \mu')b$$

$$\Leftrightarrow \bar{u}(\mu a \oplus (1 - \mu)b)$$

$$\leq \bar{u}(\mu' a \oplus (1 - \mu')b)$$

$$\Leftrightarrow \mu u(a) + (1 - \mu)u(b)$$

$$\leq \mu' u(a) + (1 - \mu')u(b)$$

$$\Leftrightarrow (\mu - \mu')(u(a) - u(b)) \leq 0.$$

Which, as $a \succ b$, is equivalent to saying that $\mu \leq \mu'$.

(Sufficiency ($\Leftarrow$)): Let $\preceq$ be a binary relation on $\mathcal{L}(A)$ satisfying conditions (i)–(iii). By (ii-1), for all $x \in A$ there exists a number $\mu_x \in [0, 1]$ such that: $x \sim \mu_x a \oplus (1 - \mu_x)b$. Note that, as $a \succ b$, (i) and (iii) ensure that this μ_x is unique. Let $u : A \to \mathbb{R}$ be the map defined by

$$u(x) := \mu_x \ \text{ s.t. } \ x \sim \mu_x a \oplus (1 - \mu_x)b.$$

Then we have that by (i) and (ii-2), $l \preceq l'$ if and only if

$$\left(\sum_{x \in A} l(x)\mu_x \right) a \oplus \left(1 - \sum_{x \in A} l(x)\mu_x \right) b$$

$$\preceq \left(\sum_{x \in A} l'(x)\mu_x \right)$$

$$a \oplus \left(1 - \sum_{x \in A} l'(x)\mu_x \right) b,$$

which by (iii) is equivalent to saying that

$$\sum_{x \in A} l(x)\mu_x \leq \sum_{x \in A} l'(x)\mu_x,$$

which in turn is equivalent to

$$\sum_{x \in A} l(x)u(x) \leq \sum_{x \in A} l'(x)u(x).$$

In other words, if and only if $\bar{u}(l) \leq \bar{u}(l')$. Thus we have $\preceq = \preceq_{\bar{u}}$. $\quad\square$

Thus Theorem 3 characterizes vNM preferences, establishing three necessary and sufficient conditions for a binary relation on $\mathcal{L}(A)$ to be within this class. Let us examine these conditions one by one. Condition (ii-1) imposes that each deterministic alternative should be indifferent to a certain lottery between the best and the worst alternative. Condition (ii-2) amounts to requiring 'respect' or consistency with basic probability calculus. Specifically, it states that indifference should prevail between any lottery and the binary one that results from replacing each alternative x in its support by its binary equivalent postulated in (ii-1). Condition (iii) seems very plausible: it just requires that of two lotteries that can only yield the best and the worst alternatives the one giving a higher probability to the best should be preferred. Finally there is condition (i) which requires the most obviously necessary conditions for a preference representable by a utility function: completeness and transitivity of preferences. Nevertheless, this is perhaps the least plausible condition if one seeks to interpret the expected utility model in positive terms, that is, as a prediction of rational 'spontaneous' behaviour: It is not credible for an individual facing the choice between any pair of lotteries, even with clear preferences on the set of deterministic alternatives, to have the sensitivity to feel an unequivocally immediate preference for one or other (think of the case of lotteries involving several maybe different alternatives), still less that he/she will not incur inconsistencies with some of the other conditions after a few choices. In fact, experiments show that this is not the case in general[8].

---

[8] For a classic example (Allais's paradox [1]) in which the expected utility model is often contradicted, see Exercise 8.

Preliminaries 17

But, inverting the point of view, it is not easy to find arguments against the rationality of these conditions, which can be used 'normatively' to guide a consistent way of choosing. In view of the proof of sufficiency in Theorem 3, an agent who finds these conditions reasonable should only specify for each deterministic alternative x the number μ_x such that $x \sim \mu_x a \oplus (1-\mu_x)b$. Then, taking $u(x) := \mu_x$, the expected utility function $\bar{u}$ would represent a vNM preference consistent with them. Thus we have the following corollary.

Corollary 4 *Let $\preceq$ be a von Neumann–Morgenstern or expected utility preference on $\mathcal{L}(A)$. If there are a best and a worst alternative in A, i.e. two alternatives $a, b \in A$ such that $a \succ b$ and $a \succeq x \succeq b$, then $\preceq = \preceq_{\bar{u}}$ for the utility function $u : A \to \mathbb{R}$ defined by $u(x) := \mu_x$ such that $x \sim \mu_x a \oplus (1 - \mu_x)b$.*

In short, conditions (i)–(iii) provide an acceptable model of rational behaviour in the face of risk. Later, when we want to incorporate players' preferences into the model of a voting situation we will do so by assuming expected utility preferences.

As shown by Example 1.2, equivalent utility functions may have non-equivalent associated expected utility functions. The following theorem establishes the relation that must exist between two utility functions for their expected utility functions to be equivalent. We omit the proof, which is an easy exercise.

Theorem 5 *Two maps $u, u' : A \to \mathbb{R}$ have equivalent associated expected utility functions, i.e. functions such that $\preceq_{\bar{u}} = \preceq_{\bar{u}'}$, if and only if there exist $\alpha \in \mathbb{R}_{++}$ and $\beta \in \mathbb{R}$ such that $u' = \alpha u + \beta$.*

Remarks. (i) The assumption that there are both most and least preferred alternatives is not crucial. It has been made only to simplify the proof of Theorem 3, but the results remain valid without this assumption. Only in Theorem 3 do conditions (ii) and (iii) need to be required for any two alternatives a, b, such that $b \preceq a$, condition (ii-1) has to be required for any x, such that $b \preceq x \preceq a$, and (ii-2) for any lottery with support between a and b.

(ii) If A is not finite other probability measures more complex than lotteries can be considered. This would involve greater technical complexity, and implicitly more technically sophisticated players (they—as the reader—should be familiar with measure theory). This is not necessary for our purpose.

(iii) It is possible to give different sets of necessary and sufficient conditions for Theorem 3 that make the assumption of vNM preferences appear less demanding[9]. We prefer the simplicity of conditions in Theorem 3, given that in any case they are both necessary and sufficient.

1.5 Some basic game theory notions

As mentioned in Section 1.4.1, game theory provides formal models, called *games*, for the analysis of what we have called game situations, in which the outcome is the result of the decisions made by the interacting agents. More than sixty years after von Neumann and Morgenstern's foundational book, the ramifications of game theory and the variety of models proposed are enormous. It is beyond the scope and possibilities of this book to even summarily overview this huge field, but in Chapters 3 and 4 some models and results from game theory are needed. This section is aimed at readers not familiar with game theory, and seeks to provide the minimal background required. To that end in this section we present a few basic game-theoretic notions. To make the section accessible to as many readers as possible and to keep the space devoted to it within reasonable limits, we avoid formal details as far as possible and concentrate on the main ideas. Readers interested in going deeper into any of them should go to the specific literature[10].

The goal of the formal models analysed by game theory is to contribute to a better understanding of game situations. If we go a step further and ask what a better understanding means, at least two answers can be given. A phenomenon can be considered as thoroughly understood if we are able to 'guess' or better predict the outcome (as meteorology seeks to do with the weather). This is a *positive* goal or a positive sort of knowledge. In other cases attempts can be made to give well-founded advice as to the best way to proceed in a given situation to achieve a given goal. This may be the case if an analyst uses game theory to found a recommendation about the best course

---

[9] See for instance [29].

[10] In recent years a number of books on game theory have been written, some of them excellent. Three in particular must be mentioned: Binmore's [13], Osborne and Rubinstein's [66], and Osborne's [65].

Preliminaries 19

of action (for the interests of whoever asks for advice). In this case the goal is *normative*, using the term without necessarily implying a moral or ethical connotation. There are still cases in which a game-theoretic recommendation can be interpreted in normative terms in a sense in which a notion of fairness is explicit or implicit. Whenever human behaviour is involved, as is the case in game theory, the distinction is often confusing, and sometimes the two points of view are complementary.

1.5.1 Equilibrium

Either point of view can lead to the notion of Nash equilibrium [61]. Assume that in a given game situation theory recommends or predicts a certain action for each of the players involved. Unless each of those actions is the best response to the other players' recommended/predicted actions the recommendation/prediction is self-contradictory. If it were not so at least one player would have incentive to act otherwise, thus breaking the recommendation/prediction. This takes us to the notion of 'equilibrium'. A profile of actions, i.e. one for each player is a *Nash equilibrium* if each player' action is the best for that player given the other players' actions. Only if this necessary condition is satisfied will no player regret following the recommendation if all the others do, and will the knowledge of the predicted behaviour of the others not cause any player to deviate.

Example 1.3: (*Prisoner's dilemma*) Two individuals face a symmetric game situation. Each has two feasible actions: cooperate (C) or defect (D), and the preferences of the players are represented by the utility functions given in the table, assuming that player 1 chooses row and player 2 column.

	C	D
C	5,5	0,6
D	6,0	1,1

If for instance player 1 chooses C and player 2 chooses D the utility 'payoffs' are 0 for player 1 and 6 for player 2. In this case the only Nash equilibrium is the pair of actions (D, D). If players cannot communicate, or communication is possible but no possibility

20 *Voting and Collective Decision-Making*

of enforcing agreements exists, (D, D) seems the most plausible outcome[11].

It should be emphasized that equilibrium is not a panacea, but a logically *necessary* condition for a consistent theory of rational behaviour in the general terms formulated.

Example 1.4: (*Battle of the sexes*) Two individuals have two strategies each: going to the cinema (C) and going to the theatre (T). Both would rather go together to either place than alone, but player 1 prefers the cinema, and player 2 the theatre. It is assumed that going separately would completely spoil the evening. Thus their preferences about the four possible situations are represented by

$$
\begin{array}{ccc}
 & C & T \\
C & 2,1 & 0,0 \\
T & 0,0 & 1,2
\end{array}
$$

Note that there are two equilibria: (C, C) and (T, T). The two equilibria of the game are the situations in which the players go together to either place, with each preferring one place to the other. Given the entire symmetry of the situation there is no argument that can discriminate either of these two equilibria as superior in any sense to the other. This simple classic example shows the possible multiplicity of equilibria even in very simple situations.

1.5.2 *Cooperative and non-cooperative game theory*

Nash established the distinction between cooperative and non-cooperative game theory, and the basic notions and methodological paradigms in each field: the notion of equilibrium [61] and the cooperative solution to the bargaining problem [60] respectively, along with what has later been called the 'Nash programme' to bridge them. The non-cooperative approach addresses game situations in which players may or may not subscribe to agreements, and proceeds by explicitly modelling the players' possible actions with some level of detail

---

[11] In this case, in addition to a Nash equilibrium (D, D) is a combination of *dominant stategies*: for both players strategy D is the best choice whatever the choice of the other.

Preliminaries 21

and trying to predict the equilibrium outcome under the given conditions. The cooperative approach addresses game situations in which players have the capacity to subscribe to agreements and means to enforce them, and proceeds by ignoring details and trying either to predict the reasonable outcome or to assess the players' expectations based on ideal rationality conditions that an agreement should satisfy. Alternatively, the cooperative approach may adopt a normative point of view, prescribing a good compromise based on suitable 'fairness' conditions. In cooperative game situations, where agreements are enforceable, both cooperative and non-cooperative approaches can be applied and, as suggested by Nash, both should be applied.

Example 1.5: (*Prisoner's dilemma in a cooperative context*) Consider the situation in Example 1.3. If players have to decide in a non-cooperative environment, i.e. when either no chance of communication exists or communication is possible but no possibility of enforcing agreements exists, (D, D) seems the most plausible outcome. But now assume that players are given the possibility of communicating and signing an agreement on the outcome, and that once signed the agreement will automatically be implemented. In this case it seems clear that the most plausible outcome is (C, C): this is better for both than (D, D), and either of them would surely refuse either of the other two alternatives (C, D) and (D, C). This simple example shows how the change of environment from non-cooperative to cooperative dramatically changes the expectations. Note also that the difference is not in the players' preferences or their readiness to cooperate but in the environment.

1.5.3 Subgame perfect equilibrium

In Examples 1.3 and 1.4 each player has only one move or one choice to make: their choices of *strategy* are simultaneous and determine an outcome. Thus the situation can be directly described in *strategic form* by listing the actions or strategies available to each player and the utility that each outcome provides for each of them. But it is often the case that the players have to make a sequence of choices in a certain order that depends on the particular rules of the game and all the previous choices by all players. In this case the situation has to be described by a decision *tree* that incorporates all possible histories of the game for all possible

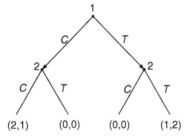

Figure 1.1. Battle of the sexes in sequential form.

sequences of decisions of the players. Games represented in this way are called *games in extensive form*. In this context a *pure strategy* of a player should specify his choice in any conceivable situation in the game (or *node* in the tree representing the game) in which that player is the one who must make a choice for the game to continue. Therefore a pure strategy profile, that is, a pure strategy for each player, completely determines the course of the game, with the only degree of freedom left being due to possible random moves that the game may include (for instance, throwing a dice). In this way, by listing all the available pure strategies for each player, a game in extensive form can be described in strategic form[12].

Example 1.6: (*Battle of the sexes in sequential form*) Let us now consider the following variation of the game of Example 1.4. Assume that player 1 chooses first, and only then can player 2 choose where to go. This new (and entirely different) game situation can be represented in extensive form by the tree shown in Figure 1.1.

In terms of pure strategies, player 1 has only two choices (*C* or *T*) but player 2 has four: *CC* (going to the cinema whatever the choice of 1), *TT* (going to the theatre whatever the choice of 1), *CT* (going with 1 whatever 1's choice), and *TC* (going alone whatever 1's choice). The following table summarizes the pure strategies available to each player.

---

[12] At least theoretically, because the number of pure strategies becomes astronomical for even relatively simple games.

Preliminaries 23

	CC	CT	TC	TT
C	2,1	2,1	0,0	0,0
T	0,0	1,2	0,0	1,2

There are three Nash equilibria: (C, CC), (C, CT), and (T, TT).

In general there may be a great many equilibria in pure strategies: i.e. pure strategy profiles such that each of them is an optimal response to the others in the same profile. Nevertheless, sometimes it is possible to discriminate between them. To illustrate this consider the three equilibria in Example 1.6. On closer examination their plausibility levels differ. Consider (T, TT). Player 1 cannot improve his situation because player 2 commits himself by the choice TT: he will go to the theatre whatever 1 does. But if player 1 happens to choose C, it would be irrational (i.e. against his preferences) on the part of player 2 to go to the theatre. Now consider (C, CC). Again there is something similar in the plan of player 2: if player 1 happens to choose T, 2 will regret not having played CT instead of CC. Thus in both equilibria one of the pure strategies has this undesirable property: there are situations (or nodes in the tree) that will never occur if both players follow the strategies that make up the equilibrium, but that would, if for whatever reasons they were reached in the course of the game, cause some of the players to change their plans, or to regret their choices if such changes were not possible. Note that the only equilibrium free from this problem is (C, CT), because it is the only *subgame perfect equilibrium* of the game.

In order to provide a general formulation we need the notion of *subgame of a game in extensive form* that we state informally below. Take any non-terminal node in the tree that describes a game in extensive form. Consider that we 'cut down' the tree exactly at this node, so that all that remains is the rest of the tree describing all the possible continuations of the game from this node on. Note that this subtree in itself specifies another game in extensive form. Any game obtained in this way is called a *subgame* of the original game. Note also that any pure strategy profile of the original game (that is, an exhaustive plan for playing the game for each player) will determine a pure strategy profile *for every subgame*.

24   *Voting and Collective Decision-Making*

Thus we have the following definition.

Definition 6 *A subgame perfect equilibrium is a strategy profile such that the restriction to any subgame is also a Nash equilibrium.*

As can easily be checked, the only subgame perfect equilibrium in Example 1.6 is (C, CT), i.e. player 1, who chooses first, chooses his preferred option, and player 2 follows 1's choice.

An important branch of game theory deals with repeated games. Take Examples 1.3 or 1.4 and assume that the same game is to be played again and again, and that at the end of each round the game recommences with probability r ($0 < r < 1$), and ends with probability $1 - r$. Alternatively, it can be assumed that after each round the game recommences but the payoffs are reduced by a discount factor of r. Even in the first case, in which the probability of a play of infinite length is 0, it is very complex to specify a pure strategy, because it requires that a choice be specified at each round t ($t = 1, 2, 3, \ldots$), which is in principle dependent on the 'history' of the game so far (i.e. the sequence of choices made by all the players so far). The implementation of such strategies entails some difficulties. For instance, it requires unlimited recall or storage capacity. There are different ways of implementing simpler strategies in these games, e.g. by using the limited capacity of finite automata. The simplest type of strategy in this context is what is called a *stationary strategy*, which consists of specifying the same choice for every round regardless of the history so far. A *stationary subgame perfect equilibrium* (*SSPE*) is a subgame perfect equilibrium in which all strategies are stationary.

1.5.4 Basic cooperative models

We end this summary overview of game-theoretic notions by introducing some basic 'cooperative games', that is, models of game situations in which the players have the capacity to subscribe agreements and the means to enforce them. As commented in Section 1.5.2, cooperative models ignore details about how the players interact and incorporate only some basic features of the situation. In this section we review three basic models that will play a role later.

Von Neumann and Morgenstern [87] introduce *transferable utility games*. A transferable utility game (or TU game, for short), is a summary of a game situation in which the only relevant information is a

Preliminaries 25

real number for each subset of players, which represents the amount of utility (assumed to be transferable between players) that the players in such a subset can guarantee for themselves if they join forces.

Formally, a *TU-game* consists of a pair (N, v), where the set $N = \{1, 2, \ldots, n\}$ labels the *players*, and v is a map $v : 2^N \to \mathbb{R}$, associating its *worth* $v(S)$ with each subset of players or *coalition* $S \subseteq N$ (with $v(\varnothing) = 0$). For short we sometimes refer to map v as a game. G_N denotes the set of all n-person (labelled by N) TU games.

A TU game v is *monotonic* if

$$(T \subseteq S) \Rightarrow (v(T) \leq v(S)).$$

This in particular entails that the worth of any coalition is positive, and that adding new members can only increase its worth. A game v is *superadditive* if two disjoint coalitions can always make at least as much by joining forces as they can separately, namely, if for all $S, T \subseteq N$, such that $S \cap T = \varnothing$,

$$v(S \cup T) \geq v(S) + v(T).$$

The situation behind a TU game v can be assumed to be the following: the players negotiate a distribution of $v(N)$, the utility that the grand coalition can obtain.

TU games in which $v(S)$ takes only the values 0 or 1 are especially simple. If in addition $v(N) = 1$, then v is called a *simple game*. The notion of simple games was also introduced by von Neumann and Morgenstern in [87], where the first example proposed is that of 'majority games'.

A more general model that includes TU games as well as bargaining problems as particular cases is that of *non-transferable utility* (NTU for short) *games*. The model consists of a pair (N, V) where $N = \{1, 2, \ldots, n\}$ is the set of players, and $V = \{V(S)\}_{S \subseteq N}$ is a collection of nonempty sets, one for each coalition $S \subseteq N$, such that for each S, $V(S) \in \mathbb{R}^S$, which represents the set of utility payoff vectors $x \in \mathbb{R}^S$ which are feasible for coalition S. In other words, $V(S)$ is the set of all payoff vectors that coalition S can guarantee by itself for its members if it forms. These sets are usually assumed to be closed, convex and *comprehensive*: i.e., $x \leq y$ and $y \in V(S) \Rightarrow x \in V(S)$. Further specifications on these sets are possible depending on the context.

26   *Voting and Collective Decision-Making*

TU games can be embedded as a subclass of NTU games. It suffices to associate with each TU game (N, v) the NTU game (N, V_v) defined by

$$V_v(S) := \left\{ x \in \mathbb{R}^S : \sum_{i \in S} x_i \le v(S) \right\}.$$

Evidently both v and V_v encapsulate the same information in different forms.

The NTU model also includes classical n-person bargaining problems (introduced in 2.1.1). These correspond to the case in which $V(N)$ is a set $D \subseteq \mathbb{R}^N$, and there is a point $d \in D$, such that for each $S \subset N$, $V(S) = \{x \in \mathbb{R}^S : x_i \le d_i \ (\forall i \in S)\}$. That is, in a bargaining problem only the grand coalition can guarantee payoffs better than those at d for its members.

1.6 Exercises

1. In weighted majorities (1.3.2), the weights and the quota usually meet the following conditions: $\frac{1}{2} \sum_{i \in N} w_i < Q < \sum_{i \in N} w_i$.

    (a) Prove that if both conditions are satisfied, then $\mathcal{W}^{(w,Q)}$ is a proper voting rule.
    (b) Is either condition alone necessary or sufficient for this?

2. Prove or disprove with a counterexample the following statements relative to weighted majority rules:

    (a) Two seats are symmetric if and only if they have the same weight.
    (b) A seat is null if and only if its weight is zero.

3. In a weighted majority what should be the weight of a seat in order for it to be a dictator's seat? What should be the weight of a seat in order for it to have a veto?

4. Let $\mathcal{W}$ be an N-voting rule. Prove that the following conditions are equivalent:

    (a) $\mathcal{W}$ is symmetric (see 1.3.1);
    (b) $\mathcal{W}$ is anonymous (that is, for any permutation $\pi : N \to N$, $\pi \mathcal{W} = \mathcal{W}$);
    (c) $\mathcal{W}$ is a q-majority voting rule for some q s.t. $\frac{1}{2} \le q < 1$.

Preliminaries 27

5. Consider an eight-seat committee divided into two subgroups: $N = A \cup B$ with $A = \{1, 2, 3, 4, 5\}$ and $B = \{6, 7, 8\}$, and two possible rules:

> Rule 1: A proposal is accepted if it has the support of at least 3 votes from A and at least 2 votes from B.
>
> Rule 2: A proposal is accepted if it has the support of at least 5 votes, of which 3 votes must be those from B.
>
> For each voting rule: (a) Give the set of winning configurations. (b) What seats are symmetric? (c) Is the dominance relationship complete? (d) Can the rule be represented by a weighted majority? If not, by a double majority?

6. The following rule, which was proposed to amend the Canadian constitution, involves the ten Canadian provinces: Quebec, Ontario, the four Atlantic provinces (New Brunswick, Nova Scotia, Prince Edward Island, and Newfoundland), the three Central provinces (Alberta, Saskatchewan, and Manitoba) and British Columbia. To pass an amendment, a proposal must get at least the support of Ontario and Quebec, two of the Atlantic provinces, and either British Columbia and a central province or all three central provinces.

(a) Give the set of winning configurations of the voting rule.
(b) Show that the dominance relationship is not complete.

7. The United Nations Security Council currently comprises fifteen members: five permanent members (China, France, Russia, United Kingdom, and United States of America) and ten non-permanent members.

(a) If we ignore the possibility of abstention, the voting rule requires the approval of its five permanent members and at least four of the ten non-permanent members in order for a decision of substance to be adopted. Give the set of winning configurations of the decision rule. Show that this rule can be represented as a weighted majority.
(b) If we take into account the possibility of abstention, a proposal can be passed if there are at least nine members in favour of the proposal and no veto member is against. How should the model be modified to distinguish between votes against and abstention?

8. (Allais's paradox): Consider the following four situations:

Option A: 100 million euros for certain.

Option B: a 10% probability of 500 million euros, an 89% probability of 100 million euros, and a 1% probability of 0 euros.

Option C: an 11% probability of 100 million euros, an 89% probability of 0 euros.

Option D: a 10% of probability of 500 million euros, a 90% probability of 0 euros.

Many individuals claim to prefer A to B, and D to C. Are these preferences compatible with the expected utility model?

9. Explain the fallacy underlying the following statement: If an individual with expected utility preferences prefers a lottery ticket in which only one out of 10 000 tickets will win 1000 euros to one euro for certain, then if each ticket cost 1 euro and he/she has 100 euros then he/she will spend it all on tickets for this lottery.

10. Discuss whether any of the following behaviour patterns of Mr X is inconsistent with vNM's model:

(a) Mr X buys a one euro lottery ticket for a draw in which only one out of 1000 tickets will win 10 euros.

(b) Mr X, who claims to prefer life to death, agrees to play Russian roulette (with one bullet in a six-bullet revolver) for the promise of a bike if he survives.

11. Let $A = \{a_1, a_2, a_3, a_4\}$, where $a_1 = 110$ euros, $a_2 = 100$ euros, $a_3 = 10$ euros, and $a_4 = 0$ euros. Two individuals have vNM preferences $\preceq_1$ and $\preceq_2$ on $\mathcal{L}(A)$ such that $a_1 \succ_i a_2 \succ_i a_3 \succ_i a_4$ $(i = 1, 2)$, and $a_3 \sim_1 \frac{3}{4}a_2 \oplus \frac{1}{4}a_4$ and $a_3 \sim_2 \frac{1}{3}a_2 \oplus \frac{4}{3}a_4$.

(a) If 1 has 25 tickets of a lottery in which one out of 100 will win 100 euros, and 2 has 10 euros. Would either of them be interested in a swap?

(b) If $a_2 \sim_1 \frac{13}{14}a_1 \oplus \frac{1}{14}a_4$ and 1 had all the tickets for this lottery, would they both be interested in the same swap (10 euros for 25 tickets)?

(c) In the conditions of (b), what is the maximum number of tickets that 1 will be willing to exchange for 10 euros? And what is the minimum number of tickets that 2 would need to be offered for 2 to be willing to pay 10 euros in exchange?

Preliminaries 29

12. An analyst is in charge of making decisions that can involve lotteries with four alternatives: a, b, c, and d. He is ordered to make decisions consistent with expected utility theory, and such that $a \succ b \succ c \succ d$.

   (a) Do these conditions determine a choice between $\frac{1}{2}a \oplus \frac{1}{2}c$ and $\frac{1}{2}b \oplus \frac{1}{2}d$?
   (b) If in addition he is also told that $b \sim \frac{2}{3}a \oplus \frac{1}{3}d$ and $c \sim \frac{1}{2}b \oplus \frac{1}{2}d$ which of the following two should he choose: $\frac{1}{6}a \oplus \frac{5}{6}b \oplus \frac{4}{6}c$ or $\frac{1}{2}b \oplus \frac{1}{2}c$?

13. An individual wants to insure a good worth w euros against a risk of damage of r euros ($r < w$). An insurance company offers a policy at a price p according to which the individual will receive r if the damage occurs. The estimated likelihood (according to both the individual and the company) of the damage occurring is 0.1%, and the company is indifferent to risk in the sense that its preferences follow the expected monetary benefit.

   (a) What is the minimum price p at which the company would be interested in offering the policy?
   (b) If the preferences of the individual are vNM and are represented for a range of monetary values between $w - r$ and w by the map $u(x) = \sqrt{\frac{x-w+r}{r}}$, within what price interval would both the company and the individual be interested in signing the policy?

2 | *Seminal papers, seminal ambiguities*

In this chapter a few important seminal papers are briefly and critically reviewed in Section 2.1. Then the basic distinction in this book between 'take-it-or-leave-it' and 'bargaining' committees is introduced in Section 2.2. The related literature is summarily reviewed in Section 2.3.

2.1 Seminal papers and seminal ambiguities

In the wake of the seminal contribution of Shapley and Shubik [78] in 1954, a copious literature on so-called 'power indices' and 'voting power' in general has been, and continues to be, produced. In this section we review only a few basic and seminal papers, Shapley and Shubik's [78] and Banzhaf's [4], as well as other previous or subsequent papers that laid the conceptual framework for later developments in voting power analysis. This will put things into historical perspective, and will also allow us to introduce some important classic models that will play a role in the book. This brief critical overview also raises some doubts about the foundations, thus motivating the endeavour and goal of this book. It is also our ambitious hope that a second reading of this chapter after reading the rest of the book will provide a test of our success. This would be the case if, to some extent, the reader had the impression that the ideas in the book had provided him / her with new 'glasses' to look at and understand the issues raised in these papers and the lights and shadows in the answers proposed in them.

2.1.1 Nash (1950): The bargaining problem

It may seem surprising to start a book on voting issues with Nash, but as will be seen later in Chapter 4 it is perfectly justified. John F. Nash is a central figure in Game Theory. A few years after von Neumann and Morgenstern's foundational book *The Theory of Games and Economic behaviour* [87], Nash established in a few papers the

Seminal papers, seminal ambiguities 31

distinction between cooperative and non-cooperative game theory (see 1.5.2), and the basic notions and methodological paradigms in the two fields: the non-cooperative equilibrium notion and the cooperative solution to the bargaining problem, respectively, along with what has later been called the 'Nash programme' to bridge them[13].

In a renowned paper [60] Nash addresses the bargaining problem, an old problem in economics that had been given up as too complex for rational analysis: What can the outcome of negotiations between two rational agents be when both can benefit from cooperating? In other words, what is the satisfaction each individual should expect to obtain from bargaining, or how much should the opportunity to engage in such a situation be worth to each of them?

In order to provide an answer the situation is idealized by several assumptions. It is assumed that both individuals are 'highly rational', i.e. that their preferences when facing risk are consistent with the von Neumann–Morgenstern utility theory reviewed in Section 1.4, which at that time had recently been introduced in [87]. In this case the preferences of each individual can be represented by a utility function determined up to the choice of a zero and a unit of scale (Theorem 5 in 1.4.4). It is also assumed that lotteries over feasible agreements are also feasible agreements and that a particular alternative representing the case of no agreement enters the specification of the situation.

The problem can thus be graphically summarized (Figure 2.1(a)) by plotting the utility vectors associated with all feasible agreements on a plane (set D) as well as the utility vector d associated with the case of disagreement. Figure 2.1(b) represents the problem obtained by adding all points which are dominated by any feasible one as feasible payoffs vectors. This alternative model, which is reasonable assuming 'free disposal' (i.e., that any level of utility inferior to a feasible one is also feasible) is used in Chapter 4.

In [60] it is assumed that the set of feasible utility vectors $D \subset \mathbb{R}^2$ is compact and convex, and contains the disagreement or *status quo* point d, and some point that strictly dominates d. The *bargaining problem* is thus summarized by the pair $B = (D, d)$. Then Nash proceeds by asking for reasonable conditions for a rational agreement,

---

[13] The collected works of Nash on game theory are reunited in [63], with an excellent introduction by Binmore. Nash's main papers on game theory and mathematics can be found in [35].

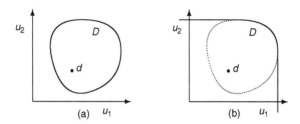

Figure 2.1. A bargaining problem: (a) Classical à la Nash model (b) Assuming 'free disposal'.

that is, a point $\Phi(B)$ or $\Phi(D,d)$ in $\mathbb{R}^2$ deserving of the name. In this way he characterizes by a set of conditions the unique 'solution' or map $\Phi : \mathfrak{B}_2 \to \mathbb{R}^2$ satisfying them, where $\mathfrak{B}_2$ denotes the set of all such bargaining problems. Namely, consistently with the interpretation of the solution as a vector of rational expectations of gain by the two bargainers, the following conditions are imposed on *rationality* grounds.

1. *Efficiency*[14]. If $(x_1, x_2), (x'_1, x'_2) \in D$ and $x_i > x'_i$ (for $i = 1, 2$), then $(x'_1, x'_2) \neq \Phi(D, d)$.

A problem (D, d) is *symmetric* if $d_1 = d_2$, and $(x_2, x_1) \in D$ whenever $(x_1, x_2) \in D$.

2. *Symmetry*. If (D, d) is symmetric, then $\Phi_1(D, d) = \Phi_2(D, d)$.

3. *Independence of irrelevant alternatives*. Given two problems with the same disagreement point, (D, d) and (D', d), if $D' \subseteq D$ and $\Phi(D, d) \in D'$, then $\Phi(D', d) = \Phi(D, d)$.

Given that von Neumann–Morgenstern utility functions are determined up to a positive affine transformation, the solution should not depend on the zero and the unit of scale chosen to represent the utilities, that is, it must be *invariant w.r.t. positive affine transformations*.

4. For any problem (D, d) and any $a_i, b_i \in \mathbb{R}\,(a_i > 0, i = 1, 2)$, if $T(D, d) = (T(D), T(d))$ is the problem that results from (D, d) by the affine transformation $T(x_1, x_2) = (a_1 x_1 + b_1, a_2 x_2 + b_2)$, then $\Phi(T(D, d)) = T(\Phi(D, d))$.

The first condition expresses that rational individuals will not accept an agreement if another better for both is feasible. The second states

---

[14] Nash did not actually name his conditions. The names we use here were given to them later.

that, given that in the model the two individuals are ideally assumed to be equally rational, when the mathematical description of the problem is entirely symmetric the solution must also be symmetric (later, in [62] Nash replaces this condition by *anonymity*, requiring that the labels, 1 or 2, identifying the players do not influence the solution). The third expresses a condition of consistency: an agreement considered satisfactory should still be considered satisfactory if it remains feasible after the feasible set shrinks (and the disagreement point remains unchanged).

Under the conditions assumed for B, these four conditions determine a unique solution $\Phi(B)$ for every bargaining problem, now known as the '*Nash solution of the bargaining problem*', which is given by

$$\text{Nash}(B) = \arg\max_{x \in D,\, x \geq d} (x_1 - d_1)(x_2 - d_2).$$

Namely, the point in D for which the product of utility gains (w.r.t. d) is maximized. The following simpler and equivalent geometrical specification of this point may prove useful. Assuming that the scales of utilities for both players have been chosen so that $d = 0$, Nash(B) is (see Figure 2.2) the point on the boundary of D which is the middle point of the segment between the intersections with the positive axes of a straight line that leaves D below it.

Although Nash only considered the two-player case, the whole construction works for the n-player case, yielding the same result. So for three players the aspect of a bargaining problem (assuming free disposal and assuming that the scales of utilities are chosen so that $d = 0$) would be as illustrated in Figure 2.3. In this case Nash(B) is the point in the boundary of D which is the baricenter of the triangle whose vertices are the intersections of a supporting hyperplane that leaves D

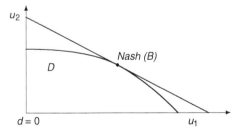

Figure 2.2. The Nash bargaining solution.

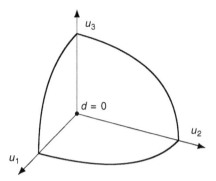

Figure 2.3. A three-person bargaining problem.

below with the positive axes (that is, if these points are P_i ($i = 1, 2, 3$): Nash(B) = $\frac{1}{3}P_1 + \frac{1}{3}P_2 + \frac{1}{3}P_3$).

In short, in a n-person bargaining problem as idealized by Nash's model, assuming that rational players' expectations should satisfy these conditions amounts to concluding that such expectations are given by

$$\text{Nash}(B) = \arg\max_{x \in D,\, x \geq d} \prod_{i=1}^{n}(x_i - d_i).$$

Note the model implicitly assumes 'complete information', that is, all the information within the model $B = (D, d)$ is shared by all the players. But note that even assuming this, Nash's characterization gives no clue about how players can interact to reach this point. Later Nash [62] re-examined the bargaining problem from a *non-cooperative* point of view, starting what is known now as 'the Nash programme', i.e. modelling the bargaining situation as a non-cooperative game in which the players' steps of negotiation (proposals and threats) become moves in a non-cooperative game, and obtaining the cooperative solution as an equilibrium[15].

2.1.2 Shapley (1953): The value of a TU game

In 1953, in the wake of Nash's success, Lloyd S. Shapley, in [76], addresses a relatively similar problem with a similar approach, but

---

[15] In fact, as a limit of equilibrium points of 'smoothed games.'

concerning a model introduced by von Neumann and Morgenstern in [87] involving n players: a *transferable utility game* (see 1.5.4). Although different stories can be provided to motivate it, there is not so clearly a real-world situation behind this model as there is behind the case of Nash's bargaining model[16].

If the situation behind a TU game (N, v) is that the players negotiate a distribution of an amount of utility $v(N)$, assumed to be 'objective and transferable', the problem can be put as follows: What is a rational agreement on how to divide $v(N)$? Answering this question entails assessing the 'value' of the game for each player. In other words, how much is the opportunity to engage in such a situation worth to each of them? Then, proceeding like Nash, Shapley asks for the following conditions[17] for a vector $\Phi(v) = (\Phi_1(v), \dots, \Phi_n(v)) \in \mathbb{R}^N$ to be considered as a rational evaluation of the prospect of playing game v.

1. *Efficiency.* $\sum_{i \in N} \Phi_i(v) = v(N)$.

Given a permutation $\pi : N \to N$ and a game v, πv denotes the permuted game defined by $\pi v(\pi(S)) := v(S)$, where $\pi(S) = \{\pi(i) : i \in S\}$. That is, πv is the game that results from v by relabelling the players according to π, so that i is in v what $\pi(i)$ is in πv.

2. *Anonymity.* For any permutation π, $\Phi_{\pi(i)}(\pi v) = \Phi_i(v)$.

A player i is a *null player* in a game v if his/her entering or leaving any coalition never changes its worth, that is, if $v(S \cup i) = v(S)$, for all S.

3. *Null player.* If i is a *null player* in a game v, then $\Phi_i(v) = 0$.

The addition of two TU games, $v + w$, can be defined by $(v + w)(S) := v(S) + w(S)$.

4. *Additivity.* $\Phi(v + w) = \Phi(v) + \Phi(w)$.

The first condition expresses that the distribution of utility is feasible and efficient in the sense that no utility is wasted. Anonymity means that if the players are relabelled their values are relabelled consistently. The third condition imposes that irrelevant players should

---

[16] In fact, TU games originally appear in [87] as a 'second order' abstraction, that is, as a model which is the result of abstracting some information from a previous and more complex model. Readers interested in the Shapley value should consult [74].

[17] In [76] the formulations and names of some of the conditions are slightly different.

receive 0. Finally, additivity, in spite of Shapley's argument that it *'is a prime requisite for any evaluation scheme designed to be applied eventually to systems of interdependent games'*, is the least compelling condition.

These conditions characterize a single map or 'value' $v \mapsto \Phi(v) \in \mathbb{R}^N$, which is now known as the *Shapley value*, or more properly, as $\Phi(v)$ is a vector, each of its components, $\Phi_i(v)$, denoted by $\mathrm{Sh}_i(v)$ here, is the Shapley value of player i in game v, and is given by

$$\mathrm{Sh}_i(v) = \sum_{S:S\subseteq N} \frac{(n-s)!(s-1)!}{n!}(v(S) - v(S\backslash i)).$$

As $v(S) - v(S\backslash i)$ is the marginal contribution of player i to the worth of coalition S, that is, the increase in worth that his/her joining $S\backslash i$ causes, $\mathrm{Sh}_i(v)$ is a weighted average of the marginal contributions of that player to the worth of all coalitions he/she belongs to. These coefficients or 'weights' admit several interpretations. Shapley proposes a bargaining model based on one of them from which the value can be derived as the expected outcome. Assume that players agree to form the grand coalition and distribute its worth in the following way: players join the coalition one at a time in a given order, all orders being equally probable, and each player receives his/her marginal contribution to the worth of the coalition formed when he/she enters. It is then easy to show that if the allocation is done in this way, $\frac{(n-s)!(s-1)!}{n!}$ is the probability of S being the coalition formed when i enters. Therefore the expected payoff (i.e., the expected marginal contribution in this probabilistic model) of each player is his/her Shapley value. It is worth stressing Shapley's comment : '[this bargaining model] *lends support to the view that the value is best regarded as an* a priori *assessment of the situation, based on either ignorance or disregard of the social organization of the players'*.

Example 2.1: Let $N = \{1,2,3\}$, and let $v : 2^N \to \mathbb{R}$ be the TU game such that $v(N) = 8$, $v(1,2) = 2$, $v(1,3) = 3$, $v(2,3) = 4$, $v(1) = v(2) = 1$, and $v(3) = 0$. In the following table the $3! = 6$ possible orders are in the left-hand column, and the marginal contributions of each player to the coalition formed when he/she enters for each order are in the other three.

Seminal papers, seminal ambiguities 37

Order	$v(S) - v(S\backslash 1)$	$v(S) - v(S\backslash 2)$	$v(S) - v(S\backslash 3)$
1, 2, 3	1	1	6
1, 3, 2	1	5	2
2, 1, 3	1	1	6
2, 3, 1	4	1	3
3, 1, 2	3	5	0
3, 2, 1	4	4	0

As each order occurs with probability $\frac{1}{6}$, the expected marginal contribution of each player is obtained by adding up each column and dividing by 6. Thus $\text{Sh}(v) = \left(\frac{14}{6}, \frac{17}{6}, \frac{17}{6} \right)$.

2.1.3 Shapley–Shubik (1954): A power index

Many collective decision procedures can be presented as simple games (see Section 1.5.4), in particular all those described as *voting rules* in Section 1.3. As defined in 1.3.1, a voting rule can be specified by the set of seats $N = \{1, 2, \dots, n\}$ and the set $W \subseteq 2^N$ of winning vote configurations, that is, those that can make a decision. So the simple TU game v_W can be associated with each voting rule W, defined by

$$v_W(S) := \begin{cases} 1, & \text{if } S \in W \\ 0, & \text{if } S \notin W. \end{cases} \tag{9}$$

In [78] Shapley and Shubik propose the Shapley value of the associated simple game as an '*a priori evaluation of the division of power among the various bodies and members of a legislature or committee system*'. Since then the Shapley value of game v_W for each $i \in N$ has been known as the *Shapley–Shubik index*.

In accordance with the interpretation of the Shapley value, the most coherent interpretation of the Shapley–Shubik index of the simple game associated with a voting rule seems to be the following: A unit of objective and transferable utility is to be distributed among n individuals, under the condition that any group of individuals that forms a winning configuration according to the specification of a given voting rule W can enforce any feasible distribution. The Shapley–Shubik index of each voter can then be interpreted as an expected share of the available unit.

On the other hand, as the marginal contribution of a player, $v_W(S) - v_W(S\backslash i)$, can only be either 0 or 1, and is 1 only when the presence/absence of a player in S makes it winning/losing, Shapley and Shubik also propose a probabilistic interpretation in terms of the likelihood of being *'pivotal'* or *'critical to the success of a winning coalition'*. They reinterpret Shapley's bargaining model assuming an *'order of voting as an indication of the relative degree of support by the different members, with the most enthusiastic members "voting" first, etc.'* Then what in the case of a TU game is the expected marginal contribution of a player, becomes now the probability of his/her being pivotal (i.e. the probability of $v_{\mathcal{W}}(S) - v_{\mathcal{W}}(S \setminus i) = 1$) if a winning coalition is formed according to this probabilistic sequential model.

Example 2.2: Let $N = \{1, 2, 3\}$, and $\mathcal{W} = \{\{1,2\}, \{1,3\}, \{1,2,3\}\}$. Then proceeding with $v_{\mathcal{W}}$ as in Example 2.1, we have:

Order	$v_{\mathcal{W}}(S) - v_{\mathcal{W}}(S \setminus 1)$	$v_{\mathcal{W}}(S) - v_{\mathcal{W}}(S \setminus 2)$	$v_{\mathcal{W}}(S) - v_{\mathcal{W}}(S \setminus 3)$
$1, 2, 3$	0	1	0
$1, 3, 2$	0	0	1
$2, 1, 3$	1	0	0
$2, 3, 1$	1	0	0
$3, 1, 2$	1	0	0
$3, 2, 1$	1	0	0

We obtain $\mathrm{Sh}_i(v) = \left(\frac{4}{6}, \frac{1}{6}, \frac{1}{6}\right)$. Note that for each row (i.e. each order) there is a single '1', corresponding to the pivotal player for that order.

A critical examination of the whole construction and its interpretation casts some doubts on the soundness of its foundations. The first source of confusion lies in the implicit identification of a voting rule with a TU-game. The specification of a voting rule (see 1.3.1) involves neither players nor their preferences (different players with different preference profiles may use a same voting rule), while a simple game is a particular type of TU game. Thus, identifying a voting rule with a TU-game amounts to assuming a very special configuration of players' preferences[18]. Second, if the compellingness of additivity is not clear in Shapley's axiomatic system, now the condition does not even make sense in the context of simple games, where the sum of two simple

---

[18] We come back to this point in Chapter 4 (see 4.2), where we consider a model of a committee consisting of a voting rule and a preference profile. In the light of this more general model, $v_{\mathcal{W}}$ appears as a particular case. Only then can this objection be fully understood.

Seminal papers, seminal ambiguities

games is not a simple TU game[19]. Third, if we turn to the pivotal interpretation, the relevance of the 'degree of support' to a proposal to be voted upon in a yes/no decision is not clear, and nor is the importance of being 'pivotal' for a given order. Why (see Example 2.2) should only the pivotal player for a given order keep all the credit and have the whole cake if other players may also be critical in the coalition formed?

In short, in addition to somewhat dubious foundations, the seminal paper contains a seminal duality or ambiguity that remained unresolved and pervaded most of the subsequent related literature: What is the meaning of Shapley–Shubik's 'power index'? Is it the 'value' or 'cooperative solution' of a sort of bargaining situation, or it is an assessment of the likelihood of being critical in the making of a decision? Is it an expected share of a prize, or it is a probability of being decisive? Or it is both these things? The same questions can be posed in regard to what is supposed to be evaluated: What is 'voting power'? On the other hand, where does the index's credibility comes from? From its axiomatic foundation or from its probabilistic interpretation?

2.1.4 Banzhaf (1965): Power as decisiveness

In [4] Banzhaf makes a devastating critique of the current practice of assigning voting weights proportional to the numbers of citizens in several legislative bodies as a means of implementing the 'one man, one vote' requirement without disturbing the existing arrangement of districts of unequal size. He provides the following examples in which some of the representatives with positive weight have null capacity to influence the outcome, or in which representatives with rather different weights have exactly the same capacity to affect it.

Example 2.3: Let $\mathcal{W}^{(w,Q)}$ be the five-person qualified majority rule with weights $w = (5, 1, 1, 1, 1)$ and $Q = 4$. In this case player 1 concentrates all decision power because this rule is 1's dictatorship. Now let $\mathcal{W}^{(w',Q')}$ with $w' = (8, 8, 8, 8, 1)$ and $Q' = 16$. In spite of the different weights the rule specified is equivalent to a simple majority rule.

---

[19] The first axiomatization of the Shapley–Shubik index, that is to say of the Shapley value in the domain of simple games, was due to Dubey [18]. It entailed additivity being replaced by a no more compelling condition (see 2.1.6).

This proves that *'voting power is not proportional to the number of votes a legislator may cast'*, and that *'the number of votes is not even a rough measure of the voting power of the individual legislator'*. To give a more precise foundation to this assertion he proposes *'to think of voting power as the ability of a legislator, by his vote, to affect the passage or defeat of a measure'*, and provides a measure of voting power based on this idea. This measure of voting power of a voter is given by the number of 'swings', that is, the number of vote combinations in which that voter is able to determine the outcome. The ratio of the power of any two voters is then given by the ratio of such combinations for each of them. He makes no explicit use of any probabilistic model, but the assumption that all vote combinations are equally probable is implicit[20].

Example 2.4: Let $N = \{1, 2, 3\}$, and $W = \{\{1, 2\}, \{1, 3\}, \{1, 2, 3\}\}$. Then we have:

Vote configuration	1's swings	2's swings	3's swings
$\{1, 2, 3\}$	1	0	0
$\{1, 2\}$	1	1	0
$\{1, 3\}$	1	0	1
$\{2, 3\}$	1	0	0
$\{1\}$	0	1	1
$\{2\}$	1	0	0
$\{3\}$	1	0	0
$\varnothing$	0	0	0
Total swings	6	2	2

Note that each row corresponds now to a possible vote configuration (order plays no role), and in some of them there are several '1', because in some vote configurations two or more players can be swingers. Note also that the ratio of 'power' according to the Banzhaf index ($3 : 1 : 1$)

---

[20] The term 'probability' never occurs in [4], but in [5] the probabilistic model is almost explicit when he asserts that *'Because a priori all voting combinations are equally possible, any objective measure of voting power must treat them as equally significant (...) no one can say beforehand which combinations will occur most often'*, and even closer when he says that equal voting power means allowing *'each voting member an opportunity to affect the outcome in an equal number of equally likely voting combinations.'*

Seminal papers, seminal ambiguities 41

is different from the ratio obtained from the Shapley–Shubik index (4 : 1 : 1) for the same voting rule.

Although he acknowledges that his definition *'is based in part on the idea of Shapley–Shubik'* he rejects their index arguing against the relevance of the order in which votes are cast in a voting situation, and asserting that their definition, *'based as it is upon mathematical game theory in which each "player" seeks to maximize his "expected winnings", seems to make unnecessary and unreasonable assumptions about the legislative process in order to justify a more complicated measure of voting power.'*

In short Banzhaf takes decisiveness as the source of power, dismissing the axiomatic approach and favouring a notion of power based on the likelihood of being decisive or critical in a decision made by vote, that is, assuming that one exerts power when one's vote is determinant.

2.1.5 *Penrose (1946), Rae (1969) and Coleman (1971)*

Independently and earlier, Penrose [68] (see also [69]) had in 1946 reached basically the same conclusions as Banzhaf. Unfortunately, in this case the seed failed to germinate and his work was widely ignored, in particular by the game-theoretic power indices main stream. Only relatively recently has his pioneering work been rediscovered and recognized.

The contribution of Coleman [15, 16], independently and coinciding in part with that of Banzhaf, and the seminal work of Rae [70] are also worth mentioning. In the next chapter their contributions are put into perspective within the conceptual framework proposed in this book.

2.1.6 *Through the axiomatic glasses: Dubey (1975), Dubey–Shapley (1979)*

In two classic papers Dubey [18], and Dubey and Shapley [20] provided the first axiomatic characterizations of the Shapley–Shubik index and the Banzhaf index. Before proceeding we need a few formal definitions. Recall (see 1.5.4) a simple game is a TU-game $v : 2^N \to \mathbb{R}$ such that $v(S)$ takes only the values 0 and 1, and such that $v(N) = 1$. But note that if $v = v_{\mathcal{W}}$ is the simple game associated with a voting rule $\mathcal{W}$ defined by (9) in Section 2.1.3, in addition to these conditions, v will satisfy the following conditions. As we assume that $(S \supseteq T \in \mathcal{W}) \Rightarrow (S \in \mathcal{W})$, then the associated game is *monotonic*. Also as we assume that $(S \in \mathcal{W}) \Rightarrow (N \setminus S \notin \mathcal{W})$, then the associated game is *superadditive*.

It is also easy to check that all simple monotonic and superadditive games are generated by (9). In other words the map $\mathcal{W} \mapsto v_{\mathcal{W}}$ is a one-to-one correspondence between the set of N-voting rules and the set of N-person simple monotonic and superadditive games, which we denote by SG_N. As in the sequel we restrict our attention to SG_N, whenever we say 'simple games' we mean 'simple *monotonic and superadditive* games'.

For any $v, w \in SG_N$, define two operations[21] on SG_N

$$(v \wedge w)(S) := \min\{v(S), w(S)\},$$

$$(v \vee w)(S) := \max\{v(S), w(S)\}.$$

Note that both $v \wedge w$ and $v \vee w$ are TU-games, but $v \vee w$ may fail to be a superadditive monotonic simple game. Dubey [18] introduces the following condition:

Transfer. A map $\Phi : SG_N \to \mathbb{R}^N$ satisfies the 'transfer' condition if for any $v, w \in SG_N$ such that $v \vee w \in SG_N$,

$$\Phi(v) + \Phi(w) = \Phi(v \wedge w) + \Phi(v \vee w). \tag{10}$$

Combining this condition with three of the conditions in Shapley's characterization gives the following result.

Theorem 7 *(Dubey [18]) The only map $\Phi : SG_N \to \mathbb{R}^N$ that satisfies efficiency, anonymity, null player, and transfer is the Shapley–Shubik index.*

Later Dubey and Shapley [20] provide an adaptation of this characterization in order to axiomatize the Banzhaf index by replacing

---

[21] In fact both operations make sense for arbitrary TU-games. As the reader may check, these operations are the exact counterparts for simple games of '$\cap$' (intersection) and '$\cup$' (union) for voting rules (see 1.3.2).

Seminal papers, seminal ambiguities

'efficiency' by the following somewhat ad hoc condition[22]:

$$\sum_{i \in N} \Phi_i(v) = \sum_{i \in N} Bz_i(v), \tag{11}$$

to obtain the following result.

Theorem 8 *(Dubey and Shapley [20]) The only* $\Phi : SG_N \to \mathbb{R}^N$ *that satisfies condition (11), anonymity, null player, and transfer, is the Banzhaf index.*

Thus from the point of view of these characterizations the Shapley–Shubik index and the Banzhaf index 'share' three axioms (anonymity, null player and transfer[23]) and differ in only one. But there are two problems with these characterizations. First, if we assume that we want to characterize either a distribution of the pie (i.e. of a unit of utility among the players), or a vector of rational expectations of shares, then 'efficiency' seems a compelling rationality condition. Moreover, if we are trying to characterize axiomatically a measure of power or of influence, whatever this might mean, then *neither* this condition *nor* (11) is compelling at all. Second, the lack of compellingness of the transfer condition in either case means a flaw in both characterizations. This condition can be seen as a sort of adaptation of 'additivity' to the narrower domain of simple games. But what is the motivation or the justification for requiring it? This is not clear at all for either a vector of rational expectations or for a measure of influence. In short, neither of

---

[22] This formulation may seem rather unsatisfactory in the sense that the index it helps to characterize appears in the axiom. Although this can be avoided by an equivalent formulation in which the right-hand side of (11) is replaced discretely by the required quantity (a function of the game v), namely

$$\sum_{i \in N} \Phi_i(v) = \frac{1}{2^{n-1}} \sum_{i \in N} \sum_{S: i \in S \subseteq N} (v(S) - v(S \setminus i)),$$

the bottom line is the same: to require the sum to be what it is for the Banzhaf index.

[23] In fact these three conditions are satisfied by all *semivalues*. Semivalues are basically the family of 'values' that result by dropping 'efficiency' in Shapley's characterizing system of his value. They were introduced by Weber [88] (see also [19]). When restricted to simple games, semivalues include the Shapley–Shubik and Banzhaf indices, and can be seen as a family of 'generalized power indices', which share with these two indices their most compelling properties (anonymity and null player) as well as transfer (see [42]).

the two above characterizations provides compelling support for either of the two indices.

Axioms, paradoxes and postulates[24]

The lack of conclusive arguments in favour of either of the two indices gave rise to a proliferation of new power indices. Several authors then provided examples of more or less counterintuitive behaviour of some of them. These examples are referred to somewhat exaggeratedly as *'paradoxes'* in the literature on power indices, where they have been widely discussed[25]. According to this point of view, each paradox entails the violation of a desirable property or *'postulate'* by a power index, and these paradoxes/postulates can be used to judge and select between power indices. This is indeed very close to the axiomatic approach, at least to its earliest versions where compellingness of the axioms was a priority[26], though no characterization has been so far provided based on really compelling 'postulates' for a measure of voting power. Nevertheless, the weakest point of the paradoxes/postulates approach lies in trying to grasp the rather abstract notion of measure of 'power' (or 'voting power' associated with a voting rule) directly, with no sufficient prior clarification of what such a 'power' may mean. Moreover, such a chimeric measure tends to be founded solely on the voting rule, disregarding any other elements from the environment.

2.2 Clear-cut models to dissipate ambiguity

Recapitulating after this brief review of the basic landmarking seminal papers, one is left with a number of doubts concerning the issues raised and the answers given to them. What is the meaning of the Shapley–Shubik index? Is it a 'value' in the cooperative-axiomatic sense à la Nash, i.e. an assessment of the expected payoff of a rational player at the prospect of engaging in a sort of bargaining situation? Or is it

---

[24] Readers not familiar with the 'voting power paradoxes' literature can skip this comment.

[25] See [22] for a discussion of the main paradoxes. See [47] (briefly commented at the end of 3.5.5) for a further critique of the whole approach.

[26] As pointed out in 2.1.1, the conditions proposed by Nash are not called 'axioms' in [60]. Only later, given their characterizing power, were they called so and 'axiomatic' such an approach.

Seminal papers, seminal ambiguities

an assessment of the likelihood of playing a critical or decisive role in the making of a decision by a vote? Or are the two interpretations compatible? Which is 'better': the Shapley–Shubik index or the Banzhaf index? What provides sounder foundations for a measure of voting power: axioms or probabilistic interpretations? In fact the tension between these two indices, like the tension between the merits of the axiomatic and probabilistic approaches, has pervaded all the subsequent related work to date. Both indices have been defended and attacked with axiomatic and probabilistic arguments.

But going further, all these question marks can be transferred to the underlying notion that is to be evaluated: What is 'power' or 'voting power' about? It is our view that a serious attempt to solve this riddle requires a more radical issue to be clarified first. To put it bluntly: What are we talking about? However provoking it may sound, this basic issue has been sidelined in much of the literature on the topic[27]. In most cases a considerable dose of ambiguity surrounds the situation under consideration. A situation in which a matter is to be decided upon by vote (or at least under conditions among which a voting rule plays a prominent role) by a collective body is the common denominator underlying this literature. But such a vague specification as this may include an extremely wide and heterogeneous constellation of voting situations: law-making in a parliament, a parliament vote for the endorsement of a government after elections, a referendum, governmental cabinet decision-making, a shareholders' meeting, an international or intergovernmental council, etc.

The only way to get rid of ambiguity and to clarify the analysis is to take the bull by the horns and start with clear-cut models of well-specified clear-cut voting situations. In accordance with this idea, in this book we take a new departure with respect to previous literature related to voting power. We distinguish neatly between two different types of voting situation that a collective body can face, or, in

---

[27] But not by all, as Peter Morriss' words testify: '*Before we can start constructing an account of power we need to know what sort of thing we are dealing with: we must decide just* what *it is that we are trying to analyse. And we must decide, as well, how we go about deciding* that. *Most writers in the social sciences pay far too little attention to these preliminary problems, with the result that they go rushing off in the wrong direction, pursuing the wrong quarry. When they eventually catch it, they may claim to have caught the beast they sought; but how do they know, if they didn't know what they were looking for?*' ([59], p. 2).

the terms chosen here, two types of committee: 'take-it-or-leave-it' committees and 'bargaining' committees. An ingredient common to both types of committee is a dichotomous voting rule (as introduced in Section 1.3) specifying the winning vote configurations. A *'take-it-or-leave-it' committee* (i) votes upon different independent proposals over time; (ii) these proposals are submitted to the committee by some external agency; and (iii) the committee is only entitled to accept or reject proposals, but cannot modify them. By contrast a *'bargaining' committee* (i) deals with different issues over time; (ii) bargains about each issue in search of a unanimous agreement, in which task it is entitled to adjust the proposal; (iii) this negotiation takes place under the condition that any winning coalition has the capacity to enforce agreements; and (iv) for each issue a different configuration of preferences emerges in the committee over the set of feasible agreements concerning the issue at stake.

Although in reality it is often the case that the same committee acts sometimes like a 'take-it-or-leave-it' committee, and others like a 'bargaining' committee, or even at times like something between the two, this clear differentiation of two clear-cut types of situation provides benchmarks for a better understanding of many less clear real-world situations. A thorough understanding of simple situations should be obtained before more complex ones are tackled. In this case this basic distinction requires different models and different conceptual analyses. It also permits more precise answers to more precisely formulated questions[28]. Moreover, as we will see, this neat double point of view dissipates ambiguities and allows for a clarification of the meaning and limits of some common places (both ideas and recommendations) sustained by inertia and ambiguity. In particular it enables us to provide coherent answers to some of the questions raised in the previous paragraphs.

2.3 Further reading

After half a century of research a huge number of papers can be seen one way or other as related to the few seminal papers briefly reviewed

---

[28] The conceptual relationship of the basic distinction in this book with the vague distinction, widely extended in the literature, between 'I-power' and 'P-power', introduced in [24] is discussed in the Conclusions at the end of the book.

Seminal papers, seminal ambiguities 47

in this chapter. It would be tiresome and futile to attempt to draw up an exhaustive list of references. On the specific topic of voting power there is Felsenthal and Machover's [22] influential book. In the following we make a personal selection of the work we consider most relevant to the issues addressed in this book. We separate the selected works into two subsections. One subsection is devoted to some of the main contributions in the axiomatic approach, the other to those related to the probabilistic approach. Some of the papers will be mentioned again in subsequent chapters. Some contributions are best left for quote and comment in later chapters, and are therefore omitted in these comments.

2.3.1 Axiomatic approach

The success of the elegant paper by Nash on the bargaining problem (immediately followed by Shapley's) enabled the cooperative 'axiomatic' approach to flourish. Each of Nash's characterizing requirements [60] seeks to embody a compelling condition about the outcome of negotiation among rational bargainers. Later this crucial aspect was often forgotten, and characterizations of these and other 'values', 'solutions' or 'power indices' proliferated. Here we give a few relevant contributions in this line of work.

The most often criticized of Nash's conditions is that of 'independence of irrelevant alternatives' and the most respectable alternative to it was 'monotonicity', which gave rise to the Kalai–Smorodinsky solution [33]. Kalai also explored the effects of dropping 'symmetry' in [32], and Roth showed how 'efficiency' and 'symmetry' can be replaced by a condition of 'individual rationality' in [72].

In an interesting paper by Roth [73] the Shapley–Shubik index and the Banzhaf index are reinterpreted as utility functions representing von Neumann–Morgenstern preferences over lotteries on 'roles' in voting procedures. In [54] Lehrer characterizes the Banzhaf index by means of a property relative to the 'amalgamation' of two players. More recently, in [39] and [40] we have provided alternative characterizations to those of [20] and [73], only to honestly conclude that there is no good reason either to reject or accept any of the two indices on pure axiomatic grounds in the framework of simple games.

48 *Voting and Collective Decision-Making*

2.3.2 Probabilistic approach

As commented, both the Shapley value and the Shapley–Shubik index admit probabilistic interpretations. A probabilistic model also underlies Banzhaf's index. This is also the case with some cooperative game-theoretic 'solutions' born out of different axiomatic explorations. But in general terms probabilistic interpretations have been overlooked by game theorists, maybe because one can always find one or more. Game theorists are in general more interested in axiomatic characterizations. Nevertheless in some cases a probabilistic model provides a clearer interpretation. Political scientists seem to have been more interested in probabilistic models. An early example of this is the collection of contributions edited by Niemi and Weisberg in 1972 [64], after the interest aroused by Rae [70]. Some important contributions that deserve to be mentioned in this respect are those of Straffin [79, 81, 82], and Weber [88, 89].

2.4 Exercises

1. A buyer and a seller discuss and bargain over the price of a good. The seller (player 1) is interested in selling at any price greater than p, and at that price would be indifferent between selling and not selling. The buyer (player 2) is interested in buying at any price lower than P and at that price would be indifferent between buying and not buying. Assuming that $p < P$ and that both players have vNM preferences, calculate the final price according to the Nash bargaining solution, assuming that their preferences on the range of prices $[p, P]$ can be represented by utility functions $u_1(x) = \frac{x-p}{P-p}$ and $u_2(x)$, for each of the following cases: (a) $u_2(x) = \frac{P-x}{P-p}$. (b) $u_2(x) = \sqrt{\frac{P-x}{P-p}}$. (c) $u_2(x) = \left(\frac{P-x}{P-p}\right)^2$.

2. Consider the following prisoner's dilemma situation in a cooperative context. Two individuals have two strategies each: cooperate (C) and defect (D). Their preferences about the four possible situations are

$$(D, C) \succ_1 (C, C) \succ_1 (D, D) \succ_1 (C, D),$$
$$(C, D) \succ_2 (C, C) \succ_2 (D, D) \succ_2 (D, C).$$

Seminal papers, seminal ambiguities 49

If lotteries on the four outcomes are admitted and both have vNM preferences on them, calculate and interpret the Nash bargaining solution in each of the following cases (in order to make the comparison easier, take $u_1(C, D) = u_2(D, C) = 0$, $u_1(D, C) = u_2(C, D) = 10$ and $d = (u_1(D, D), u_2(D, D))$ as the disagreement point in both cases):

(a) If

$$(C, C) \sim_1 \frac{4}{5}(D, C) \oplus \frac{1}{5}(C, D), \quad (D, D) \sim_1 \frac{1}{5}(D, C) \oplus \frac{4}{5}(C, D),$$

$$(C, C) \sim_2 \frac{4}{5}(C, D) \oplus \frac{1}{5}(D, C), \quad (D, D) \sim_2 \frac{1}{5}(C, D) \oplus \frac{4}{5}(D, C).$$

(b) If $\preceq_2$ is as in (a), and

$$(C, C) \sim_1 \frac{3}{5}(D, C) \oplus \frac{2}{5}(C, D), \quad (D, D) \sim_1 \frac{1}{2}(D, C) \oplus \frac{1}{2}(C, D).$$

3. Consider the following variant of the 'battle of the sexes' in a cooperative context. Two individuals have two strategies each: going to the cinema (C) and going to the theatre (T). Player 1 prefers going to the cinema, and player 2 going the theatre, but both prefer going together to either place to going alone. Thus their preferences about the four possible situations are

$$(C, C) \succ_1 (T, T) \succ_1 (C, T) \succ_1 (T, C),$$
$$(T, T) \succ_2 (C, C) \succ_2 (C, T) \succ_2 (T, C).$$

If lotteries on the four possibilities are admitted and both have vNM preferences on them, calculate and interpret the Nash bargaining solution in each of the following cases (in order to make the comparison easier, take $u_1(T, C) = u_2(T, C) = -5$ and $u_1(C, C) = u_2(T, T) = 10$ in both cases, and $d = (u_1(C, T), u_2(C, T))$ as the disagreement point):

(a) If

$$(T, T) \sim_1 \frac{2}{3}(C, C) \oplus \frac{1}{3}(T, C), \quad (C, T) \sim_1 \frac{1}{3}(C, C) \oplus \frac{2}{3}(T, C),$$

$$(C, C) \sim_2 \frac{2}{3}(T, T) \oplus \frac{1}{3}(T, C), \quad (C, T) \sim_2 \frac{1}{3}(T, T) \oplus \frac{2}{3}(T, C).$$

(b) If $\preceq_2$ is as in (a), and

$$(T,T) \sim_1 \frac{4}{5}(C,C) \oplus \frac{1}{5}(T,C), \quad (C,T) \sim_1 \frac{2}{5}(C,C) \oplus \frac{3}{5}(T,C).$$

4. Two individuals with vNM preferences bargain the division of a pie. If x ($0 \le x \le 1$) denotes 1's fraction and $1 - x$ denotes 2's fraction, and the following utility functions represent the vNM preferences of either player: $u_1(x) = ax^2 + (1-a)x$, and $u_2(x) = 1 - ax^2 - (1-a)x$, obtain and compare the divisions corresponding to the Nash bargaining solution in the following cases: (a) when $a = 0$; (b) when $a = 1$.

5. Check which of the conditions that characterize the Nash bargaining solution are satisfied by the following solutions.

   (a) The 'egalitarian' solution: choose the feasible payoff vector for which the utility gains with respect to the status quo are equal for all players and those gains are maximal. Formally,

   $$\Phi(D,d) := d + \bar{\mu}\mathbf{1},$$

   where $\bar{\mu} := \max\{\mu : d + \mu\mathbf{1} \in D\}$ and $\mathbf{1} = (1,\dots,1) \in \mathbb{R}^N$.

   (b) The 'utilitarian' solution: choose the feasible payoff vector for which the sum of the gains is maximal. Formally,

   $$\Phi(D,d) := \arg\max_{x \in D_d} \sum_{i \in N} (x_i - d_i).$$

6. Calculate the egalitarian solution and the utilitarian solution (see Exercise 5) of the bargaining problems in Exercises 2 and 3.

7. Check which of the conditions that characterize the Shapley value are satisfied by the following values.

   (a) For all $i \in N$, $\Phi_i(v) := \frac{v(N)}{n}$. (Allocate $v(N)$ in the egalitarian way.)

   (b) For all $i \in N$, $\Phi_i(v) := v(N) - v(N \setminus i)$. (Allocate to each player his/her marginal contribution to $v(N)$.)

   (c) Give 0 to every null player and allocate $v(N)$ in an egalitarian way among the non-null players. Allocate 0 to every null player and allocate $v(N)$ in an egalitarian way among the non-null players.

Seminal papers, seminal ambiguities

(d) For all $i \in N$,

$$\Phi_i(v) := \begin{cases} v(\{1\}), & \text{if } i = 1, \\ v(\{1, 2, \ldots, i\}) - v(\{1, 2, \ldots, i-1\}), & \text{if } i > 1. \end{cases}$$

(Let the players join in a fixed order $1, 2, \ldots, n$, and each player receives his/her marginal contribution to the coalition he/she joins.)

8. For each three-person voting rule, calculate the Shapley–Shubik index and compare it with the number of swings.

3 | 'Take-it-or-leave-it' committees[29]

This chapter is concerned with what was introduced in Section 2.2 as 'take-it-or-leave-it' committees. The take-it-or-leave-it scenario is explained in detail in Section 3.1. In Section 3.2 we introduce the basic notions of ex post (i.e. after a vote) success and decisiveness. Section 3.3 introduces the probabilistic representation of voters' behaviour or preferences, which provides a formal setting for addressing the likelihood of decisions being passed, the likelihood of success and that of decisiveness in Section 3.4. The normative goal leads to the assumption that all vote configurations are equally probable, which provides a common perspective in which several 'power indices' in the literature are seen as assessments of the likelihood of being decisive or of being successful in a take-it-or-leave-it committee (Section 3.5). The conceptual and analytical distinction between the notions of success and decisiveness is discussed in Section 3.6, where arguments in support of the notion of success as the relevant concept in the take-it-or-leave-it scenario are given. The question of the optimal voting rule in a take-it-or-leave-it committee is addressed in Section 3.7. Two points of view are considered: egalitarianism and utilitarianism, and the recommendations that stem from each of them are presented. The question of the optimal voting rule from either point of view is also addressed in Section 3.8 for committees of representatives.

3.1 The take-it-or-leave-it scenario

We consider voting situations in which a set of voters or committee handles collective decision-making by means of a voting rule, and is entitled only to vote for or against proposals submitted to it by an external agency. It is assumed that there is no possibility of the committee amending or modifying the proposals: hence the name

[29] The material from Sections 3.1–3.6 is partly drawn from [45] and [38].

52

'take-it-or-leave-it' committees. Moreover, we assume that there is no room either for linking decisions on different proposals. This rules out agreements among members of the committee of the type 'I'll vote "yes" on this issue even though I'd prefer it to be rejected if you vote "yes" on this other issue that is more important to me'. It is also assumed that no voter is indifferent between acceptance and rejection. In these conditions there is no room for negotiating or bargaining, nor for forming coalitions. In other words, *there is no room for strategic considerations*. The best any voter can do is to vote 'yes' or 'no' according to his/her preferred outcome (acceptance or rejection). Approximate examples of this type of situation could be a referendum or an academic committee that decides by a vote of its members on whether to admit students to a doctoral programme or a summer school without capacity constraints. In fact, such crisp conditions as the ones stated above are seldom found in real-world committees, where there is usually some margin either to link decisions that are separate and only formally independent, or to modify proposals to some extent. In other words, in real-world voting situations there is usually some room for negotiation. Nevertheless, this 'pure' take-it-or-leave-it scenario, free from ambiguity, provides a point of view that allows for a clear interpretation of some 'power indices' in the literature, as well as the existence of some relevant overlooked 'gaps' in the different aspects assessed by them. This point of view is complemented by the picture obtained from the alternative situation considered in Chapter 4, which addresses the game-theoretic analysis of 'pure' bargaining committees.

As mentioned in Section 2.2, a common ingredient in the models of both types of voting situation is the voting rule. Thus in this chapter, using the notation and terminology introduced in Section 1.3, N labels the seats of an N-voting rule $\mathcal{W}$ that specifies the outcome (acceptance or rejection) after a vote in a take-it-or-leave-it committee of n members.

In a pure take-it-or-leave-it situation several issues can be addressed. For instance, the ease with which proposals are accepted or rejected, the likelihood of a voter obtaining the result that he/she voted for and the likelihood of a voter being decisive in a vote. Obviously, the voting rule affects these probabilities. Intuition suggests that it is easier to pass a proposal under a simple majority than under the unanimity rule. Similarly, in a dictatorship the dictator always gets the result that he/she votes for and is always decisive, while the rest of the voters

54 *Voting and Collective Decision-Making*

can get the outcome they vote for only if their votes coincide with the dictator's, but they are never decisive. But dictatorship is a very special case as knowledge of the voting rule is not in general sufficient to assess the likelihood of these issues. They all depend on the voting rule and also on the voters' votes.

3.2 Success and decisiveness in a vote

To pin down these notions with more precision, let us bring the voters onto the scene and label them with the labels of their respective seats $(1, 2, \ldots, n)$. First let us consider the situation ex post, that is, once they have voted on a given proposal, a vote configuration has emerged, and the voting rule has prescribed the final outcome, i.e. passage or rejection of the proposal. A distinction can be made between voters. If the proposal is accepted (rejected), those voters who have voted in favour (against) are satisfied with the result, while the others are not. Following Barry[30] [8], we will say that they have been successful. Thus, being *successful* means obtaining the outcome – acceptance or rejection – that one voted for. We also say that a successful voter has been *decisive* in a vote if his/her vote was crucial: i.e., had he/she changed his/her vote the outcome would have been different.

Definition 9 *After a decision is made according to an N-voting rule* $\mathcal{W}$, *if the resulting configuration of votes is S,*

(i) *Voter i is said to have been successful if the decision coincides with voter i's vote, i.e. iff*

$$(i \in S \in \mathcal{W}) \text{ or } (i \notin S \notin \mathcal{W}). \tag{12}$$

(ii) *Voter i is said to have been decisive, if he/she was successful and his/her vote was critical to that success, i.e. iff*

$$(i \in S \in \mathcal{W} \text{ and } S \backslash i \notin \mathcal{W}) \text{ or } (i \notin S \notin \mathcal{W} \text{ and } S \cup i \in \mathcal{W}). \tag{13}$$

These notions are indeed '*ex post*': they depend on the voting rule used to make decisions and the resulting vote configuration *after* a vote is cast. To reflect this, we will say that '*i* is (is not) successful in

---

[30] The notion can be traced back under different names to [68] or [70] (see also [14] and [83]).

'Take-it-or-leave-it' committees   55

(W, S)', or 'i is (is not) decisive in (W, S)'. Also note that these are Boolean notions, in the sense that there is *no quantification*: a voter merely may or may not be successful or decisive in a vote.

Barry [8] also uses the notion of 'luck', considering a successful voter who is not decisive as 'lucky'. Formally, voter i is said to have been (ex post) 'lucky'[31] (for short, 'i is lucky in (W, S)'), *iff*

$$(i \in S \in W \text{ and } S \backslash i \in W) \text{ or } (i \notin S \notin W \text{ and } S \cup i \notin W).$$

Thus we have the obvious relationship:

$$i \text{ is successful in } (W, S) \Leftrightarrow \big[(i \text{ is decisive in } (W, S))$$
$$\underline{\vee}(i \text{ is 'lucky' in } (W, S))\big],$$

where '$\underline{\vee}$' stands for an exclusive 'or'.

Can these notions be extended *ex ante*, that is, once voters have occupied their seats but before the decision is made? Except for the trivial case where the voting configuration that will emerge is known with certainty (in which case ex ante becomes anticipated ex post), a meaningful assessment of success and decisiveness ex ante requires additional information, possibly imperfect, about voters' behaviour.

3.3 Preferences, behaviour and probabilities

As has been already pointed out, in a pure take-it-or-leave-it situation there is no room for strategic considerations: the best a voter can do is to vote in accordance with his/her preferred outcome. In other words, *rational behaviour follows immediately from preferences*. Uncertainty about voters' behaviour or preferences can be formally treated and represented in probabilistic terms by means of a probability distribution over all possible vote configurations. That is, we assume that we know—or at least have an estimate of—the probability of occurrence of any vote configuration that may arise. In other words, the elementary events are the vote configurations in 2^N. As their number is finite (2^n), we can represent any such probability distribution by a map

---

[31] For a thorough discussion of the different uses of the term 'luck', see [59] pp. xxxvii–xli.

$p_N : 2^N \to \mathbb{R}$, that associates with each vote configuration S its probability of occurrence $p_N(S)$, i.e. $p_N(S)$ gives the probability that voters in S will vote 'yes', and those in $N \backslash S$ will vote 'no'. To keep notation as simple as possible below, when N is clear from the context we will write p. Of course, $0 \leq p(S) \leq 1$ for any $S \subseteq N$, and $\sum_{S \subseteq N} p(S) = 1$.

The probability of i voting 'yes' is denoted by $\gamma_i(p)$, that is

$$\gamma_i(p) := \text{Prob } (i \text{ votes 'yes'}) = \sum_{S:i \in S} p(S).$$

Let P_N denote the set of all distributions of probability over 2^N. This set can be interpreted as the set of all conceivable *voting behaviours* or preference profiles of n voters within the present probabilistic setting.

The following special distributions of probability will be considered. A distribution is *anonymous* if the probability of a vote configuration depends only on the number of 'yes'-voters, that is, $p(S) = p(T)$ whenever $s = t$. A distribution is *independent* if each voter i independently votes 'yes' with probability t_i and 'no' with probability $(1 - t_i)$. The probability of the configuration S is then given by

$$p(S) = \prod_{i \in S} t_i \prod_{j \in N \backslash S} (1 - t_j).$$

As the reader can easily check, these two conditions are independent, and if a distribution is both *anonymous* and *independent* then each voter independently votes 'yes' with a probability t and 'no' with probability $(1 - t)$, so that the probability of the configuration S is then given by

$$p(S) = t^s (1 - t)^{n-s}.$$

A special case that will play a central role is when all vote configurations have the same probability, denoted by p^*. That is,

$$p^*(S) = \frac{1}{2^n} \quad \text{for all configurations } S \subseteq N.$$

This is equivalent to assuming that each voter, independently of the others, votes 'yes' with probability 1/2, and votes 'no' with probability 1/2. Thus this probability accumulates all symmetries: it is anonymous and independent, with equal inclination towards 'yes' and 'no'.

3.4 Success and decisiveness ex ante

Assume that a probability distribution over vote configurations p enters the picture as a second input besides the voting rule $\mathcal{W}$ that governs decisions in a take-it-or-leave-it committee. In a *voting situation* thus described by pair $(\mathcal{W}, p)$ the *ease of passing proposals* or probability of acceptance is given by

$$\alpha(\mathcal{W}, p) := \text{Prob (acceptance)} = \sum_{S: S \in \mathcal{W}} p(S). \tag{14}$$

Furthermore, success and decisiveness can be defined ex ante. It suffices to replace the sure configuration S by the random vote configuration specified by p in ex post definitions (12) and (13). This yields the following extension of these concepts.

Definition 10 *Let $(\mathcal{W}, p)$ be an N-voting situation, where $\mathcal{W}$ is the voting rule for making decisions and $p \in \mathbf{P}_N$ is the probability distribution over vote configurations, and let $i \in N$:*

(i) *Voter i's (ex ante) success is the probability that i is successful:*

$$\Omega_i(\mathcal{W}, p) := \text{Prob} \left(i \text{ is successful} \right) = \sum_{S: i \in S \in \mathcal{W}} p(S) + \sum_{T: i \notin T \notin \mathcal{W}} p(T).$$
$$\tag{15}$$

(ii) *Voter i's (ex ante) decisiveness is the probability that i is decisive:*

$$\Phi_i(\mathcal{W}, p) := \text{Prob} \left(i \text{ is decisive} \right) = \sum_{\substack{S: i \in S \in \mathcal{W} \\ S \setminus i \notin \mathcal{W}}} p(S) + \sum_{\substack{T: i \notin T \notin \mathcal{W} \\ T \cup i \in \mathcal{W}}} p(T).$$
$$\tag{16}$$

Note that strictly speaking i's decisiveness depends only on the other voters' behaviour, not on his/her own. To see this, voter i's decisiveness can be rewritten as

$$\Phi_i(\mathcal{W}, p) = \sum_{\substack{S: i \in S \in \mathcal{W} \\ S \setminus i \notin \mathcal{W}}} (p(S) + p(S \setminus i)).$$

Observe that for each S, $p(S) + p(S\backslash i)$ is the probability of all voters in $S\backslash i$ voting 'yes' and those in $N\backslash S$ voting 'no'. In this case, whatever voter i's vote, he/she is decisive, while Ω_i depends on all voters' behaviour. Therefore there is no way to derive one of these notions from the other, and the only relations in general are the obvious $\Phi_i(W, p) \leq \Omega_i(W, p)$ and Barry's [8] equation: 'Success' = 'Decisiveness' + 'Luck', which remains valid in a much more precise and general version:

$$\Omega_i(W, p) = \Phi_i(W, p) + \Lambda_i(W, p),$$

where $\Lambda_i(W, p)$ denotes voter i's (ex ante) 'luck' or probability of being 'lucky', that is:

$$\Lambda_i(W, p) := \sum_{\substack{S:i\in S \\ S\backslash i \in W}} p(S) + \sum_{\substack{S:i\notin S \\ S\cup i\notin W}} p(S).$$

Definition (15) of $\Omega_i(W, p)$ (the same occurs with (16) for $\Phi_i(W, p)$) aggregates as equivalent the likelihood of being successful in case of voting 'yes' and in case of voting 'no'. In some cases it is interesting to consider the case in which the relative importance that voters attach to having a proposal rejected or accepted in accordance with their preferences is not the same. We introduce the following notation:

$$\Omega_i^+(W, p) := \text{Prob }\left(i \text{ is successful \& } i \text{ votes 'yes'}\right) = \sum_{S:i\in S\in W} p(S),$$

$$\Omega_i^-(W, p) := \text{Prob }\left(i \text{ is successful \& } i \text{ votes 'no'}\right) = \sum_{T:i\notin T\notin W} p(T),$$

so that voter i's probability of success is

$$\Omega_i(W, p) = \Omega_i^+(W, p) + \Omega_i^-(W, p). \tag{17}$$

We refer to $\Omega_i^+(W, p)$ as *positive success*, and to $\Omega_i^-(W, p)$ as *negative success*. Voter i's probability of being decisive can be decomposed in a similar way.

Conditional probabilities of success and decisiveness under different conditions are also meaningful. The conditional probability of event A given event B, that is, the probability of A given that B is sure, is given by

$$P(A \mid B) = \frac{P(A \cap B)}{P(B)}.$$

Here A may stand for 'voter i is successful/decisive' and B is the condition[32]. The following questions arise naturally in this context:

Q.1: What is voter i's conditional probability of success (decisiveness), given that voter i votes in favour of (against) the proposal?

Q.2: What is voter i's conditional probability of success (decisiveness), given that the proposal is accepted (rejected)?

This makes for eight possible conditional probabilities[33]. A little notation is necessary. We will superindex the measures (Ω_i or Φ_i) with the condition. The superindex '$i+$' ('$i-$') expresses the condition 'given that i votes "yes" ("no")'. So the answers to Q.1 are given by Ω_i^{i+}, Φ_i^{i+}, Ω_i^{i-} and Φ_i^{i-}, respectively[34]. The superindex 'Acc' ('Rej') expresses the condition 'given that the proposal is accepted (rejected)'. Thus the answers to Q.2 are given by Ω_i^{Acc}, Φ_i^{Acc}, Ω_i^{Rej} and Φ_i^{Rej}, respectively.

As an illustration, we formulate two of them explicitly. Voter i's conditional probability of being decisive given that voter i votes in favour of the proposal, is given by

$$\Phi_i^{i+}(\mathcal{W},p) = \text{Prob}\ (i \text{ is decisive} \mid i \text{ votes 'yes'}) = \frac{1}{\gamma_i(p)} \sum_{\substack{S:i\in S\in\mathcal{W} \\ S\setminus i\notin\mathcal{W}}} p(S).$$

Voter i's conditional probability of success given that the proposal is accepted, is given by

$$\Omega_i^{Acc}(\mathcal{W},p) = \text{Prob}\ (i \text{ is successful} \mid \text{acceptance}) = \frac{1}{\alpha(\mathcal{W},p)} \sum_{S:i\in S\in\mathcal{W}} p(S).$$

---

[32] It is implicitly assumed that $p(B) \neq 0$ whenever we refer to a conditional probability for condition B.

[33] Of course, other questions involving different conditions (e.g. conditional to 'i and j voted the same', etc.) are possible. We highlight these particular questions because some power measures proposed in the literature can be reinterpreted as one of these conditional probabilities for a particular probability distribution.

[34] Note the difference between Ω_i^{i+} and Ω_i^+, related by

$$\Omega_i^+(\mathcal{W},p) = \gamma_i(p)\Omega_i^{i+}(\mathcal{W},p).$$

60 *Voting and Collective Decision-Making*

Table 3.1. *Ten different unconditional and conditional probabilities of success and decisiveness*

Condition:	none	i votes 'yes'	i votes 'no'	acceptance	rejection
Success	Ω_i	Ω_i^{i+}	Ω_i^{i-}	Ω_i^{Acc}	Ω_i^{Rej}
Decisiveness	Φ_i	Φ_i^{i+}	Φ_i^{i-}	Φ_i^{Acc}	Φ_i^{Rej}

The ten different unconditional and conditional probabilities of success and of decisiveness considered so far are summarized in Table 3.1.

They can all be used in principle for a *positive* or *descriptive* evaluation of a voting situation if an estimate of the voters' voting behaviour/preferences (i.e. of p) is available. In each particular real-world case the better the estimate of the probability distribution over vote configurations, the better the measure of actual success or decisiveness. In the next section, in which we set $p = p^*$ with normative purposes, we will see how seven out of these ten variants (eight out of eleven if we include $\alpha(\mathcal{W}, p)$) are related to power indices. Section 3.6 discusses the difference between success and decisiveness and their different conditional variants.

3.5 A priori assessments based on the voting rule

The probabilistic assessments considered in the previous section can be used for *normative* purposes in the evaluation of a voting rule, irrespective of which voters occupy the seats, or for the comparison of different rules in the design of decision-making procedures. In this case, the particular personality or preferences of the voters or, equivalently in a pure take-it-or-leave-it scenario, their actual patterns of behaviour, *should not* be taken into account. Then we arrive at a logical deadlock: in our setup, measurement is based on a probability distribution over vote configurations, but the relevant information for estimating this probability has to be ignored. What can be done? One way out of the difficulty is to assume that all vote configurations are equally probable a priori:

$$p^*(S) := \frac{1}{2^n} \quad \text{for any configuration } S \subseteq N.$$

'Take-it-or-leave-it' committees

This 'unbiased' choice seems consistent with the normative point of view according to which any information beyond the voting rule itself should be ignored. This a priori probabilistic model of behaviour is not beyond argument. It has often been criticized, even when a normative point of view is assumed. Other models have been considered[35], but this one seems to us reasonable and the simplest, and it makes sense when the objective is *not to assess a particular voting situation but the voting rule itself*, keeping any further information behind a 'veil of ignorance'.

For this special, totally symmetric, distribution of probability some special relations that we use later hold. One concerns $\alpha(\mathcal{W}, p^*)$ (see (14)), which can be interpreted as an index of the a priori ease of passing proposals with rule $\mathcal{W}$. For all voting rules we have

$$\alpha(\mathcal{W}, p^*) \leq \frac{1}{2}. \tag{18}$$

We also have

$$\Omega_i^+(\mathcal{W}, p^*) = 0.5\Omega_i(\mathcal{W}, p^*) + 0.5\alpha(\mathcal{W}, p^*) - 0.25, \tag{19}$$

$$\Omega_i^-(\mathcal{W}, p^*) = 0.5\Omega_i(\mathcal{W}, p^*) - 0.5\alpha(\mathcal{W}, p^*) + 0.25. \tag{20}$$

The following relationship, as will be commented later (see 3.6.1), is the source of some confusion between success and decisiveness:

$$\Omega_i(\mathcal{W}, p^*) = 0.5 + 0.5\Phi_i(\mathcal{W}, p^*). \tag{21}$$

Finally, unconditional decisiveness and conditional decisiveness given a positive vote or given a negative vote are indistinguishable:

$$\Phi_i(\mathcal{W}, p^*) = \Phi_i^{i+}(\mathcal{W}, p^*) = \Phi_i^{i-}(\mathcal{W}, p^*). \tag{22}$$

But it is worth remarking that these relationships do not hold in general[36] for $p \neq p^*$.

---

[35] See for instance [82].

[36] Relationship (22) holds for all p such that the vote of every voter is independent from the vote of the remaining voters.

Some 'power indices' in the literature can be seen as the particularization of some of the measures introduced in the previous section (Table 3.1) for this specific probability distribution. We review them here. Readers not interested in this review can skip the rest of this section and proceed to Section 3.6.

3.5.1 Rae index

Rae [70] studies the symmetric voting rule that maximizes the correspondence between a single anonymous individual vote and the collective decision. He defines an index of such a correspondence based on two assumptions[37]: the votes are independent from one another, and each voter votes 'yes' with probability 1/2, and votes 'no' with probability 1/2. Dubey and Shapley [20] suggest that the index can be generalized to any voting rule and for any voter, leading to what can be referred to as the *Rae index*, given by

$$\text{Rae}_i(\mathcal{W}) := \frac{\#\{S : i \in S \in \mathcal{W}\}}{2^n} + \frac{\#\{S : i \notin S \notin \mathcal{W}\}}{2^n}$$
$$= \sum_{S : i \in S \in \mathcal{W}} p^*(S) + \sum_{S : i \notin S \notin \mathcal{W}} p^*(S).$$

That is, Rae's index of a player i for a given rule is i's probability of success (15) for the particular distribution p^*:

$$\text{Rae}_i(\mathcal{W}) = \Omega_i(\mathcal{W}, p^*).$$

3.5.2 Banzhaf(–Penrose) index

Banzhaf's [4] original or 'raw' index (see 2.1.4) for a seat i and voting rule $\mathcal{W}$ is given by

$$\text{rawBz}_i(\mathcal{W}) := \text{number of winning configurations in which}$$
$$i \text{ is decisive.}$$

---

[37] In fact he makes a third assumption, namely that the probability of no member supporting the proposal is zero. But this must be dropped because under the other conditions the probability of no one supporting the proposal is necessarily $1/2^n$.

Dubey and Shapley [20] (see also [67]) proposed the following normalization of this index as a ratio:

$$\text{Bz}_i(\mathcal{W}) = \frac{\text{number of winning configurations in which } i \text{ is decisive}}{\text{total number of voting configurations containing } i}.$$

Therefore in the current notation the *Banzhaf index* is $\text{Bz}_i(\mathcal{W}) = \Phi_i^{i+}(\mathcal{W}, p^*)$. Thus, by (22), we have

$$\text{Bz}_i(\mathcal{W}) = \Phi_i(\mathcal{W}, p^*) = \Phi_i^{i+}(\mathcal{W}, p^*) = \Phi_i^{i-}(\mathcal{W}, p^*). \tag{23}$$

This provides three alternative interpretations of the Banzhaf index as an expectation of being decisive. Also note the relationship with the Rae index that emerges by just rewriting (21):

$$\text{Rae}_i(\mathcal{W}) = 0.5 + 0.5\text{Bz}_i(\mathcal{W}). \tag{24}$$

This relationship was anticipated by Penrose [68], who, constraining attention to weighted majority rules and assuming that all vote configurations are equally probable, writes: '*the power of the individual vote can be measured by the amount by which his chance of being on the winning side exceeds one half. The power, thus defined, is the same as half the likelihood of a situation in which an individual vote can be decisive.*' Penrose's measure of power is then $0.5\text{Bz}_i(\mathcal{W})$. For this reason the Banzhaf index is sometimes referred to as Penrose or Banzhaf–Penrose index.

3.5.3 Coleman indices

Coleman [15, 16] defines three different indices in terms of ratios. The '*power of a collectivity to act*' measures the ease of decision-making by means of a voting rule $\mathcal{W}$, and is given by

$$A(\mathcal{W}) = \frac{\text{number of winning configurations}}{\text{total number of voting configurations}}.$$

Voter i's '*Coleman index to prevent*' action (Col_i^{P}) is given by

$$\text{Col}_i^{\text{P}}(\mathcal{W}) = \frac{\text{number of winning configurations in which } i \text{ is decisive}}{\text{total number of winning configurations}},$$

while voter i's '*Coleman index to initiate*' action $(\mathrm{Col}_i^{\mathrm{I}})$ is given by

$$\mathrm{Col}_i^{\mathrm{I}}(\mathcal{W}) = \frac{\text{number of losing configurations in which } i \text{ is decisive}}{\text{total number of losing configurations}}.$$

All three indices can be reinterpreted in probabilistic terms as

$$A(\mathcal{W}) = \alpha(\mathcal{W}, p^*),$$

$$\mathrm{Col}_i^{\mathrm{P}}(\mathcal{W}) = \Phi_i^{\mathrm{Acc}}(\mathcal{W}, p^*),$$

$$\mathrm{Col}_i^{\mathrm{I}}(\mathcal{W}) = \Phi_i^{\mathrm{Rej}}(\mathcal{W}, p^*).$$

The difference between the Coleman indices and the Banzhaf index is clear. They all measure the likelihood of decisiveness assuming all vote configurations to be equally probable, but the conditions are different. Still, they are often confused. The origin of the confusion lies in the fact that their *normalizations* coincide, giving rise to the so-called 'Banzhaf–Coleman' index. In formula, we have the following relation for any voting rule $\mathcal{W}$:

$$\frac{\mathrm{Bz}_i(\mathcal{W})}{\sum_{j\in N}\mathrm{Bz}_j(\mathcal{W})} = \frac{\mathrm{Col}_i^{\mathrm{P}}(\mathcal{W})}{\sum_{j\in N}\mathrm{Col}_j^{\mathrm{P}}(\mathcal{W})} = \frac{\mathrm{Col}_i^{\mathrm{I}}(\mathcal{W})}{\sum_{j\in N}\mathrm{Col}_j^{\mathrm{I}}(\mathcal{W})}.$$

This coincidence should serve only as a warning against the common practice of normalizing these indices, since it results in their losing their probabilistic interpretation. Normalization also makes the comparison of different rules problematic: it is as if percentages of cakes of different sizes were compared. Also note that in general, for arbitrary probability distributions, the normalizations of $\Phi_i(\mathcal{W}, p)$, $\Phi_i^{\mathrm{Acc}}(\mathcal{W}, p)$, and $\Phi_i^{\mathrm{Rej}}(\mathcal{W}, p)$ do not coincide.

The Coleman indices have recently attracted more attention than was formerly been paid to them[38]. This recent upsurge in interest may be related to the intuition, or the evidence in some cases, of the different attitude of voters towards the prospect of having the proposals they support accepted, and the prospect of having the proposals they dislike rejected[39]. This nuance is missed by the Banzhaf index.

---

[38] In particular in the context of the European Council of Ministers (see for instance [53]).

[39] See for instance [56].

By (23), unconditional decisiveness of a voter, as well as conditional decisiveness given he/she votes 'yes' or given he/she votes 'no' collapse in the Banzhaf index. The Coleman's indices have sometimes been used as a remedy in a somewhat confusing attempt to distinguish what is indistinguishable from the a priori decisiveness point of view. Indeed,

$$\mathrm{Col}_i^{\mathrm{P}}(\mathcal{W}) = \Phi_i^{\mathrm{Acc}}(\mathcal{W}, p^*) \neq \Phi_i^{\mathrm{Rej}}(\mathcal{W}, p^*) = \mathrm{Col}_i^{\mathrm{I}}(\mathcal{W}).$$

This is confusing for two reasons. First, if the prospects mentioned above are to be evaluated, the right condition seems to be 'given that voter i supports (rejects) the proposal' (a condition of which a voter has more knowledge than whether the proposal will be accepted or not). Second, in Coleman indices the condition 'the proposal is accepted (rejected)' varies in probability with the rule. This makes the comparison of these indices for different rules problematic (we come back to this in 3.6.2).

3.5.4 König and Bräuninger's inclusiveness index

More recently König and Bräuninger [34] define voter i's '*inclusiveness*' as the ratio of winning configurations containing i:

$$\mathrm{KB}_i(\mathcal{W}) := \frac{\text{number of winning configurations containing } i}{\text{total number of winning configurations}},$$

which can be rewritten as

$$\mathrm{KB}_i(\mathcal{W}) = \Omega_i^{\mathrm{Acc}}(\mathcal{W}, p^*).$$

The last comments about the Coleman indices apply also to König and Bräuninger's inclusiveness. An additional weakness of König and Bräuninger's index is that information is lost by disregarding the natural pair of $\Omega_i^{\mathrm{Acc}}(\mathcal{W}, p^*)$, which is $\Omega_i^{\mathrm{Rej}}(\mathcal{W}, p^*)$.

3.5.5 Summary and remarks

The following table summarizes the relationships between these 'power indices' and the current probabilistic model. *Assuming the probability distribution $p = p^*$*, Table 3.1 becomes Table 3.2.

66 — Voting and Collective Decision-Making

Table 3.2. *Relationships between 'power indices' and the current probabilistic model*

Condition:	none	i votes 'yes'	i votes 'no'	acceptance	rejection
Success	$\mathrm{Rae}_i(\mathcal{W})$	Ω_i^{i+}	Ω_i^{i-}	$\mathrm{KB}_i(\mathcal{W})$	Ω_i^{Rej}
Decisiveness	$\mathrm{Bz}_i(\mathcal{W})$	$\mathrm{Bz}_i(\mathcal{W})$	$\mathrm{Bz}_i(\mathcal{W})$	$\mathrm{Col}_i^{\mathrm{P}}(\mathcal{W})$	$\mathrm{Col}_i^{\mathrm{I}}(\mathcal{W})$

These 'power indices,' can thus be jointly justified as a priori assessments of different aspects of the voting rule itself on the same normative grounds, based on the probability distribution that assigns the same probability to all vote configurations.

Table 3.2 still raises some further questions. First, the question of the interest for applications of the indices reviewed. In this respect the main issue is that of which notion should be given preeminence in a take-it-or-leave-it committee: success or decisiveness? In the next section we give arguments in support of success as the relevant notion in a pure take-it-or-leave-it environment. We also deal with the overlooked cells in Table 3.2, that is, $\Omega_i^{i+}(\mathcal{W}, p^*)$ and $\Omega_i^{i-}(\mathcal{W}, p^*)$.

There is also the question of the power indices that do *not* appear in Table 3.2 and their possible relation with the two-ingredient model of a take-it-or-leave-it committee. Some power indices hardly fit or do not enter the picture at all. Most of them seek to measure 'power' understood as decisiveness, which, as mentioned above, we believe to be secondary in pure take-it-or-leave-it situations. But their interpretation in this scenario is problematic (see [45]).

As briefly commented at the end of Section 2.1.6, in view of the proliferation of power indices, some authors propose the use of paradoxes/postulates to select among them. In fact, most of these postulates embody confusing desiderata in which the idea of success and decisiveness are conflated. In [47] the ex ante success and decisiveness for arbitrary probability distributions p's are tested against some of the best known voting power postulates. It is shown that in all cases in which a 'paradox' may occur it can be explained in clear and simple terms, so that the paradoxes dissipate as such. Surprisingly enough success, unavoidably intermingled with decisiveness in any pre-conceptual notion of voting power, behaves even better with respect to some postulates in principle intended for measures of decisiveness.

3.6 Success versus decisiveness

3.6.1 Success is the issue in a take-it-or-leave-it scenario

As commented in Section 2.2, considerable vagueness in the specification of the voting situation considered underlies most of the literature on 'voting power'. On such vague grounds the notion of decisiveness has *de facto* been widely accepted as the right basis for the formalization of a measure of 'voting power'. Shapley and Shubik's interpretation of their index as the probability of being 'pivotal' in the making of a decision contributed to this choice. Banzhaf's and Coleman's indices, in spite of their criticism of Shapley–Shubik's index, are also evaluations of decisiveness. Even Penrose concentrates on decisiveness as the part of success that can be credited to the voter.

In spite of this dominant view, some authors have raised doubts as to the relevance of this interpretation of 'power' as decisiveness, suggesting as more relevant the notion of satisfaction or success. That is, focusing on the likelihood of obtaining the result that one votes for irrespective of whether one's vote is crucial for it or not. Rae was the first to take an interest in a measure of success for symmetric voting rules. A few other authors have since also paid attention to the notion of success[40].

Nevertheless, in general, the notion of success has usually been either overlooked or considered as just a sort of secondary ingredient of decisiveness. The difference between the two notions should be obvious, unless firmly entrenched mental habits prevent one from perceiving it. The confusion is partly due to relationship (24) ((21) in our notation) anticipated in [68] and proved in [20]. This relationship may give the impression that success and decisiveness are two faces of the same coin[41], but it can be shown[42] that $\Omega_i(W,p) = 0.5 + 0.5\Phi_i(W,p)$ holds for all W if and *only if $p = p^*$*, i.e. under the assumption that *all vote configurations are equally probable*. Thus, in general,

$$\Omega_i(W,p) \neq 0.5 + 0.5\Phi_i(W,p),$$

---

[40] See, for instance, [14, 8, 83], and more recently [34, 10, 38] .

[41] For instance, Hosli and Machover [31] claim that '*these two concepts of voting power, far from being opposed to each other, are virtually identical, and differ only in using a different scale of measurement*'.

[42] See [38].

so success and decisiveness are not only conceptually different but also analytically independent as there is no general way to derive one concept from the other.

The following example shows how even for rather symmetric behaviour, as described by anonymous and independent probability distributions, two voting rules can be differently ranked from these two points of view.

Example 3.1: Consider a three-member committee in which each member votes 'yes' in an independent way with probability 3/4, so that $p(S) = (3/4)^s(1/4)^{n-s}$. Compare the simple majority rule $(\mathcal{W}^{SM})$ and the unanimity rule $(\mathcal{W}^N)$ for this distribution of probability. We have

$$\Omega_i(\mathcal{W}^{SM}, p) = 52/64, \quad \text{and} \quad \Omega_i(\mathcal{W}^N, p) = 43/64,$$

$$\Phi_i(\mathcal{W}^{SM}, p) = 24/64, \quad \text{and} \quad \Phi_i(\mathcal{W}^N, p) = 36/64.$$

Thus

$$\Omega_i(\mathcal{W}^{SM}, p) > \Omega_i(\mathcal{W}^N, p),$$

while

$$\Phi_i(\mathcal{W}^{SM}, p) < \Phi_i(\mathcal{W}^N, p).$$

Thus, voter i will surely prefer the simple majority if he/she prioritizes maximizing her/his likelihood of success while he/she will prefer unanimity if he/she prioritizes decisiveness.

With the conceptual and analytical difference between these two notions settled, let us come back to the basic issue: Which is more important, success or decisiveness? Once again, as argued in Section 2.2, the only way to seriously address this and other basic issues is by specifying clearly the situation that one is referring to. In this case we are concerned with a pure take-it-or-leave-it scenario. In such a context, from the voters' point of view, what really matters? Is it the likelihood of obtaining the result that one voted for? Or is it the likelihood of obtaining the result that one voted for and being crucial for it? If a voter is faced with such a choice in a pure take-it-or-leave-it situation, it seems clear that he/she will surely be more likely to prefer to obtain with higher probability the outcome that he/she votes for over

'*Take-it-or-leave-it*' committees 69

being decisive for it with a higher probability. Consider Example 3.1. If the probability distribution actually expresses the common beliefs of the members of the committee, no doubt a rational individual would prefer the decision to be made by means of the simple majority rule in spite of the fact that the probability of being decisive is lower than with the unanimity rule[43]. Why should he/she care about the likelihood of being decisive in a situation in which there is no place for strategic considerations, as argued in Section 3.1? Only the possibility of strategic use of a decisive position can make this relevant, but in a pure take-it-or-leave-it environment there is no such possibility.

In short, *in a pure take-it-or-leave-it situation success is certainly the relevant issue, while decisiveness is immaterial.* This is a departure from the dominant underlying assumption in traditional voting power literature. As we will see in the next two sections, some relatively popular recommendations about 'the best voting' rule in some contexts appear differently in this light.

3.6.2 Conditional success

With this basic issue settled, what can be said about the conditional variants of success in Tables 3.1 and 3.2? Conditional evaluations of likelihood of success can also be informative, as well as relevant for comparison of voting rules. In each vote each voter knows his/her particular vote, but he/she is in general uncertain about whether the proposal will be accepted or rejected. Therefore the information provided by Ω_i^{i+} and Ω_i^{i-} seems more interesting than that given by the other conditional variants. Moreover the condition (i.e. acceptance or rejection) under which the conditional probability is calculated for Ω_i^{Acc} or Ω_i^{Rej} varies from one rule to another, which makes comparing rules based on Ω_i^{Acc} or Ω_i^{Rej} problematic.

In sum, the three probabilities, Ω_i, Ω_i^{i+}, and Ω_i^{i-}, along with α seem to be the most relevant notions in the context of take-it-or-leave-it committees. Each of these measures provides a criterion for comparing voting rules for a given p. Measure α provides a point of view

---

[43] At least assuming that success in a positive sense (i.e. of a 'yes' vote) and success in a negative sense (i.e. of a 'no' vote) are equally valued. If, for instance, more importance is given to the success of a 'no' vote, then unanimity may be preferred (we return to this point later).

detached from any particular voter. Now consider the others. If a voter is interested in maximizing the probability of obtaining the outcome that he/she votes for, then Ω_i is the criterion for voter i. But often voters are differently concerned with the prospect of obtaining the preferred result depending on the sense of their vote, i.e. acceptance or rejection. In particular, when rejection means maintaining the *status quo* there may be a bias in either direction, giving priority to Ω_i^{i+} or Ω_i^{i-}.

The following are important simple properties for the comparison of rules. If $\mathcal{W} \subseteq \mathcal{W}'$, then for any p,

$$\alpha(\mathcal{W}, p) \leq \alpha(\mathcal{W}', p),$$

and for any i and any p,

$$\Omega_i^{i+}(\mathcal{W}, p) \leq \Omega_i^{i+}(\mathcal{W}', p) \quad \text{and} \quad \Omega_i^{i-}(\mathcal{W}, p) \geq \Omega_i^{i-}(\mathcal{W}', p).$$

An example illustrates this: as $\mathcal{W}^{\mathrm{N}} \subseteq \mathcal{W}^{\mathrm{SM}}$, whatever the estimate of p, a voter only interested in getting a proposal accepted whenever he/she favours it will prefer the simple majority to unanimity, while a voter only interested in getting a proposal rejected whenever he/she votes against it will have the reverse preference.

Note however that, depending on p, we may have

$$\Omega_i(\mathcal{W}, p) \gtreqless \Omega_i(\mathcal{W}', p) \quad \text{and} \quad \Phi_i(\mathcal{W}, p) \gtreqless \Phi_i(\mathcal{W}', p).$$

3.6.3 Summary

From Table 3.1 (or Table 3.2 if we adopt the normative a priori evaluation), we are basically left with three probabilities, Ω_i^{i+} or Ω_i^{i-} and Ω_i, along with α, as the relevant parameters for the comparison of voting rules. A voter i with an estimate of the probability distribution p, who is indifferent between the positive or negative directions of success will prefer $\mathcal{W}$ to $\mathcal{W}'$ if his/her probability of obtaining his/her preferred outcome is greater with $\mathcal{W}$ than with $\mathcal{W}'$. Thus, such a preference can be expressed by

$$\mathcal{W} \succeq_i \mathcal{W}' \quad \text{iff} \quad \Omega_i(\mathcal{W}, p) \geq \Omega_i(\mathcal{W}', p).$$

Similarly, depending on the priority given to either direction of success, other preferences can be formulated by replacing Ω_i by Ω_i^{i+} or Ω_i^{i-}.

'Take-it-or-leave-it' committees   71

3.7 The choice of voting rule: egalitarianism and utilitarianism

So far, assuming a take-it-or-leave-it environment, we have considered different points of view that allow comparisons to be made between different voting rules, as well as between different seats in a given voting rule. These comparisons are based on the voting rule and the probability distribution over vote configurations. Some of these notions help provide a foundation for normative recommendations about the choice of voting rule in such committees. This is the issue addressed in this and the next sections.

These recommendations are normative in nature. Thus, taking a detached point of view and disregarding the actual preferences and voting behaviour of the individuals occupying the seats on the committee, we make the same assumption as in Section 3.5.

Assumption 1. *A priori all vote configurations are equally probable.*

Two principles which are commonly used to make normative assessments in different contexts are those of *egalitarianism* and *utilitarianism*[44]. The former holds that an equal treatment should be given to equals, or, in utility terms, the same utility level. The latter sets out to maximize the sum of the voters' utilities. Both criteria involve interpersonal comparison of utilities. In the first case comparability is a precondition for equalization; in the second, summing up presupposes some form of homogeneity.

In the framework considered so far, a take-it-or-leave-it situation is specified by a voting rule and a probability distribution over all possible voting behaviours or preference profiles. But in order to apply any of these principles, *utility has to be introduced* and for that the utility that voters obtain in a vote has to be specified. There are four possible situations for a voter to which utilities are to be attached. Namely, one must specify

$$u_i(\mathcal{W}, S) = \begin{cases} a_i, & \text{if } i \in S \in \mathcal{W}, \\ b_i, & \text{if } i \in S \notin \mathcal{W}, \\ c_i, & \text{if } i \notin S \notin \mathcal{W}, \\ d_i, & \text{if } i \notin S \in \mathcal{W}. \end{cases}$$

---

[44] The most prominent authors related to egalitarianism and utilitarianism are John Rawls [71] and Jeremy Bentham [11] respectively.

72   *Voting and Collective Decision-Making*

Obviously, if a voter is in favour of the proposal ($i \in S$), he/she prefers the proposal to be accepted ($S \in W$) rather than rejected ($S \notin W$): that is, $a_i > b_i$. Similarly we should have $c_i > d_i$. But the comparison between either of the first two situations (success or failure for a proposal that i supports) and either of the second two (success or failure for a proposal that i rejects) is not obvious: they are necessarily associated with different proposals[45] and the importance of proposals may differ from vote to vote and from voter to voter. As an initial simplification we assume the same utility for every voter in each case (i.e. a_i, b_i, c_i, d_i are the same for all i). This can be justified in terms of the *'veil of ignorance'* [71] point of view that underlies the normative approach that we assume. The relative value of pairs a, b and c, d still remains. If obtaining the preferred outcome, whether the proposal is supported or rejected, is the goal of every voter, success is the source of utility. But as voters may value success differently in the two directions their utility may differ in the case of acceptance or rejection, that is, it may be that $a < c$, $a = c$, or $a > c$. Although a similar distinction is possible for both forms of failure, we make the simplifying assumption that both are equally valued and set their utility to 0 (i.e. $b = d = 0$).

Assumption 2[46]. *Voters have expected utility preferences, and having success means λ units of utility ($0 \le \lambda \le 1$) for any voter if the voter voted 'yes', and $1 - \lambda$ units of utility if the voter voted 'no'; not having success means zero of utility; i.e. if the rule is W and the vote*

---

[45] If we are referring, as we are here, to the same voter. Or with different voters if we refer to the same alternative.

[46] An alternative to Assumption 2 is the following. If proposals are voted against the status quo, and only modifications of the status quo matter, then one can assume $b = c$. Then setting the status quo to 0, i.e. $b = c = 0$, we have an alternative choice of utilities given by

$$u_i^{\lambda}(W, S) = \begin{cases} \lambda, & \text{if } i \in S \in W, \\ 0, & \text{if } i \in S \notin W \text{ or } i \notin S \notin W, \\ \lambda - 1, & \text{if } i \notin S \in W, \end{cases}$$

where ($0 \le \lambda \le 1$). Nevertheless, the conclusions are basically the same as under Assumption 2.

'Take-it-or-leave-it' committees 73

configuration is S, i's utility is

$$u_i^\lambda(W,S) = \begin{cases} \lambda, & \text{if } i \in S \in W, \\ 1 - \lambda, & \text{if } i \notin S \notin W, \\ 0, & \text{if } i \in S \notin W \text{ or } i \notin S \in W. \end{cases} \tag{25}$$

The parameter λ reflects the importance which is given to positive success relatively to negative success: $\lambda = 0$ means that only negative success matters, $\lambda = 1$ means that only positive success matters, $\lambda = 1/2$ means that voters are indifferent in their evaluations of positive and negative success. Indeed for $\lambda = 1/2$ we have

$$u_i^{\lambda=1/2}(W,S) = \begin{cases} \dfrac{1}{2}, & \text{if } i \in S \in W \text{ or } i \notin S \notin W \\ 0, & \text{if } i \in S \notin W \text{ or } i \notin S \in W. \end{cases}$$

Under Assumption 2, for a given W and a probability distribution over vote configurations p, the expected utility of the voting situation (W,p) for a voter i, denoted as in 1.4.4 by $\bar{u}_i^\lambda$, is given by

$$\bar{u}_i^\lambda(W,p) := E[u_i^\lambda(W,S)] = \sum_{S:i \in S \in W} p(S)\lambda + \sum_{S:i \notin S \notin W} p(S)(1 - \lambda)$$

$$= \lambda \Omega_i^+(W,p) + (1 - \lambda)\Omega_i^-(W,p). \tag{26}$$

When positive success and negative success are equally valued (i.e. when $\lambda = 1/2$), voter i's expected utility is simply half the unconditional success:

$$\bar{u}_i^{\lambda=1/2}(W,p) = \frac{1}{2}\Omega_i(W,p). \tag{27}$$

In general, under Assumption 1, setting $p = p^*$ in (26) gives voter i's *a priori* expected utility, which can be rewritten using (19) and (20) as

$$\bar{u}_i^\lambda(W,p^*) = \left(\frac{1}{2} - \lambda\right)\left(\frac{1}{2} - \alpha(W,p^*)\right) + \frac{\Omega_i(W,p^*)}{2}. \tag{28}$$

3.7.1 Egalitarianism[47]

Egalitarianism argues for equal treatment of equals behind the veil of ignorance or, in our framework under Assumptions 1 and 2, equal *a priori* expected utilities. Therefore a voting rule $\mathcal{W}$ satisfies this principle a priori if

$$\bar{u}_i^\lambda(\mathcal{W}, p^*) = \bar{u}_j^\lambda(\mathcal{W}, p^*), \quad \text{for all } i, j. \tag{29}$$

In view of (28) this is equivalent to requiring that

$$\Omega_i(\mathcal{W}, p^*) = \Omega_j(\mathcal{W}, p^*), \quad \text{for all } i, j,$$

that is, all voters should, a priori, have the same probability of obtaining the outcome that they vote for. Any symmetric rule satisfies this principle. This includes the unanimity rule and the simple majority rule, as well as all intermediate q-majority rules (see 1.3.2).

We can thus summarize the conclusions as follows:

Proposition 11 *Under Assumptions 1 and 2, whatever the parameter λ ($0 \leq \lambda \leq 1$), any symmetric rule implements the egalitarian principle a priori.*

3.7.2 Utilitarianism

The utilitarian optimum consists of maximizing aggregate utility. In our framework this would be achieved by a rule for which the aggregated a priori expected utility is maximal, i.e. by a rule $\mathcal{W}$ that solves the problem

$$\underset{\mathcal{W} \in VR_N}{\text{Max}} \sum_{i \in N} \bar{u}_i^\lambda(\mathcal{W}, p^*). \tag{30}$$

The following equivalence will help us to solve it for different values of the parameter λ (see Appendix for proof).

---

[47] The results obtained in this section and the next can be seen as particular cases of those obtained in Section 3.8 for a committee of representatives when the groups represented by the members of the committee contain just one individual each.

'Take-it-or-leave-it' committees 75

Proposition 12 *Problem (30) is equivalent to*

$$\underset{\mathcal{W}\in VR_N}{\text{Max}} \sum_{S\in\mathcal{W}} (s - (1-\lambda)n). \tag{31}$$

Therefore maximizing the aggregated expected utility means choosing $\mathcal{W}$ with as many winning configurations that satisfy $s > (1-\lambda)n$ as possible. The choice seems simple: any configuration that satisfies the condition should be winning. In fact, if $\lambda \leq 1/2$, this condition defines a q-majority voting rule with quota $q = 1 - \lambda$ that solves the problem. Thus the more importance is given to negative success, the greater the quota should be in order to implement the utilitarian principle. In particular if $\lambda = 1/2$ (i.e. equal importance is given to positive and negative success), then $q = \frac{1}{2}$. Thus the simple majority is the rule that best implements the utilitarian principle[48] if $\lambda = 1/2$. The other extreme occurs for λ close to 0 (i.e. only negative success matters), when unanimity is the best rule.

Proposition 13 *Under Assumptions 1 and 2, if $\lambda \leq \frac{1}{2}$, the voting rule that best implements the utilitarian principle a priori is the q-majority rule with quota $q = 1 - \lambda$.*

A problem appears when $\lambda > 1/2$. In this case condition $s > (1-\lambda)n$ may define an improper rule. The solution seems to be to keep the quota as low as possible, i.e. at $1/2$. The simple majority seems again to be the best rule of *all* the proper rules. The following counterexample shows that this is not true in general.

Example 3.2: Let $N = \{1, 2, 3, 4\}$ and assume that the utility of any voter is given by (25) with $\lambda = \frac{3}{4}$. Consider the simple majority $\mathcal{W}^{SM}$ and $\mathcal{W} = \mathcal{W}^{SM} \cup \{\{1, 2\}\}$. Then we have

$$\sum_{S\in\mathcal{W}} (s - (1-\lambda)n) = 1 + \sum_{S\in\mathcal{W}^{SM}} (s - (1-\lambda)n) > \sum_{S\in\mathcal{W}^{SM}} (s - (1-\lambda)n).$$

Example 3.2 provides a hint about why the simple majority rule may fail to be the utilitarian optimum: as long as it is possible to add vote configurations whose size is greater than $(1-\lambda)n$ to the set of winning

---

[48] The fact that the simple majority was the best of the symmetric rules (in a sense close to the one considered here) was conjectured in [70] and proved in [84].

76 *Voting and Collective Decision-Making*

ones without making the rule improper, the aggregated expected utility will increase. It also gives a hint about how far this can go, not very far indeed, as the following proposition shows (see proof in the Appendix).

Proposition 14 *With* $\lambda > \frac{1}{2}$, *if* $\mathcal{W}$ *is the voting rule that best implements the a priori utilitarian principle, then for all* $S \in \mathcal{W}$ *it holds that* $s \geq \frac{n}{2}$.

This means in particular that even if $\lambda > \frac{1}{2}$ for *n odd*, the simple majority implements the a priori utilitarian principle, while for *n* even, it only *almost* implements it. More precisely, for *n* even the simple majority is the best *of all symmetric rules*. Then we have the following proposition.

Proposition 15 *Under Assumptions 1 and 2, if* $\lambda > \frac{1}{2}$, *then if n is odd the simple majority is the voting rule that best implements the utilitarian principle a priori. If n is even the simple majority is the utilitarian-best of the symmetric rules.*

In short, egalitarianism and utilitarianism are compatible and easy to implement. The rule has to be symmetric in order to guarantee equal a priori expected utility for all voters. The utilitarian principle determines the choice of the quota, which varies with the importance given to positive success. The more highly positive success is valued, the smaller the quota, with a lower bound being $1/2$.

Remark. There is the question of the effect of the choice of utilities to represent the voters' vNM preferences. It should be noted that the solutions of problems (29) and (30), which yield the egalitarian and utilitarian optima, are not altered if the utilities given by (25) are replaced by

$$u_i'^{\lambda}(\mathcal{W}, S) = \alpha u_i^{\lambda}(\mathcal{W}, S) + \beta, \tag{32}$$

for some $\alpha > 0$ and some β. More precisely, this is so *as long as this is done (with the same α and β) for all voters*. Thus, as far as the exact requirement of egalitarianism is concerned, no conflict arises from any change in the form given by (32). The problem appears with comparisons between voters' expectations in case of inequality. In Section 3.8.2 we will be making such comparisons. Absolute comparisons (i.e. differences) are not altered by β if $\alpha = 1$, relative comparisons (i.e. quotients) are not altered by α if $\beta = 0$, otherwise both are dependent on both

'Take-it-or-leave-it' committees

α and β. If we want to compare the expectations of i and j, in either absolute or relative terms, then the choice of α and β in (32) matters. A reasonable solution to this problem so as to make such comparisons independent of α and β is the following. Relativize absolute comparisons w.r.t. the difference between the maximal and minimal utilities. In this way, for all α and β, we have

$$\frac{\bar{u}_i'^\lambda(\mathcal{W},p^*) - \bar{u}_j'^\lambda(\mathcal{W},p^*)}{u_{\text{Max}}'^\lambda - u_{\text{Min}}'^\lambda} = \frac{\bar{u}_i^\lambda(\mathcal{W},p^*) - \bar{u}_j^\lambda(\mathcal{W},p^*)}{u_{\text{Max}}^\lambda - u_{\text{Min}}^\lambda},$$

where, from Assumption 2 (25),

$$u_{\text{Max}}^\lambda = \text{Max}\{\lambda, 1-\lambda\} \quad \text{and} \quad u_{\text{Min}}^\lambda = 0. \tag{33}$$

Similarly, for relative comparisons take quotients of differences with the minimal utility. In this way, for all α and β, we have

$$\frac{\bar{u}_i'^\lambda(\mathcal{W},p^*) - u_{\text{Min}}'^\lambda}{\bar{u}_j'^\lambda(\mathcal{W},p^*) - u_{\text{Min}}'^\lambda} = \frac{\bar{u}_i^\lambda(\mathcal{W},p^*) - u_{\text{Min}}^\lambda}{\bar{u}_j^\lambda(\mathcal{W},p^*) - u_{\text{Min}}^\lambda}. \tag{34}$$

3.8 The choice of voting rule in a committee of representatives

Now consider a take-it-or-leave-it committee in which each member acts on behalf of a group of individuals or a constituency of a different size. Given the number of members in this committee and the sizes of each group represented, what is the most adequate voting rule for the committee?

The idea is to provide answers based on one of the two principles discussed in the previous section *with respect to those represented*. As we will see, such recommendations can be made on the basis of the number of members in the committee and the sizes of each group represented. Nevertheless, a well-founded answer requires the model to be enriched beyond these objective data. Some assumptions about the relationship between the preferences within the represented groups and the votes of their representatives is necessary. An assumption concerning the utilities of the people represented when they obtain their preferred outcome in a committee's decision is also needed. We assume that every representative always follows the majority opinion of his/her

78   *Voting and Collective Decision-Making*

group on every issue. In this way the decision-making process can be neatly modelled by a composite rule, as is done in the next section. This will allow us to make a recommendation based on Assumptions 1 and 2 *at the level of the people represented*. Note that Assumption 1 implies assuming that the voters behave independently from one another, even in the same constituency. Is this reasonable? It may be so if constituencies are seen a priori as purely administrative entities, which may not be the case. Nevertheless, this assumption seems reasonable for a normative assessment, and will enable us to make a comparison with a traditional model also based on this assumption.

First we will describe the model more precisely and then look for the rules that enable one or other of the principles to be implemented. Before proceeding, we must discard the naïve, egalitarian-sounding answer of a weighted majority with weights proportional to the groups' sizes. In this case intuition is not correct. It is easy to give examples of dictatorships that result from assigning weights on committees proportional to the group sizes, and examples in which the difference in weight is of no consequence (see Example 2.3 in 2.1.4).

3.8.1 *An ideal two-stage decision procedure*

Let n be the number of representatives on the committee, denoted by $N = \{1, 2, \ldots, n\}$, and for each $i \in N$, let m_i be the number of individuals in the group M_i represented by i. We assume these n groups to be disjoint. Let $M := \cup_{i \in N} M_i$, and let m denote the total number of individuals represented on the committee: $m = m_1 + \cdots + m_n$. Individuals in M are sometimes referred to as 'citizens'.

Each representative i is assumed to follow the majority opinion in M_i, which is equivalent to saying that on every issue the representative position is decided by a simple majority in M_i. That is, by the M_i-voting rule

$$\mathcal{W}_{M_i}^{SM} := \left\{ S_i \subseteq M_i : \#S_i > \frac{m_i}{2} \right\}.$$

Then if the voting rule in the committee of representatives is $\mathcal{W}_N$, the *two-stage idealization* of M's decision-making process is formalized by the composite M-rule (see 1.3.2)

$$\mathcal{W}_M := \mathcal{W}_N[\mathcal{W}_{M_1}^{SM}, \ldots, \mathcal{W}_{M_n}^{SM}],$$

'Take-it-or-leave-it' committees

in which each vote configuration of citizens $S \subseteq M$ determines whether the proposal is accepted or rejected. Finally, we make Assumptions 1 and 2 at the level of the citizens. That is, we assume the a priori distribution of probability p_M^*, and we assume the utilities of the individuals in M to be given by (25).

Now the model is complete and the question of the choice of the voting rule in the committee can be formally addressed. But before proceeding we must establish a few relationships that will be of use.

Observe that the voting behaviour within each group M_i, and within the committee of representatives is fully determined by p_M^*. As individuals in M vote 'yes' independently one from another with probability $1/2$, the voting behaviour in each group M_i, is $p_{M_i}^*$ [49]. Then, in the committee, as each representative i follows the majority opinion in M_i, a member i will vote independently 'yes' with probability $\alpha(W_{M_i}^{SM}, p_{M_i}^*)$, where, in view of (4) and (6),

$$
\alpha(W_{M_i}^{SM}, p_{M_i}^*) = \begin{cases} \dfrac{1}{2} & \text{if } m_i \text{ is odd} \\ \dfrac{1}{2} - \dfrac{1}{2^{m_i+1}} \binom{m_i}{m_i/2} & \text{if } m_i \text{ is even.} \end{cases} \tag{35}
$$

Note that if m_i is even and large, using Stirling's approximation (7), we have

$$
\alpha(W_{M_i}^{SM}, p_{M_i}^*) = \frac{1}{2} - \frac{1}{2^{m_i+1}} \binom{m_i}{m_i/2} \simeq \frac{1}{2} - \sqrt{\frac{1}{2\pi m_i}} \simeq \frac{1}{2}.
$$

Therefore the probability of a majority voting 'yes' in each group M_i is exactly (approximately) $1/2$ if m_i is odd (even and large). As a consequence, the voting behaviour on the committee of representatives is p_N^* exactly if all m_i are odd, or approximately if those that are even are large enough. We also have the following relationship.

Proposition 16 *Let* $W_M = W_N[W_{M_1}^{SM}, \ldots, W_{M_n}^{SM}]$. *If all* m_j *are large enough, we have*

$$
\alpha(W_M, p_M^*) \simeq \alpha(W_N, p_N^*). \tag{36}
$$

---

[49] In other terms $p_M^* = p_{M_1}^* \times \cdots \times p_{M_n}^*$.

In fact (36) is an equality if all m_j are odd, while it is a good approximation if those that are even are sufficiently large.

The following lemmas (proofs in the Appendix) will be useful later.

Lemma 17 *Let M be a population of m voters; then for m large we have for all $k \in M$*

$$\Phi_k(\mathcal{W}_M^{SM}, p_M^*) \simeq \sqrt{\frac{2}{\pi m}}. \tag{37}$$

Lemma 18 *Let $\mathcal{W}_M = \mathcal{W}_N[\mathcal{W}_{M_1}^{SM}, \ldots, \mathcal{W}_{M_n}^{SM}]$. If all m_j are large enough, for all $i \in N$, and all $k \in M_i$, we have*

$$\Phi_k(\mathcal{W}_M, p_M^*) \simeq \Phi_k(\mathcal{W}_{M_i}^{SM}, p_{M_i}^*)\Phi_i(\mathcal{W}_N, p_N^*). \tag{38}$$

Again if all m_j are odd, (38) becomes an exact equality[50].

A consequence of these two lemmas is that in this model if all groups are big enough an individual's a priori probability of being decisive is given approximately by

$$\Phi_k(\mathcal{W}_M, p_M^*) \simeq \sqrt{\frac{2}{\pi m_i}}\Phi_i(\mathcal{W}_N, p_N^*). \tag{39}$$

This quantity is small if m_i is large. In other words, in this case

$$Bz_k(\mathcal{W}_M) = \Phi_k(\mathcal{W}_M, p_M^*) \simeq 0.$$

As for an individual's success, we have that

$$\Omega_k(\mathcal{W}_M, p_M^*) \simeq 0.5,$$
$$\Omega_k^+(\mathcal{W}_M, p_M^*) \simeq 0.5\alpha(\mathcal{W}_N, p_N^*),$$
$$\Omega_k^-(\mathcal{W}_M, p_M^*) \simeq 0.5(1 - \alpha(\mathcal{W}_N, p_N^*)).$$

More precisely, using relationships (21), (19), (20) and (39), we obtain (see Appendix) the following proposition.

---

[50] Note that (38) can be equivalently expressed as

$$Bz_k(\mathcal{W}_M) \simeq Bz_k(\mathcal{W}_{M_i}^{SM})Bz_i(\mathcal{W}_N).$$

'Take-it-or-leave-it' committees 81

Proposition 19 *If* $\mathcal{W}_M = \mathcal{W}_N[\mathcal{W}_{M_1}^{SM}, \dots, \mathcal{W}_{M_n}^{SM}]$, *all* m_j *are large enough and approximation (39) is accepted, then for all* $k \in M$, *we have*

$$\Phi_k(\mathcal{W}_M, p_M^*) \leq \xi,$$

$$\Omega_k(\mathcal{W}_M, p_M^*) - 0.5 \leq 0.5\xi,$$

$$\Omega_k^+(\mathcal{W}_M, p_M^*) - 0.5\alpha(\mathcal{W}_N, p_N^*) \leq 0.25\xi,$$

$$\Omega_k^-(\mathcal{W}_M, p_M^*) - 0.5(1 - \alpha(\mathcal{W}_N, p_N^*)) \leq 0.25\xi, \tag{40}$$

where

$$\xi := \sqrt{\frac{2}{\pi \, \mathrm{Min}_{i \in N} m_i}}. \tag{41}$$

Thus, for the ideal two-stage decision procedure modelled by the composite rule $\mathcal{W}_N[\mathcal{W}_{M_1}^{SM}, \dots, \mathcal{W}_{M_n}^{SM}]$, assuming the voting behaviour described by p_M^* and all groups large enough, any individual in M has a probability of approximately one-half of obtaining his/her preferred outcome. Does this mean that a represented individual whose main concern is the probability of success would in practice be indifferent to the rule in the committee? According to the model so far described the answer seems to be yes. Now let us take utilities into consideration and see where the egalitarian and utilitarian principles take us.

3.8.2 Egalitarianism in a committee of representatives

In terms of the two-stage model, the egalitarian principle is satisfied if any two individuals in M have the same expected utility irrespective of what group they belong to, that is, under Assumptions 1 and 2 relative to the people in M, if

$$\bar{u}_k^\lambda(\mathcal{W}_M, p_M^*) = \bar{u}_l^\lambda(\mathcal{W}_M, p_M^*), \text{ for all } k, l \in M. \tag{42}$$

The individual's a priori expected utility is given by (28), which can be rewritten using (21) as

$$\bar{u}_k^\lambda(\mathcal{W}_M, p_M^*) = \tfrac{1}{4} + \tfrac{1}{4}\Phi_k(\mathcal{W}_M, p_M^*) + (\tfrac{1}{2} - \alpha(\mathcal{W}_M, p_M^*))(\tfrac{1}{2} - \lambda). \tag{43}$$

In this expression, there is just one term that is not constant for all citizens: $\frac{1}{4}\Phi_k(\mathcal{W}_M, p^*_M)$. In view of (40) this term is very small if the groups are large, and is negligible compared to the other terms. Therefore basically the a priori expected utility is the same for all individuals if all groups are large enough, namely we have

$$\bar{u}^\lambda_k(\mathcal{W}_M, p^*_M) \simeq \bar{u}^\lambda_l(\mathcal{W}_M, p^*_M) \simeq \tfrac{1}{4} + (\tfrac{1}{2} - \alpha(\mathcal{W}_M, p^*_M))(\tfrac{1}{2} - \lambda).$$

This level of utility varies in accordance with the rule used in the committee of representatives (with the term $\alpha(\mathcal{W}_M, p^*_M)$), but the egalitarian principle is thus basically satisfied. By 'basically satisfied' we mean the following, using (33) and (34) for comparisons (see 3.7.2). Whatever the rule in the committee of representatives $\mathcal{W}_N$, if all m_j are large enough, for any $k, l \in M$

$$\frac{\left|\bar{u}^\lambda_k(\mathcal{W}_M, p^*_M) - \bar{u}^\lambda_l(\mathcal{W}_M, p^*_M)\right|}{u^\lambda_{\mathrm{Max}} - u^\lambda_{\mathrm{Min}}} \simeq 0$$

and

$$\frac{\bar{u}^\lambda_k(\mathcal{W}_M, p^*_M) - u^\lambda_{\mathrm{Min}}}{\bar{u}^\lambda_l(\mathcal{W}_M, p^*_M) - u^\lambda_{\mathrm{Min}}} \simeq 1.$$

That is, the difference in utilities between two individuals in absolute terms is close to 0, and their ratio is close to 1. The following proposition gives a more precise idea of the extent to which this is so (see the proof in Appendix).

Proposition 20 *If we accept approximations (38) and (37) we have, for any $k, l \in M$,*

$$\frac{\left|\bar{u}^\lambda_k(\mathcal{W}_M, p^*_M) - \bar{u}^\lambda_l(\mathcal{W}_M, p^*_M)\right|}{u^\lambda_{\mathrm{Max}} - u^\lambda_{\mathrm{Min}}} \leq \frac{1}{2}\xi \quad and$$

$$\frac{\bar{u}^\lambda_k(\mathcal{W}_M, p^*_M) - u^\lambda_{\mathrm{Min}}}{\bar{u}^\lambda_l(\mathcal{W}_M, p^*_M) - u^\lambda_{\mathrm{Min}}} < 1 + \xi,$$

where ξ is given by (41).

'Take-it-or-leave-it' committees   83

Then we have the following claim.

Claim 21 *In the current model of a committee of representatives, for any voting rule $\mathcal{W}_N$, the egalitarian principle is basically satisfied at the individual level as long as all the groups are large in size.*

Thus, the egalitarian principle seems not to be binding after all for the choice of the rule in a take-it-or-leave-it committee of representatives. This is a very different conclusion from the one reached by the traditional 'voting power' approach. There, the so-called *'first square root rule'* (SQRR) states that the voting rule in a committee of representatives should be chosen in such a way that the Banzhaf index of each representative is proportional to the square root of the size of the group that he/she represents[51]. What leads to such contradictory conclusions in analyses based on the same two-stage idealization and the same probabilistic model?

The 'first square root rule' recommendation is based on the following notions: (i) 'voting power' is the relevant issue at stake; (ii) the Banzhaf index is the right measure of 'voting power'; and (iii) this being so, a 'fair' voting rule should give equal voting power to all individuals. That is, under these premises, for all $k, l \in M$, it should be

$$\mathrm{Bz}_k(\mathcal{W}_M) = \mathrm{Bz}_l(\mathcal{W}_M).$$

Restated in our notation what is required is

$$\Phi_k(\mathcal{W}_M, p_M^*) = \Phi_l(\mathcal{W}_M, p_M^*) \text{ for all } k, l \in M,$$

i.e. all individuals should have the same a priori probability of being decisive. The 'square root rule' is then derived as follows. Assuming that all groups are large enough to accept the approximations, for $k \in M_i$ and $l \in M_j$, using (38), the last relationship can be rewritten as

$$\Phi_k(\mathcal{W}_{M_i}^{\mathrm{SM}}, p_{M_i}^*)\Phi_i(\mathcal{W}_N, p_N^*) = \Phi_l(\mathcal{W}_{M_j}^{\mathrm{SM}}, p_{M_j}^*)\Phi_j(\mathcal{W}_N, p_N^*),$$

---

[51] Deviations from this recommendation of some voting rules in the EU Council have given rise to active criticism by some members of the academic community, as commented in Chapter 5 (see 5.2.2).

or, by (37), for m_i large enough, as

$$\sqrt{\frac{2}{\pi m_i}}\Phi_i(\mathcal{W}_N, p_N^*) = \sqrt{\frac{2}{\pi m_j}}\Phi_j(\mathcal{W}_N, p_N^*),$$

which holds if and only if

$$\frac{\Phi_i(\mathcal{W}_N, p_N^*)}{\sqrt{m_i}} = \frac{\Phi_j(\mathcal{W}_N, p_N^*)}{\sqrt{m_j}}$$

or equivalently,

$$\frac{\mathrm{Bz}_i(\mathcal{W}_N)}{\sqrt{m_i}} = \frac{\mathrm{Bz}_j(\mathcal{W}_N)}{\sqrt{m_j}}.$$

Thus, in order to equalize the Banzhaf indices of individuals in the ideal two-stage procedure modelled by $\mathcal{W}_M$, each representative's Banzhaf index in $\mathcal{W}_N$ should be proportional to the square root of his/her group's size.

On the other hand, under Assumptions 1 and 2, in view of (43) in Section 3.8.2, having equal expected utility is equivalent to having the same probability of being decisive, which entails that the egalitarian goal is equivalent to the SQRR goal. Then how can their recommendations differ?

The crucial disagreement between the approach developed here and traditional voting power lies in point (i) underlying the SQRR. That is, as argued in Section 3.6, we see no reasons to consider 'voting power' as the relevant issue at stake in a pure take-it-or-leave-it committee, nor as the source of utility[52]. Then, even though requiring equal Banzhaf indices for any two individuals in $\mathcal{W}_M$ is equivalent to requiring equal expected utility, the discrepancy appears when this condition is not met. In this case *comparisons based on expected utilities and those based on decisiveness draw different conclusions,* because comparisons in relative terms between very small numbers (likelihood of decisiveness

---

[52] Nor do we consider sound or coherent the interpretation as 'power' of the likelihood of being decisive in such committees (see 2.2). It can be argued that, given its vagueness in this point, the traditional voting power approach does not apply to take-it-or-leave-it committees. But in Chapter 4 we deal with bargaining committees and there the conclusions are even further from the SQRR.

'Take-it-or-leave-it' committees

for individuals) artificially dramatize differences between individuals. The following example illustrates this.

Example 3.3: In Chapter 5 we apply this model to different rules in the European Council of Ministers. The Council is interpreted in Section 5.2 as a take-it-or-leave-it committee of representatives of the citizens of the EU Member States. Using 2004 population figures, for the 'Nice rule', we obtain that Luxembourgian citizens (Lu) have the highest Banzhaf index, while Latvian citizens (La) have the lowest. The figures are:

$$\mathrm{Bz}_{\mathrm{La}}(\mathcal{W}_M^{\mathrm{Ni}}) = 0.00000446,$$

$$\mathrm{Bz}_{\mathrm{Lu}}(\mathcal{W}_M^{\mathrm{Ni}}) = 0.0000101,$$

with the ratio between the indices

$$\frac{\mathrm{Bz}_{\mathrm{Lu}}(\mathcal{W}_M^{\mathrm{Ni}})}{\mathrm{Bz}_{\mathrm{La}}(\mathcal{W}_M^{\mathrm{Ni}})} = 2.27.$$

Thus, according to the traditional voting power approach, a Luxembourgian citizen's 'voting power' is more than double that of a Latvian citizen's.

Nevertheless, in 2004 the smallest of the 25 member states is Malta, with a population of 380 000 individuals, which yields $\xi = 0.0013$ in (41). Thus, whatever the rule in the Council and the value of λ, for any pair of EU citizens k, l, we have

$$\frac{\left| \bar{u}_k^\lambda(\mathcal{W}_M, p_M^*) - \bar{u}_l^\lambda(\mathcal{W}_M, p_M^*) \right|}{u_{\mathrm{Max}}^\lambda - u_{\mathrm{Min}}^\lambda} \leq 0.00065,$$

and

$$\frac{\bar{u}_k^\lambda(\mathcal{W}_M, p_M^*) - u_{\mathrm{Min}}^\lambda}{\bar{u}_l^\lambda(\mathcal{W}_M, p_M^*) - u_{\mathrm{Min}}^\lambda} < 1.0013.$$

In order to illustrate the point more clearly, let us choose the following utility for the Nice rule for any citizen:

$$u_k'(\mathcal{W}_M^{\mathrm{Ni}}, S) = \begin{cases} 1, & \text{if } k \in S \in \mathcal{W}_M^{\mathrm{Ni}} \text{ or } i \notin S \notin \mathcal{W}_M^{\mathrm{Ni}} \\ -1, & \text{if } k \in S \notin \mathcal{W}_M^{\mathrm{Ni}} \text{ or } i \notin S \in \mathcal{W}_M^{\mathrm{Ni}}, \end{cases}$$

which leads to

$$\bar{u}'_k(\mathcal{W}_M^{Ni}, p_M^*) = Bz_k(\mathcal{W}_M^{Ni}).$$

Note that this corresponds to the affine transformation

$$u'_k(\mathcal{W}, S) = 4u_k^{\lambda=1/2}(\mathcal{W}, S) - 1,$$

and $u'_{Max} = 1$ and $u'_{Min} = -1$. The relative comparison of utilities according to (34) gives

$$\frac{\bar{u}'_{Lu}(\mathcal{W}_M^{Ni}, p_M^*) - \bar{u}'_{La}(\mathcal{W}_M^{Ni}, p_M^*)}{u'_{Max} - u'_{Min}} = 0.000003,$$

and

$$\frac{\bar{u}'_{Lu}(\mathcal{W}_M^{Ni}, p_M^*) - u'_{Min}(\mathcal{W}_M^{Ni}, p_M^*)}{\bar{u}'_{La}(\mathcal{W}_M^{Ni}, p_M^*) - u'_{Min}(\mathcal{W}_M^{Ni}, p_M^*)} = \frac{Bz_{Lu}(\mathcal{W}_M^{Ni}) + 1}{Bz_{La}(\mathcal{W}_M^{Ni}) + 1} = 1.000006.$$

Thus, a ratio of $2.27 : 1.$ between Banzhaf indices becomes very close to $1 : 1$ between expected utilities.

This example illustrates our point clearly. Traditional voting power comparisons are based on the Banzhaf index, which magnifies differences that are negligible in terms of expected utility. In fact, the above example is not extreme at all. One can even have

$$\frac{\bar{u}_k^\lambda(\mathcal{W}_M, p_M^*)}{\bar{u}_l^\lambda(\mathcal{W}_M, p_M^*)} \simeq 1 \quad \text{while} \quad \frac{Bz_k(\mathcal{W}_M)}{Bz_l(\mathcal{W}_M)} \simeq \infty,$$

which happens if citizen l's representative (and not k's) has a null seat[53].

Apart from magnifying the differences, a weak point of the 'square root rule' is that it does not prescribe a voting rule, but only conditions that should be met by the representatives' a priori decisiveness. Moreover, there is no guarantee that such a rule exists. Especially if the number of groups is small, it may well happen that no rule even comes close to satisfying this condition; (the number of possible rules is finite, and small when the number of seats is small).

---

[53] This is not an artificial academic example: in the European Council with six members Luxembourg had a null seat.

3.8.3 Utilitarianism in a committee of representatives

In terms of the composite model of the idealized two-stage decision procedure in which $W_M = W_N[W_1^{SM}, \ldots, W_n^{SM}]$, under Assumptions 1 and 2, the objective of the *a priori* utilitarian principle is to choose W_N so as to maximize the aggregated expected utility in M in the voting situation (W_M, p_M^*). This means maximizing

$$\sum_{k \in M} \bar{u}_k^\lambda(W_M, p_M^*) = \sum_{i \in N} \sum_{k \in M_i} \bar{u}_k^\lambda(W_M, p_M^*).$$

As the aggregated expected utility and the expected aggregated utility coincide[54], we have

$$\sum_{i \in N} \sum_{k \in M_i} \bar{u}_k^\lambda(W_M, p_M^*) = E\left[\sum_{i \in N} \sum_{k \in M_i} u_k^\lambda(W_M, S)\right].$$

Therefore the utilitarian goal is to choose W_N so as to maximize the latter expectation. In other words, to make for each vote configuration in the committee the decision for which the expectation

$$E\left[\sum_{k \in M} u_k^\lambda\right]$$

is the highest. If the vote configuration in the committee is $C \subseteq N$, given that many different vote configurations in M yield such vote configuration in the committee, the best decision is to accept the proposal if the *expected* aggregated utility *given that the vote configuration is* C is greater in case of acceptance than in case of rejection. That is, if

$$E\left[\sum_{k \in M} u_k^\lambda \mid C \;\&\; \text{accept}\right] > E\left[\sum_{k \in M} u_k^\lambda \mid C \;\&\; \text{reject}\right]. \tag{44}$$

---

[54] For any two random variables X and Y, we have: $E[X] + E[Y] = E[X + Y]$.

The following two lemmas will permit us to approximate the expectations in (44) for large groups. For this we need to know the aggregated expected utility in each group in either case (acceptance or rejection), for each vote configuration in the committee. Note that for a vote configuration C in the committee, $i \in C$ (i.e. M_i's representative votes 'yes') when a majority in group M_i votes 'yes', while if $i \in N \setminus C$ (i.e. M_i's representative votes 'no') when no majority in group M_i votes 'yes'. As an immediate consequence of the possibility of permuting aggregation and expectation, we have the following lemma.

Lemma 22 *Let $i \in N$. Under Assumption 2, the aggregated expected utility in group M_i given that the majority in M_i votes 'yes' and the proposal is accepted (rejected), is given, respectively, by*

$$E\left[\sum_{k \in M_i} u_k^\lambda \mid \#S_i > \frac{m_i}{2} \ \& \ \text{accept}\right] = \lambda E\left[\#S_i \mid \#S_i > \frac{m_i}{2}\right],$$

$$E\left[\sum_{k \in M_i} u_k^\lambda \mid \#S_i > \frac{m_i}{2} \ \& \ \text{reject}\right] = (1-\lambda)E\left[\#(M_i \setminus S_i) \mid \#S_i > \frac{m_i}{2}\right];$$

while the aggregated expected utility in group M_i, given that the majority in M_i does not vote 'yes' and the proposal is accepted (rejected), is given, respectively, by

$$E\left[\sum_{k \in M_i} u_k^\lambda \mid \#S_i \leq \frac{m_i}{2} \ \& \ \text{accept}\right] = \lambda E\left[\#S_i \mid \#S_i \leq \frac{m_i}{2}\right],$$

$$E\left[\sum_{k \in M_i} u_k^\lambda \mid \#S_i \leq \frac{m_i}{2} \ \& \ \text{reject}\right] = (1-\lambda)E\left[\#(M_i \setminus S_i) \mid \#S_i \leq \frac{m_i}{2}\right].$$

The next lemma gives approximations of the expected numbers of voters voting 'yes' and voting 'no' in a large group under the different conditions.

'Take-it-or-leave-it' committees

Lemma 23 *Let $i \in N$. Under Assumption 1, if m_i is large enough, the expected numbers of voters voting 'yes' and voting 'no' in group M_i, given that the majority in M_i votes 'yes', can be approximated, respectively, by*

$$E\left[\#S_i \mid \#S_i > \frac{m_i}{2}\right] \simeq \frac{m_i}{2} + \sqrt{\frac{m_i}{2\pi}},$$

$$E\left[\#(M_i \setminus S_i) \mid \#S_i > \frac{m_i}{2}\right] \simeq \frac{m_i}{2} - \sqrt{\frac{m_i}{2\pi}};$$

while the expected numbers of voters voting 'yes' and voting 'no' in group M_i, given that the majority in M_i does not vote 'yes', can be approximated, respectively, by

$$E\left[\#S_i \mid \#S_i \leq \frac{m_i}{2}\right] \simeq \frac{m_i}{2} - \sqrt{\frac{m_i}{2\pi}},$$

$$E\left[\#(M_i \setminus S_i) \mid \#S_i \leq \frac{m_i}{2}\right] \simeq \frac{m_i}{2} + \sqrt{\frac{m_i}{2\pi}}.$$

Now we are ready to solve the maximization problem. We consider the simplest case first, when the same importance is given to positive and negative success[55].

Case $\lambda = 1/2$: In view of the two preceding lemmas, when a majority in group M_i votes 'yes' (or, equivalently in the current model, when M_i's representative votes 'yes') the aggregated expected utility in this group *if the decision in the committee is 'yes'* is (the approximation is

---

[55] The reader may prefer to skip this case and go directly to the general case, which is discussed immediately afterwards. We deal first with this particular case because this is the most common assumption in the literature, and some readers may be interested only in this case. This will also allow us to compare the conclusion with the so-called 'second square root rule'.

good for m_i large enough),

$$E\left[\sum_{k\in M_i} u_k^{\lambda=1/2} \mid \#S_i > \frac{m_i}{2} \ \& \ \text{accept}\right] \simeq \frac{1}{2}\left(\frac{m_i}{2} + \sqrt{\frac{m_i}{2\pi}}\right);$$

while *if the decision in the committee is 'no,'* the aggregated expected utility in group M_i is

$$E\left[\sum_{k\in M_i} u_k^{\lambda=1/2} \mid \#S_i > \frac{m_i}{2} \ \& \ \text{reject}\right] \simeq \frac{1}{2}\left(\frac{m_i}{2} - \sqrt{\frac{m_i}{2\pi}}\right).$$

Similar calculations can be made for the case in which M_i's representative votes 'no'.

According to the two-stage model, a vote configuration in the committee $C \subseteq N$ occurs if for all $i \in C$, the majority in M_i votes 'yes', while for all $j \in N \setminus C$, the majority in M_j does not vote 'yes'. Thus aggregating across all groups we have that for a given vote configuration in the committee $C \subseteq N$, the aggregated expected utility in M *if the committee accepts the proposal*, given that the vote configuration in the committee is C, is (with close approximation for large enough m_i's)

$$E\left[\sum_{k\in M} u_k^{\lambda=1/2} \mid C \ \& \ \text{accept}\right]$$

$$= \sum_{i\in C} E\left[\sum_{k\in M_i} u_k^{\lambda=1/2} \mid \#S_i > \frac{m_i}{2} \ \& \ \text{accept}\right]$$

$$+ \sum_{j\in N\setminus C} E\left[\sum_{k\in M_j} u_k^{\lambda=1/2} \mid \#S_j \le \frac{m_j}{2} \ \& \ \text{accept}\right]$$

$$\simeq \frac{1}{2} \sum_{i\in C}\left(\frac{m_i}{2} + \sqrt{\frac{m_i}{2\pi}}\right) + \frac{1}{2} \sum_{j\in N\setminus C}\left(\frac{m_j}{2} - \sqrt{\frac{m_j}{2\pi}}\right)$$

$$= \frac{1}{2}\left(\frac{m}{2} + \frac{1}{\sqrt{2\pi}}\left(\sum_{i\in C}\sqrt{m_i} - \sum_{j\in N\setminus C}\sqrt{m_j}\right)\right);$$

'Take-it-or-leave-it' committees

while *if the proposal is rejected* the aggregated expected utility is

$$
E\left[\sum_{k\in M} u_k^{\lambda=1/2} \mid C \text{ \& reject}\right]
$$

$$
\simeq \frac{1}{2}\left(\frac{m}{2} + \frac{1}{\sqrt{2\pi}}\left(\sum_{j\in N\backslash C}\sqrt{m_j} - \sum_{i\in C}\sqrt{m_i}\right)\right).
$$

Thus, from the utilitarian point of view, an optimal decision in the committee is to accept the proposal if

$$
E\left[\sum_{k\in M} u_k^{\lambda=1/2} \mid C \text{ \& accept}\right] > E\left[\sum_{k\in M} u_k^{\lambda=1/2} \mid C \text{ \& reject}\right],
$$

that is, using the above approximations, if

$$
\sum_{i\in C}\sqrt{m_i} > \sum_{j\in N\backslash C}\sqrt{m_j},
$$

which, as

$$
\sum_{j\in N\backslash C}\sqrt{m_j} = \sum_{i\in N}\sqrt{m_i} - \sum_{i\in C}\sqrt{m_i},
$$

can be rewritten as

$$
\sum_{i\in C}\sqrt{m_i} > \frac{1}{2}\sum_{j\in N}\sqrt{m_j}.
$$

Thus we have the following result, always under Assumptions 1 and 2.

Proposition 24 *For $\lambda = 1/2$, if all the groups represented are large enough, the weighted majority rule in the committee $\mathcal{W}_N = \mathcal{W}^{(w,q)}$ that gives to each representative a weight proportional to the square root of the size of the group and a relative quota of 50% (i.e. $q = \frac{1}{2}$) implements the utilitarian principle with close approximation.*

Observe that the quota recommended is the same as in the case of direct voting (see Section 3.7.1), which in the symmetric direct case means a simple majority.

The rule prescribed by Proposition 24 is known in the literature as the '*second square root rule*'. Indeed, in view of (21), (23) and (27), the maximization problem that it solves is equivalent to that of maximizing

$$\sum_{i \in N} \sum_{k \in M_i} Bz_k(\mathcal{W}_M),$$

a problem that has been addressed in voting power literature (see [22, 58, 59]). Once again, as in the egalitarian case, we have the same recommendation about the choice of voting rule but based on different grounds. Here this prescription is based on a simple utilitarian principle applied to a precise model in a specific context: that of a take-it-or-leave-it committee.

General case, $\lambda \in [0, 1]$: Again using Lemmas 22 and 23, when a majority in M_i votes 'yes' the aggregated expected utility in group M_i *if the decision in the committee is 'yes'* is (approximately for m_i large enough),

$$E\left[\sum_{k \in M_i} u_k^\lambda \mid \#S_i > \frac{m_i}{2} \ \& \ \text{accept}\right] \simeq \lambda\left(\frac{m_i}{2} + \sqrt{\frac{m_i}{2\pi}}\right);$$

while *if the decision in the committee is 'no'*, the aggregated expected utility in group M_i is

$$E\left[\sum_{k \in M_i} u_k^\lambda \mid \#S_i > \frac{m_i}{2} \ \& \ \text{reject}\right] \simeq (1 - \lambda)\left(\frac{m_i}{2} - \sqrt{\frac{m_i}{2\pi}}\right).$$

Similar calculations can be made for the case in which 'yes' does not obtain a majority in M_i.

Now, as in the case $\lambda = \frac{1}{2}$, aggregating across all groups we have that for a given vote configuration in the committee $C \subseteq N$, the aggregated expected utility in M *if the committee accepts the proposal*, is (with

'Take-it-or-leave-it' committees

close approximation for large enough m_i)

$$E\left[\sum_{k\in M} u_k^\lambda \mid C \ \& \ \text{accept}\right] \simeq \lambda\left(\sum_{i\in C}\left(\frac{m_i}{2} + \sqrt{\frac{m_i}{2\pi}}\right)\right.$$

$$\left. + \sum_{i\in N\backslash C}\left(\frac{m_i}{2} - \sqrt{\frac{m_i}{2\pi}}\right)\right)$$

$$= \lambda\frac{m}{2} + \frac{\lambda}{\sqrt{2\pi}}\left(\sum_{i\in C}\sqrt{m_i} - \sum_{i\in N\backslash C}\sqrt{m_i}\right);$$

$$(45)$$

while *if the proposal is rejected* the aggregated expected utility is

$$E\left[\sum_{i\in M} u_i^\lambda \mid C \ \& \ \text{reject}\right]$$

$$\simeq (1-\lambda)\frac{m}{2} + \frac{1-\lambda}{\sqrt{2\pi}}\left(\sum_{i\in N\backslash C}\sqrt{m_i} - \sum_{i\in C}\sqrt{m_i}\right). \qquad (46)$$

Thus, from the utilitarian point of view the best decision in the committee is to accept the proposal if (44) holds, that is, after substituting and simplifying, if

$$(1-2\lambda)m\sqrt{\frac{\pi}{2}} < \sum_{i\in C}\sqrt{m_i} - \sum_{i\in N\backslash C}\sqrt{m_i}.$$

This inequality holds if and only if

$$\sum_{i\in C}\sqrt{m_i} > \frac{1}{2}\sum_{i\in N}\sqrt{m_i} + \frac{1}{2}(1-2\lambda)m\sqrt{\frac{\pi}{2}}. \qquad (47)$$

The situation is similar to that found with direct committees in Section 3.7.2. If $\lambda \leq \frac{1}{2}$ this condition defines a weighted majority rule with weights $w_i = \sqrt{m_i}$, and relative quota

$$q_\lambda = \frac{1}{2} + \frac{1}{2} \frac{(1 - 2\lambda)m\sqrt{\frac{\pi}{2}}}{\sum_{i \in N} \sqrt{m_i}}. \tag{48}$$

As expected, when the importance given to negative success increases (i.e. λ decreases), the quota increases.

Thus we have the following result (note that it includes the result obtained for $\lambda = \frac{1}{2}$ as a particular case).

Proposition 25 *Under Assumptions 1 and 2, assuming that all the represented groups are large enough, if $\lambda \leq \frac{1}{2}$, the weighted majority rule $W_N = W^{(w,q_\lambda)}$ in the committee for weights $w_i = \sqrt{m_i}$ and relative quota q_λ given by (48) implements the a priori utilitarian principle with close approximation.*

Now consider the case in which $\lambda > \frac{1}{2}$. In this case (47) may define an *improper* voting rule. The idea is then to lower the quota Q as much as possible so that $W^{(w,Q)}$, for weights $w_i = \sqrt{m_i}$, is a proper rule. Namely let

$$\bar{Q} := \text{Min} \left\{ Q \in \mathbb{R} : W^{(w,Q)} \in VR_N \right\}. \tag{49}$$

Or equivalently, take $\bar{Q}$ as the minimal $Q \geq 0$ such that

$$\sum_{i \in C} w_i > Q \Rightarrow \sum_{j \in N \setminus C} w_j \leq Q. \tag{50}$$

Then we have the following result, which shows how $W^{(w,\bar{Q})}$ is *almost* the utilitarian optimum. In the proof we use the notation

$$w(C) := \sum_{i \in C} w_i.$$

Proposition 26 *If W_N implements the utilitarian optimum according to the approximation based on (45) and (46), then for all $C \in W_N$, $\sum_{i \in C} w_i \geq \bar{Q}$.*

'Take-it-or-leave-it' committees 95

Proof. First note that, as $\lambda > \frac{1}{2}$ and $\frac{w(N)}{2}$ is among the Q that satisfy (50), we have $Q_\lambda \leq \bar{Q} \leq \frac{w(N)}{2}$, where $Q_\lambda = w(N)q_\lambda$. Then obviously

$$w(C) < \bar{Q} \Rightarrow w(N \setminus C) > \bar{Q} \geq Q_\lambda.$$

Assume that for some $C \in \mathcal{W}_N$ we have $w(C) < \bar{Q}$. We can assume C to be minimal winning. Consider the rule

$$\mathcal{W}'_N := (\mathcal{W}_N \setminus \{C\}) \cup \mathcal{W}^{N \setminus C}.$$

That is, $\mathcal{W}'_N$ is the rule that results from $\mathcal{W}_N$ by eliminating C from the set of winning configurations and adding all those containing $N \setminus C$. As C is minimal, $N \setminus C$ intersects all $T \in \mathcal{W}_N \setminus \{C\}$, and $\mathcal{W}'_N$ is a proper rule. Let us now show that $\mathcal{W}'_N$ is better than $\mathcal{W}_N$ from the utilitarian point of view. In order to compare the aggregated expected utility of a decision made by either rule, note that the decision differs only for the configuration C and for those T containing $N \setminus C$. For all the latter, as $w(T) \geq w(N \setminus C) > \bar{Q} \geq Q_\lambda$, the decision by $\mathcal{W}'_N$ (acceptance) is utilitarian-better than by $\mathcal{W}_N$ (rejection). The reverse only occurs for the configuration C. It then suffices to show that what is lost by rejecting for configuration C is outweighed by what is gained by accepting for the equally probable configuration $N \setminus C$. Again using (45) and (46), we have

$$E\left[\sum_{k \in M} u_k^\lambda \mid C \ \& \ \text{accept}\right] - E\left[\sum_{i \in M} u_i^\lambda \mid C \ \& \ \text{reject}\right]$$

$$= (2\lambda - 1)\frac{m}{2} + \frac{\lambda}{\sqrt{2\pi}}(w(C) - w(N \setminus C)) < (2\lambda - 1)\frac{m}{2},$$

while

$$E\left[\sum_{k \in M} u_k^\lambda \mid N \setminus C \ \& \ \text{accept}\right] - E\left[\sum_{i \in M} u_i^\lambda \mid N \setminus C \ \& \ \text{reject}\right]$$

$$= (2\lambda - 1)\frac{m}{2} + \frac{\lambda}{\sqrt{2\pi}}(w(N \setminus C) - w(C)) > (2\lambda - 1)\frac{m}{2}.$$

Therefore, $\mathcal{W}_N$ does not implement the utilitarian optimum according to the approximation based on (45) and (46). $\square$

Therefore a utilitarian-optimal rule (according to approximations (45) and (46)) should contain the winning configurations in $W^{(w,\bar{Q})}$ *plus* some configurations whose weight equals the quota $\bar{Q}$ if such a thing is possible. Then we have the following corollary.

Corollary 27 *Under Assumptions 1 and 2, assuming all the represented groups are large enough, if $\lambda > \frac{1}{2}$, the weighted majority rule $\mathcal{W}_N = W^{(w,\bar{Q})}$ in the committee for weights $w_i = \sqrt{m_i}$ and quota $\bar{Q}$ given by (49) implements the a priori utilitarian principle with close approximation.*

Remarks. (i) Barberà and Jackson [6] consider an even wider setting in which the representatives' vote in the committee in the two-stage decision process is an arbitrary known function of the preferences within their respective groups. Thus no voting rule governs the representatives' vote. Also the preference profile in each group concerning acceptance/rejection is in principle arbitrary, and only a probability distribution over the possible profiles is assumed to be known. In such a general setting Barberà and Jackson address the utilitarian question of decisions in the committee as a function of the vote/preference configuration that maximizes the expected aggregated utility. The generality of a setting in which the usual notion of voting rule does not constrain their model allows them to deal with ties by tossing a coin. But when they specify the conditions limiting the degrees of freedom (on preferences and decision-making process) they come very close to the conclusions obtained here.

(ii) As has been mentioned, some authors discuss the arguments in support of the a priori probability distribution p^* and favour other models. The independence of voters' behaviour is perhaps the aspect most criticized. The most important rival probabilistic model is that of '*homogeneity*'. Straffin [80] proposes the following probabilistic model for a set of voters. Let $t \in [0,1]$ be chosen from the uniform distribution on $[0,1]$, and assume that each voter votes 'yes' with probability t and 'no' with probability $(1 - t)$. This raises the question of egalitarianism and utilitarianism for alternative probabilistic models[56].

---

[56] See e.g. [9, 21, 55].

3.9 Exercises

1. Prove or disprove with a counterexample the following statements.

   (a) A voter occupying a null seat is never successful or decisive.
   (b) Whenever a proposal is accepted, a voter occupying a veto seat is successful and decisive.
   (c) Whenever a proposal is rejected, a voter occupying a veto seat is successful and decisive.

2. Assume the following three-person voting behaviour: voters 1 and 2 vote independently from each other, both with probability $1/2$, in favour of the proposal, and voter 3 votes as voter 2 does. (a) Obtain the probability distribution p that describes this. (b) If they make decisions by simple majority, calculate: α and Ω_i, Ω_i^{i+}, Ω_i^{i-}, Φ_i, Φ_i^{i+} and Φ_i^{i-}, for $i = 1, 2, 3$, for the voting situation $(\mathcal{W}^{\text{SM}}, p)$.

3. Let $\mathcal{W} \subseteq \mathcal{W}'$. (i) Prove that for any p and any i,

   $$\alpha(\mathcal{W}, p) \leq \alpha(\mathcal{W}', p),$$

   $$\Omega_i^{i+}(\mathcal{W}, p) \leq \Omega_i^{i+}(\mathcal{W}', p),$$

   $$\Omega_i^{i-}(\mathcal{W}, p) \geq \Omega_i^{i-}(\mathcal{W}', p).$$

   (ii) Show that in general the inequality may hold in either sense for Ω_i and Φ_i, and for the Coleman indices to prevent and to initiate action.

4. Consider the five-person voting situation $(\mathcal{W}^{\text{SM}}, p^*)$. Calculate $\Omega_1(\mathcal{W}^{\text{SM}}, p^*)$ and $\Phi_1(\mathcal{W}^{\text{SM}}, p^*)$, and compare them with the conditional probability of voter 1 being successful and that of his/her being decisive given that 1 and 2 voted the same way.

5. Show that symmetry is a sufficient condition for a voting rule to be a priori egalitarian (i.e. $\Omega_i(\mathcal{W}, p^*) = \Omega_j(\mathcal{W}, p^*)$ for all i, j), but this condition is not necessary.

6. Garrett and Tsebelis [26] criticize traditional power indices because voters' preferences and any other relevant contextual information are ignored. To illustrate their point they propose the following situation. Consider a seven-voter voting rule where a proposal is passed if it has the support of at least five. Voters'

unidimensional preferences are located on a real line so that only connected and minimal winning configurations occur, and all of them are equally probable. They claim that a 'more realistic power index' would be $(\frac{1}{15}, \frac{2}{15}, \frac{1}{3}, \frac{1}{3}, \frac{1}{3}, \frac{2}{15}, \frac{1}{15})$.

   (a) What is the implicit voting situation $(\mathcal{W}^{GT}, p^{GT})$?

   (b) Compute $\Phi(\mathcal{W}^{GT}, p^{GT})$ and compare this measure with what Garrett and Tsebelis propose.

7. Consider the following two weighted majorities: $\mathcal{W}^{(W,Q)}$, with $Q = 70$ and $w = (55, 35, 10)$, and $\mathcal{W}^{(w', Q)}$, with $Q = 70$ and $w' = (50, 25, 25)$.

   (a) Give the set of winning configurations for the two weighted majorities.

   (b) Compute the Banzhaf index for the two voting rules and show how the Banzhaf index of a voter who loses weight increases. Is this paradoxical?

8. Consider the following voting situation in a four-party parliament where decisions are made by a simple majority. There is a large right-wing party with 40 seats, and three left-wing parties with 20 seats each. The three left-wing parties (1, 2 and 3) always vote together, while the right-wing party (4) is always isolated, so that the probability distribution over vote configurations is given by

$$p(S) = \begin{cases} 1/2, & \text{if } S = \{1, 2, 3\} \text{ or } \{4\} \\ 0, & \text{otherwise.} \end{cases}$$

   (a) Give the set of the winning configurations (modelling the decision-making in the parliament as a four-person weighted majority rule).

   (b) Compute $\Phi_i(\mathcal{W}, p)$ and $\Omega_i(\mathcal{W}, p)$, for $i = 1, 2, 3, 4$.

   (c) Show that $\Phi_1(\mathcal{W}, p) > \Phi_4(\mathcal{W}, p)$ in spite of $w_1 < w_4$. Is this paradoxical?

9. Let the voting situation $(\mathcal{W}, p)$ with $\mathcal{W} = \{\{1, 2, 3\}, \{1, 2, 4\}, \{1, 2, 3, 4\}\}$, and

$$p(S) = \begin{cases} 9/32, & \text{if } S = \{1, 2\} \text{ or } \{3, 4\} \\ 1/32, & \text{otherwise.} \end{cases}$$

'Take-it-or-leave-it' committees   99

(a) Compute $\Phi_i(W,p)$ and $\Omega_i(W,p)$.
(b) Is the vetoer more likely to be successful than the others?

10. Prove the following statement [38]: $\Omega_i(W,p) = \frac{1}{2} + \frac{1}{2}\Phi_i(W,p)$ holds for every W if and only if $p = p^*$.

11. Prove that $\Phi_i(W,p)$, $\Phi_i^{i+}(W,p)$ and $\Phi_i^{i-}(W,p)$ coincide for every i and every voting rule W if and only if the vote of each voter is independent from the vote of all the remaining voters.

12. Consider the following variants of the model introduced in Section 3.7. Replace any voter's utility in Assumption 2 by

$$u_i(W,S) = \begin{cases} \lambda, & \text{if } i \in S \in W, \\ \alpha, & \text{if } i \notin S \notin W, \\ \beta, & \text{if } i \in S \notin W, \\ \gamma, & \text{if } i \notin S \in W. \end{cases}$$

(a) Discuss the possible relationships between λ, α, β, and γ (assuming $\lambda > \beta$, and $\alpha > \gamma$).
(b) Give voter i's expected utility ($\bar{u}_i(W,p)$) as a function of λ, α, β, and γ, and voter i's probabilities of success and of being in favour of the proposal.
(c) What is the rationale behind $\alpha = \beta = 0$ and $\gamma = \lambda - 1$?
(d) Prove that if $\alpha = \beta = 0$ and $\gamma = \lambda - 1$ then

$$\bar{u}_i(W,p) = \lambda\Omega_i^+(W,p) + (1-\lambda)\Omega_i^-(W,p) - (1-\lambda)(1-\gamma_i(p)).$$

3.10 Appendix

Proof of Proposition 12 (Section 3.7.2). In view of (28), we have

$$\text{Max} \sum_{i \in N} \bar{u}_i^\lambda(W,p^*)$$

$$= \text{Max} \sum_{i \in N} \left(\left(\frac{1}{2} - \lambda \right) \left(\frac{1}{2} - \alpha(W,p^*) \right) + \frac{\Omega_i(W,p^*)}{2} \right).$$

This sum can be rewritten as

$$= \sum_{i \in N} \frac{1}{2} \left(\frac{1}{2} - \lambda \right) + \sum_{i \in N} \left(\left(\lambda - \frac{1}{2} \right) \sum_{S:S \in W} \frac{1}{2^n} \right)$$
$$+ \frac{1}{2} \sum_{i \in N} \sum_{S:i \in S \in W} \frac{1}{2^n} + \frac{1}{2} \sum_{i \in N} \sum_{S:i \notin S \notin W} \frac{1}{2^n}.$$

As λ does not depend on the rule, the first sum can be ignored for the maximization problem. The second term is

$$\frac{1}{2^n} \sum_{i \in N} \sum_{S:S \in W} \left(\lambda - \frac{1}{2} \right) = \frac{1}{2^n} \sum_{S:S \in W} \left(\lambda - \frac{1}{2} \right) n.$$

The third term is

$$\frac{1}{2} \sum_{i \in N} \sum_{S:i \in S \in W} \frac{1}{2^n} = \frac{1}{2^n} \sum_{S:S \in W} \frac{s}{2}.$$

The fourth term is

$$\frac{1}{2} \sum_{i \in N} \sum_{S:i \notin S \notin W} \frac{1}{2^n} = \frac{1}{2^n} \sum_{S:S \notin W} \frac{n-s}{2}$$
$$= \frac{1}{2^n} \left(\sum_{S:S \subseteq N} \frac{n-s}{2} - \sum_{S:S \in W} \frac{n-s}{2} \right).$$

Also note that $\sum_{S:S \subseteq N} \frac{n-s}{2}$ does not depend on the rule. Thus, deleting this term and the multiplying factor $\frac{1}{2^n}$ we have the equivalent maximization problem:

$$\text{Max} \sum_{S:S \in W} \left(\left(\lambda - \frac{1}{2} \right) n + \frac{s}{2} - \frac{n-s}{2} \right) = \text{Max} \sum_{S:S \in W} (s - (1 - \lambda)n),$$

which is problem (31). $\qquad \square$

Proof of Proposition 14 (Section 3.7.2). Let W be a voting rule such that for some $S \in W$, it holds $s < \frac{n}{2}$. If so there must exist a minimal winning configuration $T \in W$ such that $t < \frac{n}{2}$. Let W' be the rule

$$W' := (W \setminus \{T\}) \cup W^{N \setminus T},$$

'Take-it-or-leave-it' committees

where $W \setminus \{T\}$ is the rule that results from W by eliminating T from the winning configurations, and $W^{N \setminus T}$ is the $(N \setminus T)$-unanimity rule (see Section 1.3.2). As $N \setminus T$ intersects all $S \in W \setminus \{T\}$, W' is a proper voting rule. Then we have

$$\sum_{S \in W'} (s - (1 - \lambda)n)$$

$$\geq \sum_{S \in W} (s - (1 - \lambda)n) - (t - (1 - \lambda)n) + ((n - t) - (1 - \lambda)n)$$

$$= \sum_{S \in W} (s - (1 - \lambda)n) - 2t + n > \sum_{S \in W} (s - (1 - \lambda)n).$$

Therefore W does not solve (31). In other words, W does not implement the utilitarian principle. $\square$

Proof of Lemma 17 (Section 3.8.1). $\Phi_k(W_M^{SM}, p_M^*)$ is the a priori probability of k being decisive in W_M^{SM}. In other words (assuming m odd), it gives the probability that $\frac{m-1}{2}$ voters vote 'yes' and $\frac{m-1}{2}$ voters vote 'no' in $M \setminus k$. Using Stirling's approximation (relationship (8) in 1.2.2), for m large $C_{m-1}^{\frac{m-1}{2}} \simeq 2^{m-1} \sqrt{\frac{2}{\pi(m-1)}}$. Thus, this probability approaches $\sqrt{\frac{2}{\pi(m-1)}}$ as m increases. For m large enough we can replace $m - 1$ by m, and we have (37). A similarly good approximation is obtained if m is even. $\square$

Proof of Lemma 18 (Section 3.8.1). An individual $k \in M_i$ is decisive in the ideal two-stage decision-making if k is decisive in the decision made in M_i, and M_i's representative i is decisive in the committee at the second stage. Assuming the behaviour described by p_M^*, the two events are independent. The probability of the first is given by $\Phi_k(W_{M_i}^{SM}, p_{M_i}^*)$. As representative i follows the majority opinion in M_i, i's vote is independent of the vote of the other members of the committee. If m_i is odd the probability of i voting 'yes' is exactly $1/2$, and very close to it if m_i is even but large. Thus, the probability of the latter is (approximately if m_i is even) $\Phi_i(W_N, p_N^*)$, and we have (38). $\square$

Proof of Proposition 19 (Section 3.8.1). Let $k \in M_j$. By (39), we have

$$\Phi_k(\mathcal{W}_M, p_M^*) \simeq \sqrt{\frac{2}{\pi m_i}} \Phi_i(\mathcal{W}_N, p_N^*)$$

$$\leq \sqrt{\frac{2}{\pi m_i}} \leq \sqrt{\frac{2}{\pi \, \mathrm{Min}_{i \in N} m_i}} = \xi.$$

By (21) and the same approximation, we have

$$\Omega_k(\mathcal{W}_M, p_M^*) = 0.5 + 0.5 \Phi_k(\mathcal{W}_M, p_M^*) \leq 0.5 + 0.5\xi.$$

Similarly, (19) and (20) lead to the other results. $\qquad\square$

Proof of Proposition 20 (Section 3.8.2). Assume $\bar{u}_k^\lambda(\mathcal{W}_M, p_M^*) \geq \bar{u}_l^\lambda(\mathcal{W}_M, p_M^*)$. Then by (43), (21) and (40), we have

$$\bar{u}_k^\lambda(\mathcal{W}_M, p_M^*) - \bar{u}_l^\lambda(\mathcal{W}_M, p_M^*) = \frac{1}{4} \left(\Phi_k(\mathcal{W}_M, p_M^*) - \Phi_l(\mathcal{W}_M, p_M^*) \right)$$

$$\leq \frac{1}{4} \Phi_k(\mathcal{W}_M, p_M^*) \leq \frac{1}{4}\xi.$$

By (25), $u_{\mathrm{Max}}^\lambda = \mathrm{Max}\{\lambda, 1 - \lambda\} \geq \frac{1}{2}$, $u_{\mathrm{Min}}^\lambda = 0$, and the first inequality follows.

Again using (43) we have

$$\frac{\bar{u}_k^\lambda(\mathcal{W}_M, p_M^*)}{\bar{u}_l^\lambda(\mathcal{W}_M, p_M^*)} = \frac{\frac{1}{4} + \frac{1}{4}\Phi_k(\mathcal{W}_M, p_M^*) + (\frac{1}{2} - \alpha(\mathcal{W}_M, p_M^*))(\frac{1}{2} - \lambda)}{\frac{1}{4} + \frac{1}{4}\Phi_l(\mathcal{W}_M, p_M^*) + (\frac{1}{2} - \alpha(\mathcal{W}_M, p_M^*))(\frac{1}{2} - \lambda)}$$

$$\leq \frac{\frac{1}{4} + \frac{1}{4}\Phi_k(\mathcal{W}_M, p_M^*) + (\frac{1}{2} - \alpha(\mathcal{W}_M, p_M^*))(\frac{1}{2} - \lambda)}{\frac{1}{4} + (\frac{1}{2} - \alpha(\mathcal{W}_M, p_M^*))(\frac{1}{2} - \lambda)}$$

$$\leq 1 + \frac{0.25\Phi_k(\mathcal{W}_M, p_M^*)}{\frac{1}{4} + (\frac{1}{2} - \alpha(\mathcal{W}_M, p_M^*))(\frac{1}{2} - \lambda)}.$$

In order to find the upper bound we need to know the sign of

$$\left(\frac{1}{2} - \alpha(\mathcal{W}_M, p_M^*) \right) \left(\frac{1}{2} - \lambda \right).$$

'Take-it-or-leave-it' committees 103

By (18), we have $\alpha(\mathcal{W}_M, p_M^*) \leq \frac{1}{2}$, so that if $\lambda \leq \frac{1}{2}$ the sign of this term is positive, and a lower bound of the denominator is $\frac{1}{4}$. Then we have

$$\frac{\bar{u}_k^\lambda(\mathcal{W}_M, p_M^*)}{\bar{u}_l^\lambda(\mathcal{W}_M, p_M^*)} \leq 1 + \frac{0.25\Phi_k(\mathcal{W}_M, p_M^*)}{\frac{1}{4}} \leq 1 + \xi.$$

If $\lambda > \frac{1}{2}$, the denominator has to be expanded in order to find a lower bound:

$$\frac{1}{4} - \left(\frac{1}{2} - \alpha(\mathcal{W}_M, p_M^*)\right)\left(\lambda - \frac{1}{2}\right)$$

$$= \frac{1}{2} - \frac{1}{2}\lambda - \frac{1}{2}\alpha(\mathcal{W}_M, p_M^*) + \lambda\alpha(\mathcal{W}_M, p_M^*)$$

$$= \frac{1}{2}(1 - \lambda) - \alpha(\mathcal{W}_M, p_M^*)(1 - \lambda) + \frac{1}{2}\alpha(\mathcal{W}_M, p_M^*)$$

$$= \left(\frac{1}{2} - \alpha(\mathcal{W}_M, p_M^*)\right)(1 - \lambda) + \frac{1}{2}\alpha(\mathcal{W}_M, p_M^*) \geq \frac{1}{2}\alpha(\mathcal{W}_M, p_M^*).$$

Then, if $k \in M_j$, using (39), we have

$$\frac{\bar{u}_k^\lambda(\mathcal{W}_M, p_M^*)}{\bar{u}_l^\lambda(\mathcal{W}_M, p_M^*)} \leq 1 + \frac{0.25\Phi_k(\mathcal{W}_M, p_M^*)}{0.5\alpha(\mathcal{W}_M, p_M^*)} \simeq 1 + \sqrt{\frac{2}{\pi m_j}} \frac{\Phi_j(\mathcal{W}_N, p_N^*)}{2\alpha(\mathcal{W}_M, p_M^*)}$$

$$\leq 1 + \xi \frac{\Phi_j(\mathcal{W}_N, p_N^*)}{2\alpha(\mathcal{W}_M, p_M^*)}.$$

As $\Phi_j(\mathcal{W}_N, p_N^*) = \Phi_j^{j+}(\mathcal{W}_N, p_N^*) = \sum_{\substack{S:i\in S\in\mathcal{W} \\ S\backslash i \notin \mathcal{W}}} \frac{1}{2^{n-1}}$, and $\alpha(\mathcal{W}_M, p_M^*) \simeq \alpha(\mathcal{W}_N, p_N^*)$, then as $\alpha(\mathcal{W}_N, p_N^*) = \sum_{S:i\in S\in\mathcal{W}} \frac{1}{2^n}$, we conclude that $\frac{\Phi_j(\mathcal{W}_N, p_N^*)}{\alpha(\mathcal{W}_N, p_N^*)} \leq 2$, and the result follows. $\qquad\square$

Note that we could obtain an even lower bound for the difference in utilities in absolute terms:

$$|\bar{u}_k^\lambda(\mathcal{W}_M, p_M^*) - \bar{u}_l^\lambda(\mathcal{W}_M, p_M^*)| \leq \frac{1}{4}\sqrt{\frac{2}{\pi \, \mathrm{Min}_{i\in N}m_i}} - \frac{1}{4}\sqrt{\frac{2}{\pi \, \mathrm{Max}_{i\in N}m_i}}.$$

Proof of Lemma 23 (Section 3.8.3). Assume m_i is odd, i.e. $m_i = 2r + 1$ for an integer r. Then the expected number of people voting 'yes' when a majority votes 'yes' is

$$E\left[\#S_i \mid \#S_i > \frac{m_i}{2}\right] = \frac{\sum_{S:r<s\leq m_i} \frac{1}{2^{m_i}} s}{\frac{1}{2}} = \frac{1}{2^{m_i-1}} \sum_{S:r<s\leq m_i} s$$

$$= \frac{1}{2^{m_i-1}} \left((r+1)C_{m_i}^{r+1} + (r+2)C_{m_i}^{r+2} + \cdots + mC_{m_i}^{m_i}\right)$$

$$= \frac{m_i}{2^{m_i-1}} \left(\frac{(m_i-1)!}{(m_i-r-1)!r!} + \cdots + \frac{(m_i-1)!}{0!(m_i-1)!}\right)$$

$$= \frac{m_i}{2^{m_i-1}} \left(C_{m_i-1}^{r} + C_{m_i-1}^{r+1} + \cdots + C_{m_i-1}^{m_i-1}\right). \tag{51}$$

Now, by (5) in Section 1.2.1, we have

$$C_{m_i-1}^{r} + C_{m_i-1}^{r+1} + \cdots + C_{m_i-1}^{m_i-1} = 2^{m_i-2} + \frac{1}{2}C_{m_i-1}^{r}.$$

Thus, as $r = \frac{m_i-1}{2}$, substituting in (51) and using (8) (see Section 1.2.2) we have

$$E\left[\#S_i \mid \#S_i > \frac{m_i}{2}\right] = \frac{m_i}{2^{m_i-1}} \left(2^{m_i-2} + \frac{1}{2}C_{m_i-1}^{\frac{m_i-1}{2}}\right)$$

$$\simeq \frac{m_i}{2^{m_i-1}} \left(2^{m_i-2} + \frac{1}{2}2^{m_i-1}\sqrt{\frac{2}{\pi(m_i-1)}}\right)$$

$$= \frac{m_i}{2} + m_i\sqrt{\frac{1}{2\pi(m_i-1)}}$$

$$\simeq \frac{m_i}{2} + \sqrt{\frac{m_i}{2\pi}}.$$

In the last step we have replaced $m_i - 1$ by m_i within the square root in order to simplify the expression. Similarly, it can be checked that when m_i is sufficiently large the approximation is as good for m_i even. The other approximations follow similar steps. □

4 | *Bargaining committees*

This chapter addresses voting situations in which a committee bargains in search of agreement over a set of feasible alternatives 'in the shadow of a voting rule'[57]. More specifically we consider a 'bargaining' committee that makes decisions in an environment such as the one described in Section 2.2. In particular we are interested in the role and influence of the voting rule on the outcome of negotiations in order to assess the adequacy of a voting rule in different contexts.

In Section 4.1 we describe the environment of what we call a 'bargaining committee' and in Section 4.2 a model for such a committee is presented. The situation is modelled by the two basic ingredients that specify it: the voting rule that prescribes what coalitions can enforce an agreement, and the voters' preference profile. The situation summarily described by this two-ingredient model is then analysed using two approaches. The question of what agreements are likely to arise in such situation is addressed first in Section 4.3 from a cooperative-axiomatic game-theoretic point of view, as an extension of Nash's bargaining theory. That is, by imposing reasonable conditions for an agreement among rational individuals the class of admissible agreements is drastically narrowed and characterized. The same question about reasonable agreements is then approached from a non-cooperative game-theoretic point of view in Section 4.4. That is, the decision-making process in a bargaining committee is modelled as a non-cooperative game. This is done for a variety of 'protocols', for which the stationary subgame perfect equilibria are investigated. The result is consistent with the results obtained from the axiomatic approach; that is, the same family of agreements is obtained as a limit case. In this way cooperative and non-cooperative game-theoretic support is provided for a new and richer interpretation of some power indices as measures of 'bargaining power' in a precise game-theoretic sense.

---

[57] Most of the material in this chapter is drawn from [48–51].

106   *Voting and Collective Decision-Making*

The question of the choice of voting rule in a bargaining committee is addressed in Section 4.5, with a compromise between egalitarianism and utilitarianism as the criterion applied. In Section 4.6, the same question is addressed for a bargaining committee of representatives of groups of different sizes, based on the same egalitarian/utilitarian compromise as the criterion of fairness. We propose as 'optimal' a 'neutral' voting rule in the sense that any player is indifferent between bargaining personally and leaving bargaining in the hands of a representative (at least under certain symmetry conditions relative to preferences within each group). The normative recommendation that this approach yields is different from those obtained for a take-it-or-leave-it committee in Section 3.8.

4.1 The bargaining scenario

Recall the scenario described in Section 2.2 as a *bargaining committee*. We consider a committee that makes decisions under a given voting rule under the following conditions: the committee (i) deals with different issues over time; (ii) bargains about each issue by seeking consensus on an agreement, in search of which it is entitled to adjust the proposal; (iii) this negotiation is carried out under the condition that any winning coalition (according to the voting rule) has the capacity to enforce agreements; and (iv) for every issue a different configuration of preferences emerges in the committee over the set of feasible agreements concerning the issue at stake.

A situation like this has very little in common with the one described as a take-it-or-leave-it committee, which was dealt with in Chapter 3, other than the fact that a voting rule plays a role in both cases. Apart from that the voting situation we consider now is completely different. In fact, properly speaking this is a bargaining situation, which means a game situation and calls for a game-theoretic analysis. It is worth remarking that the question of the 'power' or 'voting power' of the players involved in such a situation is premature. The natural main issue that should be addressed first is what the reasonable outcome of negotiations is in such conditions. The first main question is: What general agreements are likely to arise? Only after an answer to this basic question is obtained can one reasonably try to evaluate the relative advantage that the voting rule may give to each player.

Bargaining committees 107

4.2 A model of a bargaining committee: voting rule and voters' preferences

The situation described above is a genuine game situation, a formal model of which is obtained by incorporating the following elements. First, the set of members of the committee, or *players* for short, $N = \{1, 2, \ldots, n\}$, and the N-voting rule W under which bargaining takes place. Second, the preference profile of the members of the committee over the feasible agreements for the particular issue at stake. We assume that the players have expected utility preferences according to the von Neumann and Morgenstern model reviewed in Section 1.4.4. We assume à la Nash [60] that lotteries over feasible agreements are also feasible (or that an agreement equivalent for all players to any such lottery is always feasible). Thus we can summarize the configuration of voters' preferences over the set of feasible agreements in utility terms by the set of associated utility payoffs, exactly as in a classical n-person bargaining problem (see Section 2.1.1[58]). Thus the second ingredient of the model is the set of feasible utility vectors $D \subseteq \mathbb{R}^N$, together with the particular vector $d \in D$ associated with the *disagreement* or *status quo* that would be the payoff vector if no agreement were reached. Thus the pair (D, d) is a summary of the situation concerning the players' decisions. The problem they face is to agree on a point in D.

Under these assumptions, the situation can be summarized by a pair (B, W), where $B = (D, d)$ represents the preference profile in the committee in utility terms, and W is the N-voting rule to enforce agreements. We make the following assumptions consistent with this interpretation. We assume that D is a *closed, convex* and *comprehensive* set containing d, such that there exists some $x \in D$ s.t. $x > d$. We denote the boundary of D by ∂D. We assume also that $D_d := \{x \in D : x \geq d\}$ is *bounded* and *non-level* (i.e. $\forall x, y \in \partial D \cap D_d$, $x \geq y \Rightarrow x = y$).

Note that formally any such B is a classical n-person bargaining problem. The set of all such bargaining problems is denoted by $\mathcal{B}$.

Thus, we are concerned with pairs $(B, W) \in \mathcal{B} \times VR_N$, each of which can be referred to as a *bargaining problem B under rule W*, or for short just a *bargaining committee* (B, W).

---

[58] Readers not familiar with the material presented in Section 2.1 should read it before proceeding with this section.

It is worth remarking that this model includes classical bargaining problems and simple superadditive games as particular cases. To show this, let us see first how this class of problems can be associated with a subclass of non-transferable utility (NTU) games (Section 1.5.4).

If no player can be forced to accept a payoff below status quo level, we can associate an NTU game $(N, V_{(B,\mathcal{W})})$ with each bargaining committee $(B, \mathcal{W})$ by associating with each coalition S the set of all utility vectors feasible for S if such a coalition forms. For each $S \subseteq N$, let $\mathrm{pr}_S : \mathbb{R}^N \to \mathbb{R}^S$ denote the natural S-projection, defined by $\mathrm{pr}_S(x) := (x_i)_{i \in S}$, for all $x = (x_i)_{i \in N} \in \mathbb{R}^N$, and denote $x^S := \mathrm{pr}_S(x)$ for any $x \in \mathbb{R}^N$. Then, if $S \in \mathcal{W}$, the set of utility vectors feasible for S is the set of points in $\mathbb{R}^S$ that are the S-projection of those points in D that give to players in $N \setminus S$ at least the disagreement payoff. More precisely, for any S, the subset $V_{(B,\mathcal{W})}(S)$ of $\mathbb{R}^S$ is given by

$$
V_{(B,\mathcal{W})}(S) := \left\{ \begin{array}{ll} \mathrm{pr}_S\left(\left\{x \in D : x^{N \setminus S} \geq d^{N \setminus S}\right\}\right) & \text{if } S \in \mathcal{W}, \\ \mathrm{pr}_S(\mathrm{ch}(d)) & \text{if } S \notin \mathcal{W}, \end{array} \right.
$$

where $B = (D, d)$, and $\mathrm{ch}(d)$ denotes the comprehensive hull of $\{d\}$, that is, $\mathrm{ch}(d) = \left\{x \in \mathbb{R}^N : x \leq d\right\}$.

Classical n-person bargaining problems (see Sections 1.5.4 and 2.1.1) correspond to the case in which the voting rule is the unanimity rule, $\mathcal{W} = \{N\}$, with N as the only winning coalition, while simple superadditive TU games correspond to the case in which the configuration of preferences is TU-like in the following sense.

Definition 28 *In a bargaining committee* $(B, \mathcal{W})$ *the configuration of preferences is TU-like if* $B = \Lambda := (\Delta, 0)$*, where* $\Delta := \left\{x \in \mathbb{R}^N : \sum_{i \in N} x_i \leq 1\right\}$.

Observe that when $B = \Lambda$ the associated NTU game $V_{(\Lambda, \mathcal{W})}$ is equivalent to the *simple* TU game associated with the rule $v_{\mathcal{W}}$, given by (9) in Section 2.1.3. This two-ingredient model of a bargaining committee allows in particular for a neat distinction between voting rules and their associated simple TU games, two notions which are conceptually different (the specification of a voting rule does not involve its users' preferences, as pointed out in Section 2.1.3) but formally incorporate the same amount of information, and are often confused due to the habit of representing voting rules by simple games.

Bargaining committees

Thus the subfamily of NTU games $\{(N, V_{(B,\mathcal{W})}) : (B, \mathcal{W}) \in \mathcal{B} \times VR_N\}$ associated with what we have called bargaining committees properly contains all classical bargaining problems and all simple superadditive games.

As briefly discussed in Section 1.5.2, there are two game-theoretic approaches for modelling and analysing game situations: the cooperative and non-cooperative approaches. We first adopt a cooperative approach.

4.3 Cooperative game-theoretic approach

Nash's original two-person bargaining model (seen in 2.1.1) can be seen as consisting of two ingredients: a set of (two) players with von Neumann–Morgenstern preferences over a set of feasible agreements, and a voting procedure (unanimity) for settling agreements. As the only non-dictatorial two-person voting rule is unanimity, the second element is not explicit but tacit in Nash's model. In other words Nash's model is a particular case of the model just introduced, or, more properly speaking, the kind of situation we are interested in has been modelled by a natural generalization of Nash's model (and its traditional extension to n players), by considering n players and *an arbitrary voting rule instead of unanimity*.

The basic question that such a situation raises is what (payoff vectors associated with) agreements can reasonably arise from the interaction of rational players in search of consensus in the situation specified by the model. The importance of the issue is clear in many contexts. In contrast with the case of a 'take-it-or-leave-it' committee, only entitled to accept or reject proposals submitted to it, without capacity to modify them, it is often the case in a committee that uses a voting rule to make decisions that the final vote is merely the formal settlement of a bargaining process in which the issue to be voted upon has been adjusted to gain the acceptance of all members. In this case what general agreements are likely to arise? Or, in terms of our present model, is it possible to select a feasible agreement in D for each bargaining committee $(B, \mathcal{W})$ that can be arguably considered as a reasonable expectation for rational players confronted with the situation? Or, still in classical terms, what is the *value* for any player of the prospect of engaging in a situation such as this? Intuition suggests that the

110   *Voting and Collective Decision-Making*

voting rule under which negotiations take place may influence such expectations.

4.3.1 Rationality conditions

In order to find an answer we also follow Nash's approach. That is, by assuming conditions that can be considered desirable from the point of view of rational players that share the information encapsulated in the model (preference profile B and voting rule W) we narrow down the set of admissible agreements. The two-ingredient setting allows for the easy adaptation of the conditions used by Nash [60] and Shapley [76] in their respective setups with a similar objective.

Proceeding as in these two seminal papers we impose some conditions on a map $\Phi : B \times VR_N \to \mathbb{R}^N$, for vector $\Phi(B, W) \in \mathbb{R}^N$ to be considered as a rational agreement, or as a reasonable expectation of utility levels of a *general* agreement in a bargaining committee (B, W). As prerequisites we build the requirements of being feasible and no worse than the status quo for any player into the very notion of a solution. Namely, if $B = (D, d)$, we require: $\Phi(B, W) \in D$ *(feasibility)*, and $\Phi(B, W) \geq d$ *(individual rationality)*. Therefore we are implicitly assuming that no player can be forced to accept an agreement that is worse for him/her than the status quo[59].

In addition to this we impose the following conditions, all of them natural adaptations of Nash's and Shapley's characterizing properties (see Sections 2.1.1 and 2.1.2):

1. *Efficiency (Eff)*. For all $(B, W) \in B \times VR_N$, there is no $x \in D$ s.t. $x > \Phi(B, W)$. (Rational players will not agree on something when a better option is feasible.)

For any permutation $\pi : N \to N$, let $\pi B := (\pi(D), \pi(d))$ denote the bargaining problem that results from B by the π-permutation of its coordinates, so that for any $x \in \mathbb{R}^N$, $\pi(x)$ denotes the vector in $\mathbb{R}^N$ s.t. $\pi(x)_{\pi(i)} = x_i$.

2. *Anonymity (An)*. For all $(B, W) \in B \times VR_N$, and any permutation $\pi: N \to N$, and any $i \in N$, $\Phi_{\pi(i)}(\pi(B, W)) = \Phi_i(B, W)$, where

---

[59] A richer model would include *two* reference points: the status quo, as the initial starting point, and a vector of 'minimal rights' or minimal admissible payoffs. These two points coincide in a classical bargaining situation, but this is not necessarily so when unanimity is not required.

Bargaining committees 111

$\pi(B, W) := (\pi B, \pi W)$. (Expectations are not influenced by the players' labels but only by the structure of the problem.)

3. *Independence of irrelevant alternatives (IIA).* Let $B, B' \in \mathcal{B}$, with $B = (D, d)$ and $B' = (D', d')$, be such that $d' = d$, $D' \subseteq D$ and $\Phi(B, W) \in D'$. Then $\Phi(B', W) = \Phi(B, W)$, for any $W \in VR_N$. (An agreement that is considered satisfactory under a voting rule should also be considered satisfactory if under the same voting rule this agreement remains feasible in a smaller feasible set.)

4. *Invariance w.r.t. positive affine transformations (IAT).* For all $(B, W) \in \mathcal{B} \times VR_N$, and all $\alpha \in \mathbb{R}^N_{++}$ and $\beta \in \mathbb{R}^N$,

$$\Phi(\alpha * B + \beta, W) = \alpha * \Phi(B, W) + \beta,$$

where $\alpha * B + \beta = (\alpha * D + \beta, \alpha * d + \beta)$, denoting $\alpha * x := (\alpha_1 x_1, \ldots, \alpha_n x_n)$, and $\alpha * D + \beta := \{\alpha * x + \beta : x \in D\}$. (As seen in Section 1.4.4, utility representation of von Neumann–Morgenstern preferences is determined up to the choice of a zero and a unit of scale. Thus if the utility of each player is changed in this way the payoffs of a satisfactory agreement should change accordingly.)

5. *Null player (NP).* For all $(B, W) \in \mathcal{B} \times VR_N$, if $i \in N$ is a null player (i.e. a player occupying a null seat) in W, then $\Phi_i(B, W) = d_i$. (Null players' expectations are set to the *status quo* level, given their null capacity to influence the outcome given the voting rule according to which final agreements are enforced.)

Note that *Eff, IIA* and *IAT* are adaptations of Nash's axioms that state basically a relationship between the agreement-solution and the bargaining element B, while *An* (adapted from Nash's and Shapley's anonymity) and *NP* (from Shapley's system) concern the relationship with both elements, B and W. It may be worth remarking that *An* entails a consistent relabelling of voters in B *and* seats in W.

As we will see, these conditions are not enough to single out an agreement, so we also consider the two conditions below, which impose alternative constraints on the solution for TU configurations of preferences (i.e. when $B = \Lambda$). The first condition (*Transfer*) postulates that the effect of eliminating a minimal winning configuration from the set of winning configurations is the same whatever the voting rule. It is the adaptation to the present two-ingredient model of a condition equivalent to that of 'transfer' (see 2.1.6), introduced by Dubey

112 Voting and Collective Decision-Making

[18] in order to characterize the Shapley–Shubik index[60]. In [39] we replace it by a weaker condition (in the presence of anonymity) to characterize the Shapley–Shubik and Banzhaf indices. This is the second condition (*Symmetric gain–loss*), which requires that the effect of eliminating a minimal winning configuration from the list that specifies the voting rule is equal on any two voters belonging (not belonging) to it.

6. *Transfer (T).* For any two rules $W, W' \in VR_N$, and all $S \in M(W) \cap M(W')$ $(S \neq N)$:

$$\Phi(\Lambda, W) - \Phi(\Lambda, W \setminus \{S\}) = \Phi(\Lambda, W') - \Phi(\Lambda, W' \setminus \{S\}). \tag{52}$$

6^*. *Symmetric gain–loss (SymGL).* For any voting rule $W \in VR_N$, and all $S \in M(W)$ $(S \neq N)$,

$$\Phi_i(\Lambda, W) - \Phi_i(\Lambda, W \setminus \{S\}) = \Phi_j(\Lambda, W) - \Phi_j(\Lambda, W \setminus \{S\}),$$

for any two voters $i, j \in S$, and any two voters $i, j \in N \setminus S$.

4.3.2 Axiomatic characterizations

Denote by $\mathrm{Nash}(B)$ the Nash bargaining solution of an n-person bargaining problem $B = (D, d)$ (as in 2.1.1), that is

$$\mathrm{Nash}(B) = \arg \max_{x \in D_d} \prod_{i \in N} (x_i - d_i).$$

And denote by $\mathrm{Nash}^w(B)$ the w-weighted asymmetric Nash bargaining solution [32] of the same problem for a vector of non-negative weights $w = (w_i)_{i \in N}$, that is

$$\mathrm{Nash}^w(B) = \arg \max_{x \in D_d} \prod_{i \in N} (x_i - d_i)^{w_i}.$$

---

[60] Formulation (52) of this condition is equivalent (see [39]) to the more traditional form for simple games (see (10) in 2.1.6), which once rewritten in terms of the current model becomes

$$\Phi(\Lambda, W) + \Phi(\Lambda, W') = \Phi(\Lambda, W \cup W') + \Phi(\Lambda, W \cap W').$$

Bargaining committees 113

Basically, asymmetric Nash bargaining solutions emerge by dropping the requirement of symmetry or anonymity in the Nash system, hence their name. Obviously, the bigger the weight w_i the better for player i. The lack of symmetry may be due to an asymmetric environment (which is not included in the model) that favours different players differently. Binmore ([12], p. 78) uses the term *'bargaining power'* to refer to the players' weights and interprets the asymmetric Nash solutions as reflecting the different bargaining powers of the players *'determined by the strategic advantages conferred on players by the circumstances under which they bargain'*. Note that if we accept this interpretation then this notion of bargaining power is purely relative in the sense that a w-weighted asymmetric Nash bargaining solution, $\text{Nash}^w(B)$, does not vary if all the weights are multiplied by the same positive constant. In particular when the bargaining problem is $\Lambda = (\Delta, 0)$, then it is easy to check that

$$\text{Nash}^w(\Lambda) = \overline{w}, \tag{53}$$

where $\overline{w}$ is w's normalization, that is, $\overline{w} = w/\sum_{i \in N} w_i$.

The following result shows how conditions 1–5 considered in the previous section drastically restrict the possible answers to the question raised.

Theorem 29 *(Laruelle and Valenciano [48][61]) A value* $\Phi : \mathcal{B} \times VR_N \to \mathbb{R}^N$ *satisfies efficiency (Eff), anonymity (An), independence of irrelevant alternatives (IIA), invariance w.r.t. affine transformations (IAT) and null player (NP), if and only if*

$$\Phi(B, \mathcal{W}) = \text{Nash}^{\varphi(\mathcal{W})}(B), \tag{54}$$

for some map $\varphi : VR_N \to \mathbb{R}^N$ *that satisfies anonymity and null player.*

The interpretation is clear. If these conditions are accepted as desirable requirements for an agreement to be considered acceptable, they fail to characterize a single agreement for each problem, but restrict

---

[61] In fact the result proved in [48] is slightly different because there we do not assume non-levelness of D_d. This forces us to assume there a stronger version of *NP*, in which *only* null players have null expectations (though in exchange *Eff* is not needed). Thus this is an alternative version of the result proved there that can be proved assuming non-levelness of D_d as we do here.

114   *Voting and Collective Decision-Making*

drastically the structure of the solution. Namely, these conditions yield (54), a remarkable formula in which the impact of the voting rule is, so to say, 'separated' as exclusively affecting the 'bargaining power' (in the precise game-theoretic sense explained above) of each member of the committee. More precisely, such bargaining power is an anonymous function of the voting rule that gives power zero to the members occupying null seats, *whatever the preference profile.*

Note that in view of (54) and (53), we have in particular for a TU-like preference profile

$$\Phi(\Lambda, \mathcal{W}) = \text{Nash}^{\varphi(\mathcal{W})}(\Lambda) = \overline{\varphi}(\mathcal{W}),$$

where $\overline{\varphi}(\mathcal{W}) = \varphi(\mathcal{W}) / \sum_{i \in N} \varphi_i(\mathcal{W})$. That is, if the weights $\varphi(\mathcal{W})$ are normalized so as to add up to one, they coincide with $\Phi(\Lambda, \mathcal{W})$. Therefore, as $\text{Nash}^{\varphi(\mathcal{W})}(B) = \text{Nash}^{\overline{\varphi}(\mathcal{W})}(B)$, formula (54) can be rewritten

$$\Phi(B, \mathcal{W}) = \text{Nash}^{\Phi(\Lambda, \mathcal{W})}(B). \tag{55}$$

Remark. Therefore in our setting the old striking duality of the Shapley–Shubik index, mentioned in Section 2.1.3, which can be interpreted either as a piece of 'cake' or (on less clear grounds) as a measure of 'voting power' is clarified. This happens on clear grounds for *any* Φ *that satisfies the above conditions.* Namely, for any Φ that satisfies the above conditions, when the configuration of preferences is TU-like it holds that for any voting rule $\mathcal{W}$, vector $\Phi(\Lambda, \mathcal{W})$, which is a vector of expected utilities (pieces of a 'cake'), also gives the bargaining powers in the precise game-theoretic sense.

Nevertheless these conditions do not provide a crisp answer to the question of reasonable agreement. But in view of the above discussion, any map $\Phi(\Lambda, \cdot) : VR_N \to \mathbb{R}^N$ that satisfies efficiency, anonymity and null player would fit into formula (55) and yield a solution $\Phi(B, \mathcal{W})$ that satisfies the four conditions. In other words: assuming *Eff, An, IIA, IAT* and *NP, the solution, given by* (55), *will be unique as soon as* $\Phi(\Lambda, \cdot)$ *is specified.*

The conditions on $\Phi(\Lambda, \cdot)$ (efficiency, anonymity and null player) bring to mind the Shapley value or, more specifically in the context of simple games, the Shapley–Shubik index. But there are other alternatives; for instance, the normalization of any semivalue meets these

Bargaining committees 115

conditions, as do some other power indices, such as the *Holler–Packel index* (see [30]).

Denote by Sh(W) the Shapley–Shubik index of a voting rule W, i.e. the Shapley value of the associated simple game v_W. We have the following result (see [48]).

Proposition 30 *Let* $\Phi : \mathcal{B} \times VR_N \to \mathbb{R}^N$ *be a value that satisfies Eff, An, NP and T, then for any voting rule* $W \in VR_N$, $\Phi(\Lambda, W) = \mathrm{Sh}(W)$.

Then as an easy corollary of Theorem 29 and Proposition 30 we have the following theorem.

Theorem 31 *(Laruelle and Valenciano [48]) There exists a unique value* $\Phi : \mathcal{B} \times VR_N \to \mathbb{R}^N$ *that satisfies efficiency (Eff), anonymity (An), independence of irrelevant alternatives (IIA), invariance w.r.t. affine transformations (IAT), null player (NP) and transfer (T), and it is given by*

$$\Phi(B, W) = \mathrm{Nash}^{\mathrm{Sh}(W)}(B). \tag{56}$$

Note that (56) yields for $W = \{N\}$ (or any *symmetric* voting rule):

$$\Phi(B, W) = \mathrm{Nash}(B),$$

while when $B = \Lambda$, for any rule W, it yields

$$\Phi(\Lambda, W) = \mathrm{Sh}(W).$$

Therefore when the solution (56) is restricted to bargaining problems it yields the Nash bargaining solution, and when restricted to TU-like committees it yields the Shapley–Shubik index. Moreover, *NP* and *T* become empty requirements when W is fixed as the unanimity rule $W = \{N\}$ (or any *symmetric* voting rule). Thus the characterizing axioms in Theorems 29 and 31 *become Nash's axiomatic system* when restricted to $\Phi(\cdot, W) : \mathcal{B} \to \mathbb{R}^N$ for any fixed symmetric rule. On the other hand, as conditions *IIA* and *IAT* become empty requirements when fixing $B = \Lambda$, Proposition 30 can also be rephrased like this: the characterizing axioms in Theorem 31 when restricted to $\Phi(\Lambda, \cdot) : VR_N \to \mathbb{R}^N$ *become Shapley–Dubey's characterizing system of the Shapley–Shubik index* in W.

In other words, Theorem 31 integrates Nash's and Shapley–Dubey's [20] characterizations into one, but goes further beyond these previous characterizations, yielding a surprising solution to the more complex problem under consideration given by (56).

Remark. In Proposition 30, and in Theorem 31, transfer (T) can be replaced by the weaker (in the presence of anonymity) condition of *SymGL*. Thus we have still an alternative characterization of (56) given by the following theorem.

Theorem 32 *There exists a unique value* $\Phi : \mathcal{B} \times VR_N \to \mathbb{R}^N$ *that satisfies Eff, An, IIA, IAT, NP and SymGL, and it is given by (56).*

4.3.3 Discussion

As briefly reviewed in Section 2.1.3, the Shapley–Shubik index results from applying the Shapley value to the simple game (a particular type of TU-game) associated with a voting rule. Recall that the Shapley value (see 2.1.2) is meant to be a 'value' in the sense of Nash's bargaining solution. That is, a rational expectation of utility for a rational player engaging in *a sort of bargaining situation* described by a TU-game. Thus the Shapley–Shubik index presupposes a sort of bargaining situation described by the TU-game associated with the voting rule. But why the one described by this game? In the light of the richer model we have introduced here we see that this amounts to assuming a very particular preference profile in the committee: a TU-like preference profile. The simple game associated with a voting rule is often presented in the literature as merely an alternative way of presenting the same information: the voting rule itself. But, as has been pointed out by various authors, this representation has certain conceptual implications. In terms of the model presented here a TU preference profile is only a particular case. In other words, from the point of view provided by Theorem 29, the Shapley–Shubik index is just one of the candidates to fit formulae (54) and (55). Even the duality of the Shapley–Shubik index alluded to in Section 2.1.3 (piece of a 'cake' and measure of 'power') is shared by all the reasonable candidates to fit formula (54).

Now there is the question of the compellingness of the characterizing conditions, and consequently that of the results obtained: Theorems 29 and 31. The conditions in Theorem 29 are the result of integrating the (in our view) most compelling ones in the classical characterizations

Bargaining committees 117

of the Nash bargaining solution and the Shapley value. But these conditions are not enough to single out an agreement for each bargaining committee. We see no drawback here though, nor do we consider this lack of uniqueness surprising. After all, the model only incorporates the basic elements of the situation. In such situations, even assuming a given profile of preferences and a given voting rule, there are other details that would surely influence the outcome of negotiations. Most importantly, the particular 'protocol' or set of more or less clear rules according to which negotiations proceed in the committee is crucial. This will be seen more clearly in the next section, in which we adopt a non-cooperative approach, and consider a variety of such protocols.

As for Theorem 31, it gives 'axiomatic' support to (56), and consequently to the Shapley–Shubik index as a measure of bargaining power in a wider setting than the classical setup of simple games. But there is still the question of the compellingness of the 'transfer' condition, and the same doubts about this condition raised in the traditional setting of simple games in Section 2.1.6 remain in the current setup[62]. The discussion in the preceding paragraph sheds some light on this problem. It seems clear that there is not sufficient information within the current model to expect a unique compelling answer based on its two elements. In the next section we describe a very simple protocol that would yield the solution given by (56), thus providing non-cooperative foundations for it.

4.4 A non-cooperative model of a bargaining committee

We now explore the non-cooperative foundations of formulae (54) and (56). As Binmore [13] puts it: *'Cooperative game theory sometimes provides simple characterizations of* what *agreement rational players will reach, but we need non-cooperative game theory to understand*

---

[62] In [50] we consider a wider model admitting random voting rules. In this wider setting transfer can be derived from two relatively compelling conditions. One requires basically that when the preference profile is TU-like the expected payoff vector when a coin is to be tossed to choose between two voting rules is the same as the average between the expectations in either case. The other requires that, for any given preference profile, the expectations for two random voting rules such that both give the same probability of being winning to each coalition are the same. In other words, the expected payoffs depend only on the probabilities of each coalition being winning. But the latter condition is not beyond controversy as it means ignoring part of the information explicit in a random voting rule.

why.' In our case non-cooperative modelling requires further specification beyond the only two elements, B and W. Some assumptions are necessary about the way in which bargaining takes place in the committee. How are the proposals for agreement submitted and by whom? If consensus is sought, how are partial disagreements dealt with? How is enforcing power used by winning coalitions?

The mere formulation of these questions evidences the complexity of the situation we want to model. The answers are not obvious, and they surely differ in different real-world contexts. A positive approach would require us to have, if possible, the particular details that answer these questions for the particular committee we are dealing with. But we are not interested in a prediction for a particular committee. We are interested rather in a term of reference model in which the necessary details are at once simple and sufficiently specified, and in which the only source of 'bias' or asymmetry lies in the ingredients that specify the model so far: B and W. The two elements are usually asymmetric, as the proximity between players' preferences may differ, and often the voting rule is not symmetric. But if our ultimate goal is to establish a recommendation for the choice of a voting rule, it seems that such a recommendation should not depend on the preference configuration in the committee. This preference profile is different for each issue, while the voting rule is usually the same, at least for a specified variety of issues. Therefore it seems that our model of a *bargaining protocol* should not depend on the preference profile. On the other hand, a model consistent with the results obtained axiomatically, in which the bargaining power is a function of the voting rule, calls for bargaining protocols dependent on the voting rule.

Thus *we assume that in order to make a proposal the proposer needs the support of a winning coalition*. In this way the voting rule may be determinant for the chances of each player playing the role of proposer, and if the voting rule is not symmetric players may not have the same chances of playing that role.

The basic idea for the bargaining protocols that we consider is this: A player, with the support of a winning coalition to play the role of proposer, makes a proposal for agreement. If it is accepted by all players, the game ends. If any player rejects it then with some probability negotiation ends in failure (i.e. the *status quo* prevails), otherwise a new proposer and a winning coalition supporting him/her are chosen. Thus the negotiating process ends either when consensus is reached or,

Bargaining committees 119

if failure occurs, in the *status quo*. This still leaves many possibilities open: How is the supporting coalition formed? How is the proposer chosen by such a coalition? In particular this model accounts for the non-uniqueness of the answer provided by (54). Different specifications concerning these points yield different outcomes. As we will see, (56) appears as a special case with a sort of 'focal' appeal given the simplicity of the particular protocol associated, which confers on it some normative value as a term of reference.

In order to see the effect of the likelihood of being the proposer and the effect of the way in which disagreement is dealt with, we consider first a strictly probabilistic bargaining protocol in which no voting rule enters the model.

4.4.1 *Probabilistic protocols*

For each $p = (p_1, \ldots, p_n) \in \mathbb{R}_+^N$ s.t. $\sum_{i \in N} p_i = 1$, and each $r \in \mathbb{R}$ ($0 < r < 1$), assume the following strictly *probabilistic protocol* for a committee with a given preference profile $B = (D, d)$:

(p, r)-**Protocol:** A proposer $i \in N$ is chosen with probability p_i and makes a feasible proposal $x \in D_d$.

(i) If all the players accept it the game ends with payoffs x.
(ii) If any player does not accept it:
with probability r the process recommences,
with probability $1 - r$ the game ends in failure or 'breakdown' with payoffs d.

In this model p and r are exogenous, that is, they are the parameters that specify the model. The different likelihood of being a proposer should originate from some asymmetry in the environment outside the model. The interpretation of r is clear: it represents the patience of the committee in seeking consensus. The bigger r is, the smaller the risk of breakdown is, and the greater the chances of continuing to bargain in search of consensus after a disagreement.

We have the following result for this family of protocols; one for each probability distribution p and each r.

Theorem 33 *(Laruelle and Valenciano [51]) Let $B = (D, d)$ be the preference profile of an N-person committee satisfying the conditions specified in Section 4.2. Under a (p, r)-protocol: (i) there exists a*

120   *Voting and Collective Decision-Making*

stationary subgame perfect equilibrium SSPE; (ii) as $r \to 1$ any SSPE payoff vector converges to the w-weighted Nash bargaining solution of B with weights given by $w_i = p_i$.

We give here an outline of the proof in [51] that provides some interesting insights, in particular regarding the nature of the stationary subgame perfect equilibria (see 1.5.3) for each r.

A stationary strategy profile should specify for each player i the proposal that he/she will make whenever he/she is chosen to be the proposer, and what proposals he/she will accept from others. A proposal by i can be specified by a vector $\pi^i = (y_i, (x^i_j)_{j \in N \setminus i}) \in D_d$, where y_i is the payoff i will propose for him/herself, and x^i_j the payoff i will propose for $j \neq i$. Acceptance and refusal by i of a proposal by another player should depend only on the utility he/she receives. This can be specified by the minimal level of utility for which he/she will accept it. In *SSP* equilibrium every player should be offered at least what he/she expects if he/she refuses. We can assume $d = 0$ without loss of generality, and consistently in what follows we write D_0 instead of D_d. Then it should be that for all i and all $j \neq i$,

$$x^i_j \geq (1 - r)0 + rp_j y_j + r \sum_{k \in N \setminus j} p_k x^k_j.$$

As the proposer will seek the biggest payoff compatible with this condition, from the non-levelness D_0 we can assume equality. As the right-hand side of the equation does not depend on i, we can drop the superindex in x^i_j and x^k_j, and rewrite the above condition as an equation:

$$x_j = rp_j y_j + r \sum_{k \in N \setminus j} p_k x_j = rp_j y_j + r(1 - p_j)x_j,$$

that can be rewritten for all j as

$$rp_j y_j = (1 - r + rp_j)x_j. \tag{57}$$

Note that if $p_j = 0$ then $x_j = 0$, while if $p_j \neq 0$ (57) can be rewritten

$$y_j = \theta_j(r)x_j \quad (\text{where} \quad \theta_j(r) := \frac{1 - r + rp_j}{rp_j} > 1). \tag{58}$$

Bargaining committees 121

Observe that in this case (i.e. if $p_j \neq 0$) $y_j > x_j$. That is, being the proposer is desirable. In fact the proposer would make the best of this advantage by maximizing his/her payoff under the constraint of feasibility, that is, for all j

$$y_j = \max\left\{y \in \mathbb{R} : (x_{-j}, y) \in D\right\}, \tag{59}$$

where (x_{-j}, y) denotes the point whose j-coordinate is y and all other coordinates are equal to those of x (this maximum exists from the compactness of D_0). As players with probability 0 of being the proposer will receive 0 according to (57), one can constrain attention to those players with a positive probability of being the proposer. To simplify the notation, instead of dealing with this subset as $N' = \{i_1, \ldots, i_{n'}\} \subseteq N$, one can take $N' = N$.

We then have a system with $2n$ equations ((58) and (59)) with $2n$ unknown (($x_1, \ldots, x_n$) and ($y_1, \ldots, y_n$)) specifying a stationary strategy profile: each j whenever chosen as proposer will propose $\pi^j = (y_j, x_{-j})$. That is, he/she will propose y_j for him/herself and x_i for each $i \neq j$, and accept only proposals that give him/her at least x_j. The problem is to prove that a solution for this system exists. This can be proved by a fixed-point argument[63]. Then it only remains to show that the limit of *SSPE* ex ante payoffs (i.e. the expected payoffs before the proposer is chosen) as $r \to 1$ is Nash$^{\mathrm{P}}(B)$. We omit the details that can be seen in [51].

Interpretation of the *SSPE*. Let us examine the equations (58) and (59) solved by a *SSPE*. That is for all $j \in N$,

$$\begin{cases} y_j = \theta_j(r)x_j & \text{(with} \quad \theta_j(r) := \frac{1-r+rp_j}{rp_j} > 1) \\ y_j = \max\left\{y \in \mathbb{R} : (x_{-j}, y) \in D\right\} \end{cases}$$

(i) According to the first equation, *the relative advantage of the proposer diminishes as r increases*. Namely, $\theta_j(r) \to 1$ as $r \to 1$, where

---

[63] If B is the normalized TU bargaining problem $\Lambda = (\Delta, 0)$, equation (59) becomes

$$y_j = 1 - \sum_{k \in N \setminus j} x_k,$$

so that a linear system results that, as can be easily proved, yields as its unique solution: $x_j = rp_j$, and $y_j = 1 - r + rp_j$.

$\theta_j(r) = \frac{y_j}{x_j}$ is the ratio between player j's expected payoff when he/she is the proposer and when the proposer is someone else.

(ii) Nevertheless, as each player j is the proposer with probability p_j, ex ante (i.e. before the proposer is chosen), the expected *SSPE* payoffs for each r, are given by

$$\sum_{j \in N} p_j \pi^j = \sum_{j \in N} p_j(y_j, x_{-j}). \tag{60}$$

Thus *the probability of being the proposer has a determinant impact on the expected SSPE payoffs*, which according to Theorem 33 converge to $\text{Nash}^p(B)$ as $r \to 1$ (see Figure 4.1).

(iii) Note that the 'agreement' given by (60) *is not 'efficient' in general*, as it is the p-weighted average (i.e. a convex combination) of n points in ∂D: $\pi^1, \pi^2, \ldots, \pi^n$, namely the continuation *SSPE* payoffs after the choice of a proposer corresponding to the n different possible proposers. Thus, in general the *SSPE* ex ante payoffs are not 'efficient', as they are at the interior of D, though the bigger the r the closer they are to ∂D (see Figure 4.1).

(iv) By contrast, as for every proposer the continuation *SSPE* payoffs after the choice of a proposer are in ∂D, *if B is the TU-bargaining*

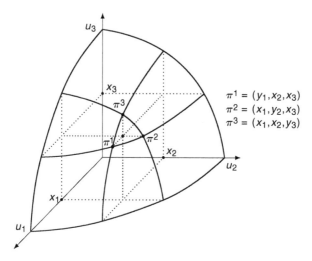

Figure 4.1. Continuation payoffs after the choice of proposer in a three-person problem.

problem $\Lambda = (\Delta, 0)$ *the SSPE ex ante payoffs are 'efficient'* (i.e. they are in ∂D) *and the same for every r*, and given by $\text{Nash}^p(\Lambda) = p$.

4.4.2 Bargaining protocols under a voting rule

What we have called a (p, r)-protocol is entirely specified in probabilistic terms. On the other hand, a comparison of the results given by Theorem 33 with formula (54) suggests a way of bridging these results obtained from different approaches. The basic idea is, as anticipated above, to link the probability of being the proposer, which is the source of bargaining power in a (p, r)-protocol, with the voting rule, which is the only element of the bargaining environment included in the model of a bargaining committee. But there are many ways of selecting a proposer based on the voting rule. That is, there are infinite ways of mapping voting rules into probability distributions over players. The question is whether there are any especially simple reasonable proposer selection protocols based on the voting rule within the plethora of possibilities consistent with formulae (54) and (56).

A general principle that seems reasonable is the following: In order to play the role of proposer the support of a winning coalition that he/she belongs to is needed. In order to consider in full generality ways of going from voting rules to probabilities respecting this principle we can abstract away protocol details. We consider maps $P : VR_N \to \mathcal{P}_{N \times 2^N}$, where $\mathcal{P}_{N \times 2^N}$ denotes the set of probability distributions over $N \times 2^N$, and use the notation $p_{\mathcal{W}}$ to denote $P(\mathcal{W})$. That is, under rule $\mathcal{W}$,

$$p_{\mathcal{W}}(i, S) = \text{Prob } (i \text{ is the proposer with the support of } S).$$

If we want $p_{\mathcal{W}} : N \times 2^N \to [0, 1]$ to respect the principle stated as well as the null player principle, the following should be required

$$(p_{\mathcal{W}}(i, S) \neq 0) \;\Rightarrow\; (i \in S \in \mathcal{W} \text{ and } S \setminus i \notin \mathcal{W}). \tag{61}$$

That is, *the proposer has to be decisive in the winning coalition that supports him/her*. In order to preserve the principle of anonymity the following must be required for any permutation π,

$$p_{\mathcal{W}}(i, S) = p_{\pi \mathcal{W}}(\pi i, \pi S). \tag{62}$$

Then any $p : VR_N \to \mathcal{P}_{N \times 2^N}$ satisfying (61) and (62) 'abstracts' a proposer's selection protocol determined by the voting rule in a bargaining committee which gives the probabilities of being the proposer by

$$p_i^{\mathcal{W}} := \sum_{S:i \in S} p_{\mathcal{W}}(i, S).$$

Any such protocol combined with the $(p^{\mathcal{W}}, r)$-protocol will yield a particular case of (54) in the limit (in the sense of Theorem 33). But, as has been stated, any map satisfying these conditions just 'abstracts' a proposer's selection protocol, and we are interested in the explicit protocols, not in their abstract summary by a vector of probabilities p. Still, a great variety of protocols are compatible with the above conditions.

We consider a general relatively simple way of selecting a player i to play the role of proposer and a winning coalition S containing him/her such that $i \in S \in \mathcal{W}$, and $S \setminus i \notin \mathcal{W}$. It seems natural to form a coalition in support of a proposer prior to the choice of the proposer. This entails a coalition formation process that can be encapsulated in a black-box-like probability distribution. Let p denote a probability distribution over coalitions described by a map $p : 2^N \to [0, 1]$ that, in order to be consistent with the anonymity assumption, assigns the same probability to all coalitions of the same size. In other words $p(S)$ depends only on s. Thus we can write p_s instead of $p(S)$.

(S-i)-**Protocols** (Choose first S, then i). Assume a given probability distribution over coalitions p (satisfying the above conditions), and the following protocol: Choose a coalition S according to p. Choose a player i in S at random. If $S \in \mathcal{W}$ and $S \setminus i \notin \mathcal{W}$, player i is the proposer, otherwise recommence until a proposer is chosen.

The probability of player i being the proposer after the first two steps is given by

$$\sum_{\substack{S:i \in S \in \mathcal{W} \\ S \setminus i \notin \mathcal{W}}} \frac{1}{s} p_s = \sum_{S:i \in S} \frac{1}{s} p_s (v_{\mathcal{W}}(S) - v_{\mathcal{W}}(S \setminus i)), \tag{63}$$

but in general no player is chosen as proposer after a single round. Nevertheless the actual probabilities of being proposer after applying an (S-i)-protocol are proportional to the probabilities given by (63),

Bargaining committees

which, as can easily be checked, yields the family of normalized semi-values. In particular the two best known semivalues result for the following probabilities.

Shapley–Shubik index. If $p_s = \frac{1}{n+1} \frac{1}{\binom{n}{s}}$, then the probability of player i being the proposer under $(S\text{-}i)$-protocol is given by the Shapley–Shubik index of the voting rule, that is, $p_i^{\mathcal{W}} = Sh_i(\mathcal{W})$. Thus in terms of $(S\text{-}i)$-protocols the Shapley–Shubik index emerges for the familiar probabilistic model of choosing a size at random, and then a coalition of that size at random.

Normalized Banzhaf index. If $p_s = k\frac{s}{2^n}$, where k is a constant resulting from normalization, then the probability of player i being the proposer under $(S\text{-}i)$-protocol is given by the normalized Banzhaf index of the voting rule. Note that in this protocol the probability of a coalition is weighted by its size[64].

A more general way of selecting a proposer is the following.

(i, S)-**Protocols** (Choose i and S simultaneously). As already pointed out, any $\mathcal{W} \mapsto p_{\mathcal{W}}$ such that $p_{\mathcal{W}}(i, S)$ satisfies (61) and (62) abstracts a protocol that, combined with the resulting (p, r)-protocol, yields a particular case of (54) in the limit. This also includes as particular cases some power indices less familiar than Shapley–Shubik's and Banzhaf's that lie outside the family of normalized semivalues, such as *Deegan–Packel's* [17] and Holler–Packel's [30] indices.

But again the Shapley–Shubik index emerges associated with a very simple selection procedure:

Shapley–Shubik's Protocol (formulation 1). (i) Choose an order in N at random, and let the players join a coalition in this order until a winning coalition S is formed. (ii) Then the last player entering S is the proposer.

Under this protocol:

Prob $(i$ is the proposer$) = Sh_i(\mathcal{W})$.

The simplicity of this procedure within the family of protocols described above is worth remarking on. First, the formation of the

---

[64] Note that if $p_s = \frac{1}{2^n}$ for all S, i.e. if all coalitions are equally probable, then the probability of a player being chosen as the proposer is *not* the normalized Banzhaf index of that player.

126   *Voting and Collective Decision-Making*

coalition appears in this case as a sequential process, which seems at once natural and the simplest way. Alternatively and equivalently it can be described as choosing one player at random to join the coalition at each step. One may wonder why the 'swinger' is chosen as the proposer rather than any other player who is decisive in S. But it does not make any difference if the second step is replaced by this: Choose one of the players decisive in S at random. It can be easily seen that the procedure is equivalent. Thus the protocol can be specified alternatively as follows:

Shapley–Shubik's Protocol (formulation 2). (i) Starting from the empty coalition, choose one player at random each time from the remaining players until a winning coalition S is formed. (ii) Then choose one of the players decisive in S at random.

Thus, *under this protocol each player has a probability of being the proposer equal to his/her Shapley–Shubik index for the current voting rule.*

Summing up we can combine any of the above proposer selection protocols with the probabilistic (p, r)-protocol considered in the previous section. In view of Theorem 29 and the above discussion we have the following results, which are the non-cooperative counterpart of (54) and (56).

Theorem 34 *Let $(B, \mathcal{W})$ be an N-person bargaining committee with preference profile $B = (D, d)$ satisfying the conditions specified in Section 4.2. Under any $(S\text{-}i)$ or (i, S)-protocol for selecting the proposer combined with the resulting (p, r)-protocol: (i) for all r $(0 < r < 1)$, there exists a stationary subgame perfect equilibrium (SSPE); (ii) as $r \to 1$, any SSPE payoff vectors converge to the weighted Nash bargaining solution of B with weights given by the probabilities of being the proposer determined by $\mathcal{W}$ and the proposer selection protocol; (iii) under an $(S\text{-}i)$-protocol, these weights are given by a normalized semivalue of the voting rule (i.e. of the simple TU-game $v_{\mathcal{W}}$).*

Theorem 35 *Under the Shapley–Shubik protocol combined with the resulting (p, r)-protocol: (i) parts (i) and (ii) of Theorem 34 hold, and the weights in the limit are given by the Shapley–Shubik index of the voting rule $\mathcal{W}$; (ii) if $B = \Lambda$, also the SSPE payoffs are given by the Shapley–Shubik index of the voting rule $\mathcal{W}$, for all $r(0 < r < 1)$.*

Bargaining committees 127

Remarks. In the light of this bargaining model the voters' conventional 'voting power' or decisiveness becomes 'bargaining power' in a specific game-theoretic sense. Thus, the old conceptual ambiguity commented on in Section 2.2 concerning the game-theoretic notion of 'value' when applied to simple games representing voting rules, and its alternative interpretation as 'decisiveness', or likelihood of playing a crucial role in a decision, is clarified.

(i) In a bargaining committee, according to this model, *the source of (bargaining) power is the likelihood of being the proposer, related to the likelihood of being decisive via the protocol.*

(ii) By part (ii) of Theorem 35, in the case of a committee with a TU preference profile, i.e. if $B = \Lambda$, the ex ante *SSPE* payoffs are given by the Shapley–Shubik index of the voting rule W, *whatever r ($0 < r < 1$)*. Thus the limit result for $r \to 1$ is trivial in this case. But observe that the non-cooperative 'implementation' of the Shapley–Shubik index of the voting rule W (or equivalently, of the Shapley value of the associated simple game v_W) is different from previous ones. In this model $\mathrm{Sh}(W)$ represents an expectation in a precise sense, in which no player (unless the rule is a dictatorship) has a chance of getting the whole cake, although the proposer would benefit (decreasingly as r gets bigger) from this role. Observe also that when $r \to 0$, in the limit the proposer will have the whole cake, though the ex ante expectations are the same. In other words, for $r \to 0$, in the limit we have a reinterpretation of the original Shapley model applied to the simple game associated with the voting rule.

(iii) Theorem 35-(ii) is the non-cooperative counterpart of the fact pointed out in Section 4.3.2 that $\mathrm{Nash}^{\mathrm{Sh}(W)}(B) = \mathrm{Sh}(W)$ when $B = \Lambda$. In cooperative terms it was emphasized there that the relevant point is not this particular case, but the fact that $\mathrm{Sh}(W)$ appears in (56) setting the bargaining weights *for all B*, thus with a new meaning: the bargaining power that the voting rule confers to the players. Now in this non-cooperative model this interpretation is corroborated and clarified: this is so (in the limit for $r \to 1$) for a specific and particularly simple protocol.

4.4.3 Discussion

Theorems 34 and 35 provide a non-cooperative interpretation of formulae (54) and (56), originally obtained from a cooperative-axiomatic approach. Nevertheless the non-cooperative model admits many variations that may be worth investigating. Here are some of the possible lines of further research.

As briefly commented in Section 4.3.1, in our model of a bargaining committee the status quo is a reference point that at the same time sets a level of utility below which no player can be forced to accept. Even if such a limit exists, it is sometimes below the status quo, so that players can be worse off within certain limits if forced into this situation by a winning coalition. Thus a richer model would include two different points: the initial starting point or status quo and a vector of minimal admissible payoffs. Another way of enriching the model is by admitting partial agreements. That is, in our models the outcome is either general consensus or breakdown: why not admit the possibility of partial consensus even if general consensus is sought?[65] Finally, in this model all symmetric rules appear as equivalent and yield the Nash bargaining solution. But intuition suggests that the difficulty of reaching agreements is not the same under a unanimity rule and under a simple majority. A model accounting for this seems desirable.

4.5 Egalitarianism and utilitarianism in a bargaining committee

In Section 3.7 we addressed the question of the voting rule that best implements the egalitarian and utilitarian principles in a take-it-or-leave-it committee. To this end, utilities were introduced in the model in a very simple way assuming a strong degree of symmetry. Then it was seen that any symmetric rule implements the egalitarian principle, and of those rules it is the simple majority that best implements the utilitarian principle under certain conditions.

Unlike the case of a take-it-or-leave-it committee, in a bargaining committee the preference profile, given in utility terms, is one of the ingredients of the model. Moreover, this element, $B = (D, d)$, separated from the voting rule, is precisely the only ingredient in a classical bargaining problem and, as is well known, in such an environment

---

[65] The closest model to the (p, r)-protocols is that of Rubinstein [75], of which it may be considered an extension. In [28] a bargaining model is provided in the NTU framework in which consensus is sought and there is a risk of breakdown. Other interesting non-cooperative models are [3, 7, 57] .

Bargaining committees 129

utilitarianism and egalitarianism conflict. Given an n-person bargaining problem $B = (D, d)$, the egalitarian optimum is at the point in D for which the gains of utility with respect to the status quo d are equal for all players and those gains are maximal: that is, the point

$$d + \bar{\mu}\mathbf{1} \quad \text{where} \quad \bar{\mu} := \max\{\mu : d + \mu\mathbf{1} \in D\}, \tag{64}$$

where $\mathbf{1} = (1, \ldots, 1) \in \mathbb{R}^N$. By contrast, the utilitarian optimum would be reached at the feasible point for which the sum of the gains is maximal, that is, at

$$\arg\max_{x \in D_d} \sum_{i \in N} (x_i - d_i). \tag{65}$$

In general these two points are different, and both depend on D and d. Therefore the idea of looking for the voting rule that best implements either principle independently of the preference profile does not make sense, nor does it make sense to look for such rules for each preference profile. In fact, as pointed out by Shapley [77], *the Nash bargaining solution can be seen as a compromise between these two principles* in the following sense. A compromise between the different points given by (64) and (65), can be this: find a system of weights $\lambda = (\lambda_i)_{i \in N} \in \mathbb{R}_+^N$, such that the following two problems *have the same solution*. First, find the point $d + \bar{\mu}\lambda$ such that

$$\bar{\mu} = \max\{\mu : d + \mu\lambda \in D\},$$

and, second, find the point

$$\arg\max_{x \in D_d} \sum_{i \in N} \lambda_i(x_i - d_i).$$

As Shapley [77] points out, such a system of weights $(\lambda_i)_{i \in N}$ for which the solution to both problems is the same does exist, and it turns out that for these weights *the common solution is given by the Nash bargaining solution*, that is by Nash(B).

Therefore if we accept this compromise between the egalitarian and utilitarian principles as a '*fair*' deal, and we accept (54) as the normative term of reference (supported by Theorems 29 and 34) of a rational agreement in a bargaining committee $(B, \mathcal{W})$, then any symmetric

130   *Voting and Collective Decision-Making*

voting rule implements such a compromise, because in this case all components of $\varphi(\mathcal{W})$ in (54) are equal, so that it yields Nash(B).

4.6 The neutral voting rule in a committee of representatives

Now we turn our attention to the normative issue of the choice of voting rule in a committee of representatives in which each member acts on behalf of a group of different size. In Section 3.8 we addressed this issue for the case of a take-it-or-leave-it committee. We now address the case in which the committee of representatives acts as a bargaining committee. As we will see the conclusions are different.

Assume that each member i of a bargaining committee of n members, labelled by N, represents a group M_i of size m_i. Let's assume that these groups are disjoint, so that if $M = \cup_{i \in N} M_i$, and the cardinality of M is $m = \sum_{i \in N} m_i$. Denote by $\mathcal{M}$ the partition $\mathcal{M} = \{M_1, M_2, \dots, M_n\}$. It seems intuitively clear that if the groups are of different sizes a symmetric voting rule is not adequate for such a committee, at least if a principle of equal representation (whatever this might mean in this context) is to be implemented. This raises the issue of the choice of the 'most adequate' voting rule under these conditions. The main difficulty in providing an answer is to specify precisely what is meant by 'adequate', 'right', or 'fair'. To begin with, 'adequate', 'right', or 'fair' in what sense and from which or whose point of view?

It seems clear that it should be so from the point of view of the people represented. The basic idea, which we further specify and justify presently, is this: A voting rule is 'fair' if any individual of any group is indifferent between bargaining directly with the other people in M (assuming such 'mass bargaining' were possible and yielded the M-person Nash bargaining solution), and leaving bargaining in the hands of a representative picked arbitrarily from the group. Even if this sounds Utopian (and as indeed it *is* in general), we will show that it is implementable in a precise sense if a certain level of symmetry (not uniformity!) of preferences within each group is assumed.

In general, a bargaining committee of representatives will negotiate about different issues over time under the same voting rule. In each case, depending on the particular issue, a different configuration of preferences will emerge in the population represented by the members of the committee. Thus it does not make sense to make the choice of the voting rule dependent on the preference profile, nor does it make

Bargaining committees 131

sense to assume unanimous preferences within every constituency. On the other hand, if there is no relationship at all between the preferences of the individuals within each group it is not clear on what normative grounds the choice of a voting rule for the committee of representatives should be founded[66].

In order to find an answer we assume that the configuration of preferences in the population represented is symmetric *within each group* in the following sense. Assume that $B = (D, d)$ $(d \in D \subseteq \mathbb{R}^M)$ is the m-person bargaining problem representing the configuration of vNM preferences of the m individuals in M about the issue at stake in the committee. We say that a permutation $\pi : M \to M$ respects $\mathcal{M}$ if for all $i \in N$, $\pi(M_i) = M_i$. We say that B is *$\mathcal{M}$-symmetric* if for any permutation $\pi : M \to M$ that respects $\mathcal{M}$, it holds that $\pi d = d$, and for all $x \in D$, $\pi x \in D$. In other words, B is $\mathcal{M}$-symmetric if for any group (M_i) the disagreement payoff is the same for all its members $(d_k = d_l$, for all $k, l \in M_i)$, and with the payoffs of the other players in $M \backslash M_i$ fixed in any way, the set of feasible payoffs for the players in that group (M_i) is symmetric. Notice that this does not mean at all that all players within each group have the same preferences. In fact it includes all symmetric situations ranging from unanimous preferences to the 'zero-sum' case of strict competition within each group. But note that if the payoffs of all the players in $M \backslash M_i$ are fixed, the outcome of bargaining within M_i (under unanimity and assuming anonymity) would yield the same utility level for all players in M_i. Thus $\mathcal{M}$-symmetry in B entails the following consequences.

Let M, N and $\mathcal{M}$ be as above, and let $B = (D, d)$ be $\mathcal{M}$-symmetric. Assuming as a term of reference that the players in M negotiate directly under unanimity, according to Nash's bargaining model the outcome would be Nash(B). Or, in other terms, Nash(B) can be considered as a normative term of reference representing an egalitarian-utilitarian compromise as discussed in Section 4.5. As B is $\mathcal{M}$-symmetric, it must be that

$$\text{Nash}_k(B) = \text{Nash}_l(B) \qquad (\forall i \in N, \forall k, l \in M_i).$$

---

[66] An extreme example can illustrate this: Assume all individuals in group M_i have identical preferences, and all in group M_j but individual $k \in M_j$ have also the same preferences (but different from those in M_i), while k has identical preferences to those in M_i. In a case like this individual k would prefer representative i to be more powerful than his/her own representative j.

132   *Voting and Collective Decision-Making*

Namely, in each group all players would receive the same pay-off according to Nash's bargaining solution. Therefore the optimal solution of the maximization problem

$$\arg\max_{x\in D_d} \prod_{l\in M}(x_l - d_l)$$

that yields Nash(B) coincides with the optimal solution of the same maximization problem when the set of feasible payoff vectors is constrained to yield the same payoff for any two players in the same group. Formally, denote by B^N the N-bargaining problem $B^N = (D^N, d^N)$, where

$$D^N := \big\{(x_1,\ldots,x_n)\in\mathbb{R}^N : \underbrace{(x_1,\ldots,x_1,}_{m_1-times} \quad\ldots\quad, \underbrace{x_n,\ldots,x_n)}_{m_n-times} \in D\big\},$$

and by d^N the vector in $\mathbb{R}^N$ whose i-component is, for each $i \in N$, equal to d_k (the same for all $k \in M_i$). Namely, B^N is the bargaining problem that would result by taking one individual from each constituency as a representative for bargaining on its behalf, under the commitment of later bargaining symmetrically within that constituency after the level of utility of the other constituencies has been settled. We have that, for all $i \in N$ and all $k \in M_i$,

$$\mathrm{Nash}_k(B) = \arg_k \max_{x\in D_d} \prod_{l\in M}(x_l - d_l)$$

$$= \arg_i \max_{x\in D^N_{d^N}} \prod_{j\in N}(x_j - d_j)^{m_j} = \mathrm{Nash}_i^{\overline{m}}(B^N),$$

where $\overline{m} = (m_1,\ldots,m_n)$. That is to say, for the configuration of preferences or M-bargaining problem B, a player k in M would obtain the same utility level by direct (m-player unanimous) bargaining that a representative would obtain by bargaining on behalf of him/her (and of all the players in the same group) under the configuration of preferences B^N *if each representative were endowed with a bargaining power proportional to the size of the group.*

The problem then is how to 'implement' such a weighted Nash bargaining solution. In other words, and more precisely, *how to implement a bargaining environment that confers the right bargaining power on each representative.* In view of Theorem 29, if a 'power index'

Bargaining committees 133

(i.e. a map $\varphi : VR_N \rightarrow \mathbb{R}^N$ that is efficient, anonymous and ignores null players) is considered to be the right assessment of bargaining power in a committee, and for some N-voting rule $\mathcal{W}$ it holds that

$$\frac{\varphi_i(\mathcal{W})}{m_i} = \frac{\varphi_j(\mathcal{W})}{m_j} \qquad (\forall i, j \in N), \tag{66}$$

then *this rule would exactly implement such an environment.* In particular, if such an index is the Shapley–Shubik index (Theorem 31), an optimal voting rule would be one for which

$$\frac{\text{Sh}_i(\mathcal{W})}{m_i} = \frac{\text{Sh}_j(\mathcal{W})}{m_j} \qquad (\forall i, j \in N). \tag{67}$$

In view of the underlying interpretation of 'fairness' as a compromise between egalitarianism and utilitarianism, it could be also adequate to call it 'neutrality', and to call a voting rule satisfying it 'neutral'.

Then we conclude that *if:* (i) the term 'bargaining power' is interpreted in the precise game-theoretic sense formerly specified (i.e. bargaining weights); (ii) (54) is accepted as a reasonable expectation in a bargaining committee supported by Theorems 29 and 34; and (iii) 'fairness' or 'neutrality' is understood as the egalitarian–utilitarian compromise given by the Nash bargaining solution; *then* the above discussion and the formulae (66) and (67) that it yields can be summarized in the following theorem.

Theorem 36 *A fair or neutral voting rule in a bargaining committee of representatives is one that gives each member a bargaining power proportional to the size of the group that he/she represents.*

From the point of view of application there are still some issues to be resolved. There is the question of the 'right' power index (i.e. the right $\varphi(\mathcal{W})$ in formula (54)) for assessing the bargaining power that the voting rule confers to each member of the committee. As discussed in Sections 4.3 and 4.4, this issue cannot be settled unless additional assumptions about the bargaining protocol in the committee are made. Nevertheless, as we have seen in Section 4.4.2, the Shapley–Shubik index emerges associated with a particularly simple bargaining protocol and consequently, in the absence of further information, it can be taken as a term of reference for a normative assessment. In any case, it is

134   *Voting and Collective Decision-Making*

worth stressing the clear message of Theorem 36, somewhat consistent with intuition and different from previous recommendations[67].

4.7 Exercises

1. Let $\Phi : \mathcal{B} \times VR_N \to \mathbb{R}^N$ be a solution satisfying the conditions of feasibility and individual rationality, that is, such that $\Phi(B, W) \in D_d$. Prove that if Φ also satisfies Independence of Irrelevant Alternatives, then for any two problems $B = (D, d)$ and $B' = (D', d')$ such that $d = d'$ and $D_d = D'_{d'}$, and any rule W, it holds that

$$\Phi(B, W) = \Phi(B', W).$$

2. Consider a two-person bargaining committee (B, W), where $B = (D, d)$, $d = (0, 0)$, and D is the comprehensive hull of D_d, given by

$$D_d = \{(x_1, x_2) \in \mathbb{R}^2_+ : x_1^2 + x_2^2 \leq 1\}.$$

Discuss the possible solutions under the conditions of Theorem 29 for the possible voting rules (dictatorship or unanimity).

3. Consider a three-person bargaining committee (B, W), where $B = (D, d)$, $d = (0, 0, 0)$ and

$$D = \{(x_1, x_2, x_3) \in \mathbb{R}^3 : x_1 + x_2 + x_2 \leq 3\}.$$

Discuss the possible solutions under the conditions of Theorem 29 in the following cases. (a) Player 1 is a dictator. (b) They decide by simple majority. (c) There is an oligarchy of players 1 and 2.

4. Let $W = \{\{1, 2\}, \{1, 3\}, \{1, 2, 3\}\}$. Calculate the solution for a bargaining committee (B, W) according to Theorem 31, in the following cases:

(a) B is as in the preceding exercise.

---

[67] In [10] a curious antecedent of this recommendation is given: *'In Franklin v. Kraus (1973), the New York Court of Appeals again approved a weighted voting system that made the Banzhaf power index of each representative proportional to his district's size.'*

Bargaining committees 135

(b) $B = (D, d)$, $d = (0, 0, 0)$, and D is the comprehensive hull of D_d, given by

$$D_d = \{(x_1, x_2, x_3) \in \mathbb{R}^3_+ : x_1^2 + x_2^2 + x_3^2 \le 9\}.$$

(c) Compare the proportion between the solution payoffs of the vetoer (player 1) and that of any of the other two in either case.

5. Let $B = (D, d)$ be as in Exercise 3. Determine the stationary subgame perfect equilibrium strategy profile for a (p, r)-protocol in which each player has probability $\frac{1}{3}$ of being the proposer: that is, $p = (\frac{1}{3}, \frac{1}{3}, \frac{1}{3})$. (a) If $r = \frac{1}{2}$. (b) If $r = \frac{3}{4}$.

6. Let (B, W) be a three-person bargaining committee, such that $B = (D, d)$ is as in Exercise 3 and $W = \{\{1, 2\}, \{1, 3\}, \{1, 2, 3\}\}$. Determine the stationary subgame perfect equilibrium strategy profile for the Shapley–Shubik Protocol combined with the resulting (p, r)-protocol for $r = \frac{3}{4}$.

7. Let W be the four-person voting rule whose minimal winning vote configurations are $M(W) = \{\{1, 2\}, \{1, 3\}, \{2, 3, 4\}\}$. If W is the voting rule in a bargaining committee of representatives, and the total number of people represented is 12,000, what should the number of people represented by each member be for W to be the 'neutral rule' (according to Theorem 36 and assuming the Shapley–Shubik index is the adequate measure of bargaining power)?

5 | *Application to the European Union*

In this chapter we apply the models developed in the preceding chapters to the European Council of Ministers. We submit the different voting rules that are or have been used in the Council, as well as some others that have been proposed, to cross-examination from the different points of view provided by the two basic models discussed in Chapters 3 and 4.

The different voting rules used in the Council are described in Section 5.1. In Section 5.2 we apply the model of a take-it-or-leave-it committee. In Section 5.2.1 we examine some relevant probabilities based on the a priori model of voting behaviour for the different rules. Then, in Section 5.2.2, we incorporate utilities into the model and assess the different rules in the Council from the egalitarian and utilitarian points of view, as a committee of states and as a committee of representatives. Finally, in Section 5.3 we apply the bargaining committee model.

The reader will not find any categorical normative recommendations along the lines of 'this is the best rule for the Council' or 'this is the rule that should be used by the Council'. None of the models applied captures all the complexity of the real situation. But they all help to understand it, as this application gives some insights into how the rules may affect the working of the Council. On the other hand, applying concepts and theoretical constructions also helps gain a deeper understanding of them.

5.1 Voting rules in the European Council

The rules that we consider here are rules that have been used in the Council at some time, more precisely between 1958 and 2005; the number of members in the Council increasing with the enlargements over this period. In 2005, the 25 members in decreasing order of population size were (with their abbreviated forms): Germany (*Ge*),

Application to the European Union 137

United Kingdom (*UK*), France (*Fr*), Italy (*It*), Spain (*Sp*), Poland (*Pl*), Netherlands (*Ne*), Greece (*Gr*), Czech Republic (*CR*), Belgium (*Be*), Hungary (*Hu*), Portugal (*Pr*), Sweden (*Sw*), Austria (*Au*), Slovakia (*Sk*), Denmark (*De*), Finland (*Fi*), Ireland (*Ir*), Lithuania (*Li*), Latvia (*La*), Slovenia (*Sn*), Estonia (*Es*), Cyprus (*Cy*), Luxembourg (*Lu*) and Malta (*Ma*).

We denote the set of Council members by N_n, where the subscript n refers to the number of states. During the period considered, we have, always in decreasing population order:

From 1958 to 1972:

$$N_6 = \{Ge, Fr, It, Ne, Be, Lu\};$$

from 1973 to 1980:

$$N_9 = \{Ge, UK, Fr, It, Ne, Be, De, Ir, Lu\};$$

from 1981 to 1985:

$$N_{10} = \{Ge, UK, Fr, It, Ne, Gr, Be, De, Ir, Lu\};$$

from 1986 to 1994:

$$N_{12} = \{Ge, UK, Fr, It, Sp, Ne, Gr, Be, Pr, De, Ir, Lu\};$$

from 1995 to 2003:

$$N_{15} = \{Ge, UK, Fr, It, Sp, Ne, Gr, Be, Pr, Sw, Au, De, Fi, Ir, Lu\};$$

and in 2004 and 2005:

$$N_{25} = \{Ge, UK, Fr, It, Sp, Pl, Ne, Gr, CR, Be, Hu, Pr, Sw,$$
$$Au, Sk, De, Fi, Ir, Li, La, Sn, Es, Cy, Lu, Ma\}.$$

Three main rules are used in the Council: simple majority, unanimity, and the so-called qualified majority. The simple majority is the default voting rule unless the Treaty provides otherwise, which it usually does. In practice the Council decides by simple majority only in a limited number of mainly procedural matters. Unanimity is used for quasi-constitutional or politically sensitive matters, and a qualified majority is used for all other cases. Successive modifications of the Treaty have resulted in an extension of the use of the qualified majority voting in comparison to the unanimity voting.

The simple majority $(\mathcal{W}_n^{\mathrm{SM}})$ and unanimity $(\mathcal{W}_n^{\mathrm{U}})$ are symmetric rules that were introduced in 1.3.2 for n seats. Note that we always have

$$\mathcal{W}_n^{\mathrm{U}} \subset \mathcal{W}_n^{\mathrm{SM}}, \tag{68}$$

that is, it is always in principle more difficult to pass proposals under unanimity than under a simple majority.

The *qualified majority* $(\mathcal{W}_n^{\mathrm{QM}})$ is a weighted majority used up to enlargement to the N_{25} Council. For $n = 6, 9, 10, 12$, and 15 we have

$$\mathcal{W}_n^{\mathrm{QM}} = \left\{ S \subseteq N_n : \sum_{i \in S} w_i(N_n) \geq Q(N_n) \right\},$$

with weights and quotas given by

$$w(N_6) = (4, 4, 4, 2, 2, 1), \ Q(N_6) = 12,$$

$$w(N_9) = (10, 10, 10, 10, 5, 5, 3, 3, 2), \ Q(N_9) = 41,$$

$$w(N_{10}) = (10, 10, 10, 10, 5, 5, 5, 3, 3, 2), \ Q(N_{10}) = 45,$$

$$w(N_{12}) = (10, 10, 10, 10, 8, 5, 5, 5, 5, 3, 3, 2), \ Q(N_{12}) = 54,$$

$$w(N_{15}) = (10, 10, 10, 10, 8, 5, 5, 5, 5, 4, 4, 3, 3, 3, 2), \ Q(N_{15}) = 62.$$

Galloway ([25], p. 63) justifies the choice of the weights and quotas as follows:

'The system was constructed so as to ensure a certain relationship between member states based on a system of "groups" or "clusters" of large, medium and small member states, with states in each cluster having an identical number of votes. (...)

- *Apart from an adjustment in voting weights to accommodate new categories of member states at the first enlargement in 1973, the system has undergone straightforward extrapolation at each successive enlargement.*
- *The system of "clusters" was maintained. With each successive enlargement, new member states were categorized in accordance with the same principle, although additional categories had to be inserted into the system as required on the basis of member states'*

size (e.g. Denmark and Ireland were allocated three votes each, Spain eight votes and Austria and Sweden four votes each).'

Remarks. (i) Luxembourg had a null seat in W_6^{QM}. Thus Luxembourg's probability of being decisive was zero in the N_6 Council (whatever the voting behaviour of the others).

(ii) Luxembourg's seat, like Denmark's and Ireland's seats, are symmetric in W_{10}^{QM}, in spite of their having different numbers of votes: 2 for Luxembourg, and 3 each for Ireland and Denmark. These three states thus had the same probabilities of being decisive or successful in the N_{10} Council for any anonymous probability distribution.

(iii) We always have

$$W_n^U \subset W_n^{QM}. \tag{69}$$

As the simple majority obviously contains a larger number of winning configurations than the qualified majority, there may also exist some inclusion between these rules, but this is not always true. We only have

$$W_n^{QM} \subset W_n^{SM} \quad \text{for } n = 9, \text{ 12, and 15.} \tag{70}$$

The inclusion does not hold for the N_6 nor the N_{10} Councils[68].

The Treaty of Nice has substantially modified the qualified majority rule for the N_{25} Council in two ways. First, the system of weights was redesigned. Second, an additional clause was added: to be adopted, a proposal needs the support of a majority of member states. Thus the qualified majority is no longer a weighted majority, but a double (weighted) majority. We refer to this rule as *'the Nice rule'* (W_{25}^{Ni}):

$$W_{25}^{Ni} = \left\{ S \subseteq N_{25} : \sum_{i \in S} w_i(N_{25}) \geq 232 \text{ and } s \geq 13 \right\},$$

where

$$w(N_{25}) = (29, 29, 29, 29, 27, 27, 13, 12, 12, 12, 12,$$
$$12, 10, 10, 7, 7, 7, 7, 7, 4, 4, 4, 4, 4, 3).$$

[68] Consider for example $S = \{Ge, It, Fr\}$. We have $S \in W_6^{QM}$ but $S \notin W_6^{SM}$.

The choice of this rule was the result of difficult and painful bargaining among member states in December 2000. It soon came to be considered as not very satisfactory. In 2001, a Convention was launched to reform the Nice Treaty and to consider the possibility of writing a Constitution.

The Convention finished its work in July 2003, and came up with a substitute to the Nice rule. This alternative rule, which we refer to as *'the Convention rule'* $(\mathcal{W}_n^{Cv})$, is described as follows (article 24): *'When the European Council of the Council of Ministers takes decisions by qualified majority, such a majority shall consist of the majority of Member States, representing at least three fifths of the population of the Union.'* For the N_{25} Council, we have:

$$\mathcal{W}_{25}^{Cv} = \{S \subseteq N_{25} : \sum_{i \in S} m_i \geq 0.6 \, m \text{ and } s \geq 13\},$$

where m_i denotes state i's population and m the total population in the EU. In 2005, these figures were[69]:

$82,500,800$ (*Ge*), $60,561,200$ (*UK*), $60,034,500$ (*Fr*), $58,462,400$ (*It*), $43,038,000$ (*Sp*), $38,173,800$ (*Pl*), $16,305,500$ (*Ne*), $11,075,700$ (*Gr*), $10,529,300$ (*CR*), $10,445,900$ (*Be*), $10,220,600$ (*Hu*), $10,097,500$ (*Pr*), $9,011,400$ (*Sw*), $8,206,500$ (*Au*), $5,411,400$ (*Sk*), $5,384,800$ (*De*), $5,236,600$ (*Fi*), $4,109,200$ (*Ir*), $3,425,300$ (*Li*), $2,306,400$ (*La*), $1,997,600$ (*Sn*), $1,347,000$ (*Es*), $749,200$ (*Cy*), $455,000$ (*Lu*), $402,700$ (*Ma*).

An Intergovernmental Conference then took place between October 2003 and June 2004 and concluded its work with the signing of the Constitution in October 2004. In article I-25 of the Constitutional Treaty a winning configuration is defined as containing *'at least 55% of the members of the Council, comprising at least fifteen of them and representing Member States comprising at least 65% of the population of the Union. A blocking minority must include at least four Council members, failing which the qualified majority shall be deemed attained.'* We will refer to this rule as *'the Constitution rule'* $(\mathcal{W}_n^{Cs})$.

[69] EUROSTAT (the statistical office of the European Commission), 2005.

Application to the European Union 141

For the N_{25} Council, we have[70]

$$\mathcal{W}_{25}^{Cs} = \left\{ S \subseteq N_{25} : \left(\sum_{i \in S} m_i \geq 0.65 \, m \text{ and } s \geq 15 \right) \text{ or } (s \geq 22) \right\}.$$

It was decided during the Intergovernmental Conference that the weights chosen in Nice would be used until 2009. By then if the Constitution is ratified that rule will be replaced by the Constitution rule. But the fate of the Constitution is now unclear after the 'no' votes by the Dutch and French to the Constitutional Treaty.

Remarks. (i) The main innovation of the Convention rule (and afterwards of the Constitution rule) is that they depend only on population figures and percentage of member states. They can thus be extended mechanically at each new enlargement.

(ii) For the N_{25} Council, neither the Convention rule nor the Constitution rule has been used. Still, as they competed to become the rule for the Council, they were widely discussed in the media. As such, it seems that they deserve a formal study[71]. They are also useful as terms of comparison for the evaluation of the Nice rule[72].

(iii) In the Constitution rule, any member may request verification that the Member States constituting the qualified majority represent at least 62% of the total population of the Union. This clause, sometimes called the population safety net will not be considered here.

(iv) By construction, the sets of winning configurations of the Nice rule, the Constitution rule and the Convention rule are all included in the list of winning configurations of the simple majority. We have

$$\mathcal{W}_{25}^U \subset \mathcal{W}_{25}^{EU} \subset \mathcal{W}_{25}^{SM} \quad \text{for} \quad \mathcal{W}_{25}^{EU} \in \{\mathcal{W}_{25}^{Ni}, \mathcal{W}_{25}^{Cs}, \mathcal{W}_{25}^{Cv}\}. \tag{71}$$

No inclusion relation holds between the Constitution, the Convention and the Nice rules (see Exercise 2).

---

[70] As 55% of 25 is 13.75, the clause concerning 55% of members states is inoperative, as at least 15 member states are needed.

[71] Moreover this is not the first time that a system of double majority was proposed: prior to the Treaty of Nice the Commission proposed a system close to the Convention rule (with relative quotas of both population and members being set to 50%). See [41].

[72] For other studies of the N_{25} Council, see for instance [23] or [36].

142 *Voting and Collective Decision-Making*

The models developed in Chapters 3 and 4 can be used to compare the rules presented above (we refer to any of these rules as $\mathcal{W}_n^{\mathrm{EU}}$). Special emphasis is given to the comparison of the Nice rule, the Convention rule and the Constitution rule, as they were competitors for use as the new qualified majority.

5.2 The Council as a take-it-or-leave-it committee

In practice, the Council usually makes a formal vote when it has practically reached a unanimous agreement[73]. It seems clear that the effective work of the Council is closer to what has been described as the environment of a bargaining committee than to that of a take-it-or-leave-it committee. Thus the bargaining committee model seems more adequate for the Council. Still, with the successive enlargements informal bargaining may become more and more difficult. With larger numbers of member states, the need for an effective vote may perhaps arise more frequently. In any case, the take-it-or-leave-it committee model, or more precisely some of the relevant probabilistic measures based on this model, provide an interesting assessment of various issues related to the voting rules used at different times in the Council.

In the take-it-or-leave-it model, some relations hold independently of voting behaviour. This happens when there is an inclusion between the sets of winning configurations of two rules. In this case there are some conclusions that do not depend on the voting behaviour. To complete the picture and get numerical values, a probability distribution has to be chosen. In Chapter 3 we have advocated in favour of p^* for a normative a priori evaluation of voting rules[74]. But one should always

---

[73] The Council publishes a monthly document listing legislative and non-legislative acts of the Council including the results of votes since 1999. These results can be found at www.consilium.europa.eu

[74] The specific context of the European decision-making process may justify other normative assumptions. For instance, any proposal that reaches the Council can be expected to have the support of more than half the member states (otherwise it would have been blocked in the Commission). A vote configuration with a number of 'yes'-voters smaller than half the members can be assumed to have a zero probability. Then settting an equal probability to all other vote configurations we have the probability distribution

$$\tilde{p}_n(S) := \begin{cases} 1/r \text{ if } s > \frac{n}{2} \\ 0 \text{ otherwise,} \end{cases}$$

where r represents the number of vote configurations where $s > \frac{n}{2}$. (See [37].)

Application to the European Union 143

keep in mind that assessments and recommendations based on p^* have no predictive power[75].

With the voting rule, and the a priori distribution of probability p^*, the take-it-or-leave-it model is complete. We first apply the criteria based on probabilities (ease of passing proposals, probability of success and its conditional variants), then the criteria based on utilities (egalitarianism and utilitarianism).

5.2.1 Criteria based on probabilities

Using the inclusions between the sets of winning configurations for the EU rules (that is, (68), (69), (70) and (71)), we obtain the following relations that do not depend on the probability distribution p_n.

For $n = 9, 12, 15$, and for any i and any p_n:

$$\alpha(W_n^U, p_n) \leq \alpha(W_n^{QM}, p_n) \leq \alpha(W_n^{SM}, p_n),$$

$$\Omega_i^{i+}(W_n^U, p_n) \leq \Omega_i^{i+}(W_n^{QM}, p_n) \leq \Omega_i^{i+}(W_n^{SM}, p_n),$$

$$\Omega_i^{i-}(W_n^U, p_n) \geq \Omega_i^{i-}(W_n^{QM}, p_n) \geq \Omega_i^{i-}(W_n^{SM}, p_n).$$

For $n = 6, 10$, and for any i and any p_n:

$$\alpha(W_n^U, p_n) \leq \min\{\alpha(W_n^{QM}, p_n), \alpha(W_n^{SM}, p_n)\},$$

$$\Omega_i^{i+}(W_n^U, p_n) \leq \min\{\Omega_i^{i+}(W_n^{QM}, p_n), \Omega_i^{i+}(W_n^{SM}, p_n)\},$$

$$\Omega_i^{i-}(W_n^U, p_n) \geq \max\{\Omega_i^{i-}(W_n^{QM}, p_n), \Omega_i^{i-}(W_n^{SM}, p_n)\}.$$

For the N_{25} Council, and any $W_{25}^{EU} \in \{W_{25}^{Ni}, W_{25}^{Cs}, W_{25}^{Cv}\}$, we have

$$\alpha(W_{25}^U, p_{25}) \leq \alpha(W_{25}^{EU}, p_{25}) \leq \alpha(W_{25}^{SM}, p_{25}),$$

$$\Omega_i^{i+}(W_{25}^U, p_{25}) \leq \Omega_i^{i+}(W_{25}^{EU}, p_{25}) \leq \Omega_i^{i+}(W_{25}^{SM}, p_{25}),$$

$$\Omega_i^{i-}(W_{25}^U, p_{25}) \geq \Omega_i^{i-}(W_{25}^{EU}, p_{25}) \geq \Omega_i^{i-}(W_{25}^{SM}, p_{25}),$$

---

[75] For instance, the claim that the Council (under the N_{27} Nice rule) '*is likely to become immobilized by the extreme difficulty of getting acts approved*' ([23], p. 19) is based on the computation of the a priori ease of passing proposals: $\alpha(W, p^*)$. This risk is rightly dismissed by practitioners, arguing that votes are taken once member states have basically agreed on the proposal (confirming the appropriateness of the bargaining model). Nevertheless, such figures as $\alpha(W, p^*)$ and others are expressive in comparisons if used with care.

for any i and any p_{25}. Also note that unanimity gives a veto right to any state:

$$\Omega_i^{i-}(W_n^U, p_n) = 1.$$

This is certainly why the unanimity is used for quasi-constitutional or politically sensitive matters: any state can be sure that it will not be forced to accept a decision that it does not favour.

These results confirm the intuition, but do not permit us to compare the Nice rule, the Constitution rule and the Convention rule. The normative distribution of probability p_n^* permits us to complete the ranking.

A priori ease of passing proposals

For any voting rule W^{EU} considered in the Council, the results of computing the *a priori ease of passing proposals*, given by

$$\alpha(W_n^{EU}, p^*) = \sum_{S:S \in W_n^{EU}} p^*(S),$$

are given in Table 5.1.

It is worth making some comments on these figures. Not surprisingly, for any number of member states, the a priori ease of passing proposals is always largest under the simple majority, and smallest under unanimity. The a priori ease of passing proposals is around 50% under the simple majority[76]. At the other extreme, the ease of passing proposals under unanimity is very small, and is divided by 2 each time a new member is added to the Council: it is only 1.6% for the N_6 Council, and is negligible for the N_{25} Council[77]. Under a qualified majority, the a priori ease of passing proposals also decreases at each enlargement of the Council: it is around 21.9% in the N_6 Council and around 7.8% in the N_{15} Council. The Nice rule accentuates this trend still further, while the other rules would reverse it. Under the Constitution rule the ease of passing proposals is around 10% (very close to what was obtained for the N_{12} Council), while it would be 22.5% under the Convention rule (higher than in the initial

---

[76] Recall that (see (35), in 3.8.1) the a priori ease of passing a proposal is exactly 50% if n is odd, and smaller if n is even (although it tends to 50% when n is large).

[77] In Table 5.1 read $3E - 8$ as $3 \times 10^{-8} = 0.00000003$.

Application to the European Union

Table 5.1. *A priori ease of passing proposals:* $\alpha(\mathcal{W}_n^{\text{EU}}, \text{p}_n^*)$

$n =$	6	9	10	12	15	25
$\mathcal{W}_n^{\text{SM}}$	0.344	0.500	0.377	0.387	0.500	0.500
$\mathcal{W}_n^{\text{U}}$	0.016	0.002	0.001	2E-4	3E-5	3E-8
$\mathcal{W}_n^{\text{QM}}$	0.219	0.146	0.137	0.098	0.078	-
$\mathcal{W}_n^{\text{Ni}}$	-	-	-	-	-	0.036
$\mathcal{W}_n^{\text{Cs}}$	-	-	-	-	-	0.101
$\mathcal{W}_n^{\text{Cv}}$	-	-	-	-	-	0.225

N_6 Council). The ranking of these three rules from this point of view is thus

$$\alpha(\mathcal{W}_{25}^{\text{Ni}}, p_{25}^*) < \alpha(\mathcal{W}_{25}^{\text{Cs}}, p_{25}^*) < \alpha(\mathcal{W}_{25}^{\text{Cv}}, p_{25}^*).$$

A priori integration and sovereignty indices

Ex ante success decomposes into two parts: positive success and negative success (see (17) in 3.4). A priori, i.e. for $p = p^*$, we have

$$\Omega_i(\mathcal{W}, p^*) = \frac{1}{2}\Omega_i^{i+}(\mathcal{W}, p^*) + \frac{1}{2}\Omega_i^{i-}(\mathcal{W}, p^*)$$

for any $i \in N_n$. In the European context, a priori success conditional to a positive vote, that is

$$\Omega_i^{i+}(\mathcal{W}_n^{\text{EU}}, p^*),$$

can be interpreted as an '*a priori integration index*'. Indeed, the more '*pro-integration*' a state, the more sensitive it should in principle be to this form of success than to the other (i.e. $\Omega_i^{i-}(\mathcal{W}_n^{\text{EU}}, p^*)$). The values of $\Omega_i^{i+}(\mathcal{W}_n^{\text{EU}}, p^*)$ are given in Table 5.2.

The same can be said here as for the a priori ease of passing proposals. For any number of states, for any state, the largest integration index is obtained under the simple majority (around 50%), and the smallest under unanimity. The integration indices steadily decrease over time under unanimity and the qualified majority (with the exception of Luxembourg in the enlargement from the N_9 Council to the N_{10}

Table 5.2. *A priori integration indices:* $\Omega_i^{i+}(\mathcal{W}_n^{EU}, p_n^*)$

$\mathcal{W}_{n=6,9,10,12,15,25}^{SM}$	$\mathcal{W}_6^{SM}$	$\mathcal{W}_9^{SM}$	$\mathcal{W}_{10}^{SM}$	$\mathcal{W}_{12}^{SM}$	$\mathcal{W}_{15}^{SM}$	$\mathcal{W}_{25}^{SM}$		
any $i \in N_n$	0.500	0.637	0.500	0.500	0.605	0.581		
$\mathcal{W}_{n=6,9,10,12,15,25}^{U}$	$\mathcal{W}_6^{U}$	$\mathcal{W}_9^{U}$	$\mathcal{W}_{10}^{U}$	$\mathcal{W}_{12}^{U}$	$\mathcal{W}_{15}^{U}$	$\mathcal{W}_{25}^{U}$		
any $i \in N_n$	0.031	0.004	0.002	5E-4	6E-5	6E-08		
$\mathcal{W}_{n=6,9,10,12,15,25}^{QM}$	$\mathcal{W}_6^{QM}$	$\mathcal{W}_9^{QM}$	$\mathcal{W}_{10}^{QM}$	$\mathcal{W}_{12}^{QM}$	$\mathcal{W}_{15}^{QM}$	$\mathcal{W}_{25}^{Ni}$	$\mathcal{W}_{25}^{Cs}$	$\mathcal{W}_{25}^{Cv}$
Germany	0.375	0.250	0.234	0.168	0.134	0.063	0.180	0.379
UK	-	0.250	0.234	0.168	0.134	0.063	0.159	0.335
France	0.375	0.250	0.234	0.168	0.134	0.063	0.159	0.334
Italy	0.375	0.250	0.234	0.168	0.134	0.063	0.158	0.332
Spain	-	-	-	0.157	0.124	0.062	0.144	0.304
Poland	-	-	-	-	-	0.062	0.144	0.303
Netherlands	0.312	0.203	0.188	0.134	0.107	0.050	0.129	0.266
Greece	-	-	0.188	0.134	0.107	0.048	0.126	0.258
Czech	-	-	-	-	-	0.048	0.126	0.258

Belgium	0.312	0.203	0.188	0.134	0.107	0.048	0.126	0.258
Hungary	-	-	-	-	-	0.048	0.126	0.258
Portugal	-	-	-	0.134	0.107	0.048	0.126	0.258
Sweden	-	-	-	-	0.102	0.046	0.125	0.256
Austria	-	-	-	-	0.102	0.046	0.125	0.255
Slovakia	-	-	-	-	-	0.043	0.123	0.251
Denmark	-	0.188	0.162	0.123	0.096	0.043	0.123	0.251
Finland	-	-	-	-	0.096	0.043	0.123	0.251
Ireland	-	0.188	0.162	0.123	0.096	0.043	0.122	0.249
Lithuania	-	-	-	-	-	0.043	0.122	0.248
Latvia	-	-	-	-	-	0.040	0.121	0.246
Slovenia	-	-	-	-	-	0.040	0.121	0.246
Estonia	-	-	-	-	-	0.040	0.121	0.245
Cyprus	-	-	-	-	-	0.040	0.120	0.244
Luxembourg	0.219	0.156	0.162	0.108	0.089	0.040	0.120	0.243
Malta	-	-	-	-	-	0.039	0.120	0.243

Council[78]). The decrease is significant in magnitude. Under a qualified majority the probability for large states falls from 37.5% in N_6 to 13.4% in N_{15}, while Luxembourg's probability falls from 21.9% to 8.9%. The Nice rule reinforces this decrease still further, while the Constitution rule and the Convention rule would reverse the trend. The indices under the Convention rule would be larger than those obtained under the qualified majority for the N_9 Council. For any state i, we have

$$\Omega_i^{i+}(W_{25}^{Ni}, p_{25}^*) < \Omega_i^{i+}(W_{25}^{Cs}, p_{25}^*) < \Omega_i^{i+}(W_{25}^{Cv}, p_{25}^*).$$

Interestingly enough, the ranking given by the integration index is always identical *for all states* whatever their size. The Convention rule can be said to be the most advanced from the integrationist point of view the Nice rule the least; with the Convention rule as a compromise between them. Note that the integration index ranks rules in the same way as the a priori ease of passing proposals does.

Inversely, the more jealous a state is of its national sovereignty, the more concerned it is to avoid having a decision that it does not favour imposed upon it. The probability of a proposal being accepted given that a state i votes 'no', is given by

$$\frac{1}{1 - \gamma_i(p)} \sum_{S: i \notin S \in W} p(S).$$

As we have

$$\frac{1}{1 - \gamma_i(p)} \sum_{S: i \notin S \in W} p(S) = 1 - \Omega_i^{i-}(W, p),$$

the a priori success conditional to a negative vote, that is

$$\Omega_i^{i-}(W_n^{EU}, p^*),$$

can be interpreted as an '*a priori sovereignty index*'. The more jealous of its national sovereignty a state is, the more it would prefer this

---

[78] In the N_{10} Council Luxembourg's, Ireland's and Denmark's seats are symmetric.

Application to the European Union 149

form of success to the other. The values of $\Omega_i^{i-}(W_n^{\text{EU}}, p^*)$ are given in Table 5.3.

The comments to be made here are the opposite of those made for the integration index or the ease of passing proposals. For any number of states, for any state, the largest sovereignty index is obtained under unanimity, which gives a veto right to all states. The sovereignty index is smallest under the simple majority, with one exception: Luxembourg has a larger sovereignty index under the simple majority than under the qualified majority in the N_6 Council.

Under the qualified majority, sovereignty indices are quite large (more than 80%[79]) and they increase over time up to the last enlargement, with the exception of Denmark and Ireland from the N_9 Council to the N_{10} Council. Sovereignty indices continue to increase under the Nice rule: large member states' sovereignty indices are around 99% (with the smallest state, Malta, having around 97%). These indices are very close to 1. In this sense, it can be said that, a priori, states almost have a veto right under the Nice rule. Again the Constitution rule and the Convention rule reverse the trend. Under the Constitution rule, the range of probabilities is between 79% (Malta) and 93% (Germany). Under the Convention rule, sovereignty indices would be smaller than under the qualified majority in the N_6 Council. For any state i, we have

$$\Omega_i^{i-}(W_{25}^{\text{Ni}}, p_{25}^*) > \Omega_i^{i-}(W_{25}^{\text{Cs}}, p_{25}^*) > \Omega_i^{i-}(W_{25}^{\text{Cv}}, p_{25}^*).$$

Thus, the ranking given by the sovereignty index is the same for all states (with the exception of the ranking between the simple and qualified majorities in the N_6 Council). This ranking is opposite to the one given by the a priori ease of passing proposals or the integration index.

A priori success

Any state's unconditional a priori success is given by the average of its integration index and its sovereignty index. The numerical results are given in Table 5.4.

Any state's a priori success is around 50% under unanimity. It is larger under the simple majority, although it also tends to 50% when

---

[79] These indices have to be compared with integration indices smaller than 40%.

Table 5.3. *A priori sovereignty indices:* $\Omega_i^{i-}(\mathcal{W}_n^{\mathrm{EU}}, p_n^*)$

$\mathcal{W}_{n=6,9,10,12,15,25}^{\mathrm{SM}}$	$\mathcal{W}_6^{\mathrm{SM}}$	$\mathcal{W}_9^{\mathrm{SM}}$	$\mathcal{W}_{10}^{\mathrm{SM}}$	$\mathcal{W}_{12}^{\mathrm{SM}}$	$\mathcal{W}_{15}^{\mathrm{SM}}$	$\mathcal{W}_{25}^{\mathrm{SM}}$		
any $i \in N_n$	0.812	0.637	0.746	0.726	0.605	0.581		
$\mathcal{W}_{n=6,9,10,12,15,25}^{\mathrm{U}}$	$\mathcal{W}_6^{\mathrm{U}}$	$\mathcal{W}_9^{\mathrm{U}}$	$\mathcal{W}_{10}^{\mathrm{U}}$	$\mathcal{W}_{12}^{\mathrm{U}}$	$\mathcal{W}_{15}^{\mathrm{U}}$	$\mathcal{W}_{25}^{\mathrm{U}}$		
any $i \in N_n$	1	1	1	1	1	1		
$\mathcal{W}_{n=6,9,10,12,15,25}^{\mathrm{QM}}$	$\mathcal{W}_6^{\mathrm{QM}}$	$\mathcal{W}_9^{\mathrm{QM}}$	$\mathcal{W}_{10}^{\mathrm{QM}}$	$\mathcal{W}_{12}^{\mathrm{QM}}$	$\mathcal{W}_{15}^{\mathrm{QM}}$	$\mathcal{W}_{25}^{\mathrm{Ni}}$	$\mathcal{W}_{25}^{\mathrm{Cs}}$	$\mathcal{W}_{25}^{\mathrm{Cv}}$
Germany	0.937	0.957	0.961	0.972	0.979	0.992	0.978	0.930
UK	-	0.957	0.961	0.972	0.979	0.992	0.957	0.886
France	0.937	0.957	0.961	0.972	0.979	0.992	0.956	0.884
Italy	0.937	0.957	0.961	0.972	0.979	0.992	0.956	0.883
Spain	-	-	-	0.961	0.969	0.990	0.942	0.854
Poland	-	-	-	-	-	0.990	0.941	0.854
Netherlands	0.875	0.910	0.914	0.938	0.952	0.978	0.927	0.817
Greece	-	-	0.914	0.938	0.952	0.977	0.924	0.809
Czech	-	-	-	-	-	0.977	0.924	0.809

Belgium	0.875	0.910	0.914	0.938	0.952	0.977	0.924	0.809
Hungary	-	-	-	-	-	0.977	0.924	0.808
Portugal	-	-	-	0.938	0.952	0.977	0.924	0.808
Sweden	-	-	-	-	0.946	0.975	0.923	0.807
Austria	-	-	-	-	0.946	0.975	0.922	0.806
Slovakia	-	-	-	-	-	0.972	0.921	0.802
Denmark	-	0.894	0.889	0.927	0.94	0.972	0.921	0.801
Finland	-	-	-	-	0.94	0.972	0.921	0.801
Ireland	-	0.894	0.889	0.927	0.94	0.972	0.920	0.799
Lithuania	-	-	-	-	-	0.972	0.920	0.799
Latvia	-	-	-	-	-	0.968	0.919	0.797
Slovenia	-	-	-	-	-	0.968	0.919	0.796
Estonia	-	-	-	-	-	0.968	0.918	0.796
Cyprus	-	-	-	-	-	0.968	0.918	0.795
Luxembourg	0.781	0.863	0.889	0.912	0.934	0.968	0.918	0.794
Malta	-	-	-	-	-	0.967	0.918	0.794

Table 5.4. *A priori success:* $\Omega_i(\mathcal{W}_n^{\mathrm{EU}}, p_n^*)$

$\mathcal{W}_{n=6,9,10,12,15,25}^{\mathrm{SM}}$	$\mathcal{W}_6^{\mathrm{SM}}$	$\mathcal{W}_9^{\mathrm{SM}}$	$\mathcal{W}_{10}^{\mathrm{SM}}$	$\mathcal{W}_{12}^{\mathrm{SM}}$	$\mathcal{W}_{15}^{\mathrm{SM}}$	$\mathcal{W}_{25}^{\mathrm{SM}}$		
any $i \in N_n$	0.656	0.637	0.623	0.613	0.605	0.581		
$\mathcal{W}_{n=6,9,10,12,15,25}^{\mathrm{U}}$	$\mathcal{W}_6^{\mathrm{U}}$	$\mathcal{W}_9^{\mathrm{U}}$	$\mathcal{W}_{10}^{\mathrm{U}}$	$\mathcal{W}_{12}^{\mathrm{U}}$	$\mathcal{W}_{15}^{\mathrm{U}}$	$\mathcal{W}_{25}^{\mathrm{U}}$		
any $i \in N_n$	0.516	0.502	0.501	0.500	0.500	0.500		
$\mathcal{W}_{n=6,9,10,12,15,25}^{\mathrm{QM}}$	$\mathcal{W}_6^{\mathrm{QM}}$	$\mathcal{W}_9^{\mathrm{QM}}$	$\mathcal{W}_{10}^{\mathrm{QM}}$	$\mathcal{W}_{12}^{\mathrm{QM}}$	$\mathcal{W}_{15}^{\mathrm{QM}}$	$\mathcal{W}_{25}^{\mathrm{Ni}}$	$\mathcal{W}_{25}^{\mathrm{Cs}}$	$\mathcal{W}_{25}^{\mathrm{Cv}}$
Germany	0.656	0.603	0.598	0.567	0.556	0.528	0.579	0.654
UK	-	0.603	0.598	0.567	0.556	0.528	0.558	0.610
France	0.656	0.603	0.598	0.567	0.556	0.528	0.558	0.609
Italy	0.656	0.603	0.598	0.567	0.556	0.528	0.557	0.607
Spain	-	-	-	0.559	0.547	0.526	0.543	0.579
Poland	-	-	-	-	-	0.526	0.543	0.578
Netherlands	0.594	0.557	0.551	0.536	0.530	0.514	0.528	0.542
Greece	-	-	0.551	0.536	0.530	0.513	0.525	0.534
Czech	-	-	-	-	-	0.513	0.525	0.533

Belgium	0.594	0.557	0.551	0.536	0.530	0.513	0.525	0.533
Hungary	-	-	-	-	-	0.513	0.525	0.533
Portugal	-	-	-	0.536	0.530	0.513	0.525	0.533
Sweden	-	-	-	-	0.524	0.510	0.524	0.531
Austria	-	-	-	-	0.524	0.510	0.524	0.530
Slovakia	-	-	-	-	-	0.507	0.522	0.526
Denmark	-	0.541	0.525	0.525	0.518	0.507	0.522	0.526
Finland	-	-	-	-	0.518	0.507	0.522	0.526
Ireland	-	0.541	0.525	0.525	0.518	0.507	0.521	0.524
Lithuania	-	-	-	-	-	0.507	0.521	0.524
Latvia	-	-	-	-	-	0.504	0.520	0.522
Slovenia	-	-	-	-	-	0.504	0.520	0.521
Estonia	-	-	-	-	-	0.504	0.519	0.520
Cyprus	-	-	-	-	-	0.504	0.519	0.519
Luxembourg	0.5	0.510	0.525	0.510	0.511	0.504	0.519	0.519
Malta	-	-	-	-	-	0.503	0.519	0.519

n is large. When the number of states is smaller than 25 we have

$$\Omega_i(W_n^U, p_n^*) < \Omega_i(W_n^{QM}, p_n^*) < \Omega_i(W_n^{SM}, p_n^*)$$

for any state i, except Luxembourg in the N_6 Council, where we have

$$\Omega_{Lu}(W_6^{SM}, p_6^*) > \Omega_{Lu}(W_6^U, p_6^*) > \Omega_{Lu}(W_6^{QM}, p_6^*).$$

Under a qualified majority the a priori success decreases over time[80]. This trend is confirmed under the Nice rule, but reversed under the Convention rule. Under the Constitution rule there is no trend: the likelihood of success of medium states would decrease, while that of large and small states would increase.

For the N_{25} Council, for any state i, we have

$$\Omega_i(W_{25}^U, p_{25}^*) < \Omega_i(W_{25}^{Ni}, p_{25}^*) < \Omega_i(W_{25}^{Cs}, p_{25}^*) < \Omega_i(W_{25}^{Cv}, p_{25}^*).$$

But if we compare the Convention rule and the simple majority, the ranking differs according to the size of the states:

$$\Omega_i(W_{25}^{Cv}, p_{25}^*) > \Omega_i(W_{25}^{SM}, p_{25}^*) > \Omega_i(W_{25}^{Cs}, p_{25}^*)$$

for large states (if $i = Ge, UK, Fr, It$) while the reverse holds for the remaining states. In other words, if states rank rules with a priori success as their criterion, large states should prefer the Convention to the simple majority, while the other states would prefer the simple majority. Note that for Germany the probability of success is very similar under these two rules.

Thus if states rank rules with a priori success as their criterion, the ranking is generally the same for all states with a few exceptions (in the N_6 and N_{25} Councils).

Probabilistic criteria: summary conclusions

In the public debate, the choice of the rule in the Council is often presented as a zero-sum game between states. In particular, it is often claimed that large states are less and less well-represented, or that they have lost power in favour of medium or small states. Similarly,

---

[80] An exception is Luxembourg, whose a priori success increases with the first two enlargements. Recall however that in the N_6 Council, Luxembourg had a null seat. In the N_{10} Council, Luxembourg, Ireland and Denmark had symmetric seats.

Application to the European Union 155

the discussions prior to the Nice summit were in terms of balance of representation between large, medium and small states.

The analysis above offers a different point of view for comparing rules: The a priori probabilities of success (conditional in one sense or other, or unconditional) of each state are evaluated for different rules. These are absolute values[81] that can be compared over time, and between different rules.

The analysis leads to the following conclusions (recalling the caveat for any descriptive interpretation). The variation over time is similar for all states: a decreasing trend for the integration index or a priori success, and an increasing trend for the sovereignty index. The Convention rule would reverse this trend for the integration index, a priori success and the sovereignty index. The Constitution rule would increase the integration index and decrease the sovereignty index. Concerning the choice between the three new rules for the N_{25} Council, all states have the largest integration index and largest a priori success under the Convention rule, and all states have the largest sovereignty index under the Nice rule. For both indices, the Constitution rule gives intermediate values to all states.

It is indeed remarkable that the ranking between rules according to these indices does not depend on the size of states: the ranking between rules is identical for all states (with only two exceptions). The difference in ranking between rules depends on the criterion chosen (ease of passing proposals, or integration index versus sovereignty index). From these points of view, the Constitution rule can be seen as a compromise between the Nice rule, which is more 'sovereignist' and less confident about integration, and the Convention rule, which is more resolutely integrationist and less jealous of sovereignty.

Of course, inter-state comparisons are also relevant. The relative position of one state compared to another state also matters. In particular, the issue remains of assessing the differences between states and their justification on grounds of differences in population size. Egalitarianism and utilitarianism provide standpoints that allow for comparisons from the point of view of both states and citizens.

---

[81] Most power indices are usually expressed in relative terms, which make comparisons between different rules unsound (see the comment on the normalization of the Banzhaf–Coleman index, Section 3.5.3).

5.2.2 Criteria based on utilities

There is a well known duality in the way in which the Council is seen. It is sometimes seen as a committee of states, hence the symmetric simple majority or the unanimity rules for certain matters, and other times as a committee of representatives of their respective populations, hence the different asymmetric qualified majority rules. We thus apply both the models presented in Sections 3.7 and 3.8.

In the model in Section 3.7 each member of the committee acts on his/her own behalf and has his/her own utility function. According to this model for any rule in the Council, $\mathcal{W}_n^{\text{EU}}$, state i's ($i \in N_n$) a priori expected utility can be defined as (see (26) in 3.7):

$$\bar{u}_i^\lambda(\mathcal{W}_n^{\text{EU}}, p_n^*) = \lambda \Omega_i^+(\mathcal{W}_n^{\text{EU}}, p_n^*) + (1 - \lambda)\Omega_i^-(\mathcal{W}_n^{\text{EU}}, p_n^*).$$

In the European context, λ can be interpreted as the importance given to the 'integration index' relative to the 'sovereignty index': $\lambda > 0.5$ means a more *pro-integration* view, while $\lambda < 0.5$ means a more *pro-sovereignty* view. In fact, λ can be regarded as representing the 'bias' of a state between these two extremes. If $\lambda = 0.5$ both views are equally important and what matters is obtaining the preferred outcome. The formula above presupposes the same bias λ for all states.

In the model in Section 3.8 each member of the committee acts on behalf of a group of a different size, in which each individual has his/her own utility function. Let $M(t)$ be the set of European citizens in year t, distributed across n states, $M(t) = M_1(t) \cup \ldots \cup M_n(t)$. As in Section 3.8, we assume that each minister in the EU Council follows the majority will in his/her state. Or, equivalently, decisions within state i are made by a simple majority, which we denote[82] by $\mathcal{W}_{m_i}^{\text{SM}_t}$. The composite rule

$$\mathcal{W}_m^{\text{EU}_t} = \mathcal{W}_n^{\text{EU}}[\mathcal{W}_{m_1}^{\text{SM}_t}, \ldots, \mathcal{W}_{m_n}^{\text{SM}_t}], \tag{72}$$

models the EU Council's decision-making as a two stage EU-citizens' decision. Then EU's citizen k's ($k \in M$) a priori expected utility is

---

[82] According to the convention previously adopted the notation should be $\mathcal{W}_{m_i(t)}^{\text{SM}}$, but no confusion can arise with this simpler notation if we recall that the number of citizens in a state varies with t. Similarly we write p_m^* instead of $p_{m(t)}^*$, or $\mathcal{W}_m^{\text{EU}_t}$ or $\mathcal{W}_{m(t)}^{\text{EU}}$.

Application to the European Union 157

(assuming the same bias λ for all citizens) given by

$$\bar{u}_k^\lambda(W_m^{\mathrm{EU}_t}, p_m^*) = \lambda \Omega_k^+(W_m^{\mathrm{EU}_t}, p_m^*) + (1 - \lambda)\Omega_k^-(W_m^{\mathrm{EU}_t}, p_m^*).$$

Egalitarian principle

The egalitarian principle requires that a priori all voters have the same expected utility. Symmetric rules implement the principle. Thus, the simple majority and unanimity satisfy the egalitarian principle at state level. The qualified majority does not: only states with symmetric seats have the same expected utility. That is, states with the same number of votes or Luxembourg, Denmark and Ireland on the N_{10} Council.

Of course, the purpose of the qualified majority is to take into account the differences in terms of populations, and thus the egalitarian principle should be checked at citizen level. For any pair of citizens k and l, we obtain that the egalitarian principle is thus basically satisfied at citizen level whatever the rule (see (42) in 3.8.1):

$$\bar{u}_k^\lambda(W_m^{\mathrm{EU}_t}, p_m^*) \simeq \bar{u}_l^\lambda(W_m^{\mathrm{EU}_t}, p_m^*).$$

More precisely, applying Proposition 20 in 3.8.2 (adopting the same approximations), the maximal ratio between two citizens, whatever the year considered and whatever the importance given to the integration index relative to the sovereignty index, is

$$\frac{\bar{u}_k^\lambda(W_m^{\mathrm{EU}_t}, p_m^*)}{\bar{u}_l^\lambda(W_m^{\mathrm{EU}_t}, p_m^*)} < 1 + \xi(t),$$

where $\xi(t)$, given by (41), depends on the smallest population figure in year t. For the years considered, $\xi(t)$ is always smaller than 0.0015, which means that the citizen with the largest expected utility never has more than 0.15% more than the expected utility of any other citizen. In Table 5.5 an upper bound $\delta(n)$ is given for each n (i.e. each period with a given number of member states), namely

$$\delta(n) = \mathrm{Max}_t \left[1 + \xi(t)\right],$$

where the maximum is taken for those years t in which the Council had n members.

158   *Voting and Collective Decision-Making*

Table 5.5. *Maximum ratio between citizens' expected utilities (upper bound).*

$n =$	6	9	10	12	15	25
$\delta(n)$	1.00143	1.00135	1.00132	1.00132	1.00125	1.00126

Comparison with the square root rule

We can compute a similar ratio for the Banzhaf index, that is

$$\Delta(W_n^{\text{EU}}) = \text{Max}_t \left[\frac{\text{Max}_k \text{Bz}_k(W_m^{\text{EU}_t})}{\text{Min}_l \text{Bz}_l(W_m^{\text{EU}_t})} \right],$$

where the maximum is taken for any year t such that the Council had n members. The results are given in Table 5.6.

This ratio is certainly not close to 1, (it can even be infinity in the N_6 Council!), and is always much larger than 2; (the sole exception being the qualified majority in the N_9 Council). If citizens' representation were measured by the Banzhaf index, this would mean large inequalities between citizens from different states. During the debates that followed the Treaty of Nice some scientists claimed that: '*The basic democratic principle that the vote of any citizen of a Member State ought to be worth as much as for any other Member State is strongly violated both in the voting system of the Treaty of Nice and in the rules given in the draft Constitution.*'[83] The rationale for their claim is basically that, for instance,

$$\Delta(W_{25}^{\text{Ni}}) = 2.27$$

$$\Delta(W_{25}^{\text{Cs}}) = 4.35,$$

and these values were considered as much too large. By focusing on the Banzhaf indices, as discussed in Example 3.3 in Section 3.8.2, their approach magnifies the differences between citizens from different countries. As was argued there, using the probability of being decisive as a measure of representation (i.e. of the vote of any citizen

---

[83] Open letter addressed to the governments of the EU member states. The letter (that as the reader may guess, we refused to sign), as well as the list of scientists who signed it, can be found, for instance, at www.esi2.us.es/˜mbilbao/pdffiles.letter.pdf.

Application to the European Union   159

Table 5.6. *Maximum ratio between citizens' Banzhaf indices*

$n =$	6	9	10	12	15	25
$\Delta(\mathcal{W}_n^{SM})$	13.4	13.3	13	14.4	14.2	14.4
$\Delta(\mathcal{W}_n^{QM})$	∞	1.78	3.75	2.02	2.87	–
$\Delta(\mathcal{W}_n^{Ni})$	-	–	–	–	–	2.27
$\Delta(\mathcal{W}_n^{Cs})$	-	–	–	–	–	4.35
$\Delta(\mathcal{W}_n^{Cv})$	-	–	–	–	–	2.88
$\Delta(\mathcal{W}_n^{U})$	13.4	13.3	13	14.4	14.2	14.4

of a Member State's '*worth*') in a take-it-or-leave-it environment is misleading. These values have to be compared with the corresponding number in Table 5.5, which is

$$\delta(25) = 1.000126.$$

The reason why there is such a big a difference between these figures is clear: in the a priori probabilistic model, a citizen's expected utility depends only slightly on his/her decisiveness.

Utilitarian principle

The voting rules that implement the utilitarian principle in different conditions were discussed in Sections 3.7.2 and 3.8.3. Here we consider the rules that have actually been used in the Council. To compare rules from a utilitarian point of view, the criterion is the sum[84] of expected utilities. That is, $\mathcal{W}$ is better than $\mathcal{W}'$ ($\mathcal{W} \succ \mathcal{W}'$) if

$$\sum_i \bar{u}_i^\lambda(\mathcal{W}, p^*) > \sum_i \bar{u}_i^\lambda(\mathcal{W}', p^*).$$

This can be applied at state level or at citizen level.

If the Council is interpreted as a committee of 'equals', then, according to Propositions 13 and 15 in Section 3.7.2,

$\mathcal{W}^{SM}$ is the best rule if $\lambda \geq 0.5$,

$\mathcal{W}^{U}$ is the best rule if $\lambda = 0$.

---

[84] Here we only compare rules with identical numbers of voters. If this is not the case, average expected utility would be a better criterion.

For $0 < \lambda < 0.5$, the utilitarian-best (i.e. the $(1 - \lambda)$-majority rule) is not used in the Council. We compare the expected utilities for the three rules actually used: W_n^{SM}, W_n^{QM} and W_n^{U}, and also W_{25}^{Ni}, W_{25}^{Cs}, and W_{25}^{Cv} for the N_{25} Council.

Let us detail the calculations for N_6 Council, at state level. Plugging the values of the a priori success and the a priori ease of passing proposals (Tables 5.1 and 5.4) into (28) in Section 3.7 we obtain the aggregated expected utility for the simple majority, the qualified majority and unanimity:

$$\sum_{i \in N_6} \bar{u}_i^{\lambda}(W_6^{SM}, p_6^*) = 2.44 - 0.94\lambda,$$

$$\sum_{i \in N_6} \bar{u}_i^{\lambda}(W_6^{QM}, p_6^*) = 2.67 - 1.69\lambda,$$

$$\sum_{i \in N_6} \bar{u}_i^{\lambda}(W_6^{U}, p_6^*) = 3 - 2.91\lambda.$$

The largest sum is obtained with the simple majority for $\lambda = 1$, and with the unanimity rule for $\lambda = 0$. For intermediate values, as λ increases from 0 to 1 (i.e. the relative weight of the integration index w.r.t. the sovereignty index increases), the performance of the three rules (W_6^{U}, W_6^{QM} and W_6^{SM}) is reversed. A comparison of these sums leads to

$$W_6^{U} \succ W_6^{QM} \succ W_6^{SM} \quad \text{if } \lambda < 0.27,$$
$$W_6^{U} \sim W_6^{QM} \succ W_6^{SM} \quad \text{if } \lambda = 0.27,$$
$$W_6^{QM} \succ W_6^{U} \succ W_6^{SM} \quad \text{for } 0.27 < \lambda < 0.28,$$
$$W_6^{QM} \succ W_6^{U} \sim W_6^{SM} \quad \text{if } \lambda = 0.28,$$
$$W_6^{QM} \succ W_6^{SM} \succ W_6^{U} \quad \text{for } 0.28 < \lambda < 0.31,$$
$$W_6^{QM} \sim W_6^{SM} \succ W_6^{U} \quad \text{if } \lambda = 0.31,$$
$$W_6^{SM} \succ W_6^{QM} \succ W_6^{U} \quad \text{for } \lambda > 0.31.$$

We can thus conclude that for the N_6 Council, if the choice is between simple majority, unanimity and qualified majority, the utilitarian principle is best satisfied by unanimity if $\lambda < 0.27$, by a qualified majority only for λ within the narrow interval $0.27 < \lambda < 0.31$, and by a simple majority if $\lambda > 0.31$.

Application to the European Union 161

We can proceed similarly for the N_9, N_{10}, N_{12} and N_{15} Councils. The results can be summarized as follows. If the choice is between a simple majority, unanimity and a qualified majority, the utilitarian principle is best satisfied by

$$W_n^U \quad \text{if } \lambda < a_n,$$
$$W_n^{QM} \quad \text{for } a_n < \lambda < b_n,$$
$$W_n^{SM} \quad \text{if } \lambda > b_n,$$

with

$$a_9 = 0.27, \ a_{10} = 0.28, \ a_{12} = 0.27, \ a_{15} = 0.28$$
$$b_9 = 0.40, \ b_{10} = 0.37, \ b_{12} = 0.38, \ b_{15} = 0.42.$$

Therefore the qualitative results are similar in all cases: the simple majority is the best rule for a large range of values of λ (above b_n, which is around 0.40). Unanimity is the best rule for a range of values of λ (below a_n, which is close to 0.30). And the qualified majority is better than unanimity and the simple majority only for a small range of values of λ (a_n and b_n are quite close).

For the N_{25} Council, if the choice is between simple majority, the Convention rule, the Constitution rule, the Nice rule and unanimity, the utilitarian principle is best satisfied by

$$W_{25}^U \quad \text{if } \lambda < 0.32,$$
$$W_{25}^{Ni} \quad \text{for } 0.32 < \lambda < 0.37,$$
$$W_{25}^{Cs} \quad \text{for } 0.37 < \lambda < 0.42,$$
$$W_{25}^{Cv} \quad \text{for } 0.42 < \lambda < 0.44,$$
$$W_{25}^{SM} \quad \text{if } \lambda > 0.44.$$

Note that the Constitution rule is once again in an intermediate position (in this case the range of λ for which it is the best) between the Nice and Convention rules, as it was with criteria based on probabilistic indices. Of the three rules, the Constitution rule was the one finally chosen. This can be interpreted as a choice based on the utilitarian principle (from the point of view of the Council as a committee of 'equal states') in the following terms: in the light of the current model, the European Union's choice can be rationalized from the utilitarian

162   *Voting and Collective Decision-Making*

point of view by assuming that the common view is a slightly biased *pro-sovereignty* view, with $0.37 < \lambda < 0.42$.

We can proceed in a similar way at citizen level using the model introduced in Section 3.8.3, in which the EU Council works as a two stage EU-citizens' decision-maker. Now in (72) $W_m^{EU_t}$ can be either $W_m^{SM_t}$, $W_m^{QM_t}$ or $W_m^{U_t}$, depending on whether the rule in the Council is the simple majority, a qualified majority or unanimity. We obtain that the utilitarian principle is best satisfied at citizen level under

$$W_m^{U_t} \quad \text{if } \lambda < a_m^t,$$
$$W_m^{QM_t} \quad \text{for } a_m^t < \lambda < b_m^t,$$
$$W_m^{SM_t} \quad \text{if } \lambda > b_m^t,$$

with $a_m^t \in [0.499960, 0.499973]$, and $b_m^t \in [0.499987, 0.499992]$. Thus for any year considered the interval within which a qualified majority is the best of the three rules is very narrow as $a_m^t \simeq b_m^t \simeq 0.5$. Thus at citizen level, of the rules that have been used in the Council, the one that best satisfies the utilitarian principle is

$$W_m^{U_t} \quad \text{if } \lambda < 0.5$$
$$W_m^{SM_t} \quad \text{if } \lambda \geq 0.5.$$

In conclusion, the aggregated expected utility is almost never highest under a qualified majority (be it under the Nice rule, the Convention rule, or the Constitution rule for the N_{25} Council). In fact, according to the a priori model, as the relative weight given to positive success w.r.t. negative success increases, at about $\lambda = 0.5$ there is a brusque shift, and the simple majority becomes better than unanimity. Thus, from this point of view, the qualified majority is a compromise between these two extremes that can be justified in optimality terms only for a value of λ close to 0.5, but which makes sense as an intermediate rule between the two extreme rules between which optimality switches depending on the bias.

Criteria based on utilities: summary conclusions

Unanimity and simple majority rules obviously implement the egalitarian principle at state level. At citizen level, expected utility based on the a priori model is basically the same for all citizens, irrespective of their

Application to the European Union 163

nationality. Therefore the egalitarian principle is basically satisfied at citizen level for the different rules. From the utilitarian point of view, a qualified majority (i.e. the Nice, Constitution or Convention rule) is the best rule at state level only for a narrow range within a slightly biased *pro-sovereignty* view (common to all states), and practically never at citizen level. Nevertheless, all the three qualified majority rules make sense as intermediate between the two extreme rules between which optimality switches depending on the bias.

5.3 The Council as a bargaining committee

As has been already said, the Council works more like what has been described as a bargaining committee. The minutes of the Council suggest that often the formal vote takes place once the Council has found a unanimous agreement. In fact, the confirmation by David Galloway[85] that this is very often the case in the decisions made by a qualified majority, along with the fact that the redistribution of weights in the Council is obviously the most problematic issue at each enlargement, are at the origin of the model presented in Chapter 4. He also pointed out[86] that '*weights do matter because negotiators know that they can be outvoted*'. In reference to the way in which negotiations in the EU's Council usually proceed, Galloway also pointed out the capacity of experienced negotiators to 'guess', at a certain stage of the bargaining process after some negotiating rounds, '*where more or less the final agreement will lie*'.

To apply the model developed in Chapter 4, we assume that this 'final agreement' is:

$$\Phi(B, \mathcal{W}_n^{EU}) = \text{Nash}^{\text{Sh}(\mathcal{W}_n^{EU})}(B),$$

that is, we measure the bargaining power (in the precise game-theoretic sense of giving the weights of the asymmetric Nash bargaining solution) by the Shapley–Shubik index. As discussed in Sections 4.3 and 4.4, there are no conclusive arguments in support of this index in this

---

[85] An experienced EU practitioner, working for the Council for 20 years. See [25] for an account of the 2000 Nice summit from the point of view of a well-informed insider.

[86] In the course of a face-to-face interview on 23.06.02.

context, given that everything depends on the bargaining protocol. Nevertheless, we take this index as a term of reference in view of the very simple underlying protocol that supports it.

As explained in Section 4.5, the Nash bargaining solution can be seen as a compromise between the (generally incompatible) egalitarian and utilitarian goals. At state level, according to this model the implementation of the Nash solution is guaranteed by any symmetric rule, where all states have the same bargaining power. In particular, the simple majority and unanimity satisfy the condition

$$\mathrm{Sh}_i(\mathcal{W}_n^{\mathrm{SM}}) = \mathrm{Sh}_i(\mathcal{W}_n^{\mathrm{U}}) = \frac{1}{n} \quad \text{(for any } i \in N).$$

Under a qualified majority, states with symmetric seats have the same bargaining power, but in general different states have different bargaining powers as shown in Table 5.7. Thus it can be said that under the simple majority and under unanimity the final agreement that should be reached can be expected to be a compromise between egalitarianism and utilitarianism at state level.

Of course the objective of the qualified majority is to take into account the differences in terms of populations between the different states. For an assessment from this point of view, we use the model of a bargaining committee of representatives discussed in Section 4.6. With the notation introduced in Section 5.2.2, let $M(t)$ be the set of European citizens in year t, distributed in n states, $M(t) = M_1(t) \cup \ldots \cup M_n(t)$. Thus each minister i represents a group of size $m_i(t)$ in the EU Council. Then the 'neutral' rule in the Council, according to the model in Section 4.6, would be such that any state's bargaining power is proportional to the size of the group that he/she represents. That is, such that

$$\frac{\mathrm{Sh}_i(\mathcal{W}_n^{\mathrm{EU}})}{m_i(t)} = \frac{\mathrm{Sh}_j(\mathcal{W}_n^{\mathrm{EU}})}{m_j(t)},$$

for any two countries i, j. If the rule satisfies this property, in the conditions and sense explained in Section 4.6, any citizen is indifferent between bargaining directly within $M(t)$, and leaving bargaining in the hands of his/her minister.

The simple majority and unanimity would be neutral if the population were the same in all states. Table 5.8 gives states' bargaining

Table 5.7. *Shapley–Shubik index for the qualified majority*

$W^{QM}_{n=6,9,10,12,15,25}$	W^{QM}_6	W^{QM}_9	W^{QM}_{10}	W^{QM}_{12}	W^{QM}_{15}	W^{Ni}_{25}	W^{Cs}_{25}	W^{Cv}_{25}
Germany	0.233	0.179	0.174	0.134	0.117	0.093	0.157	0.163
UK	-	0.179	0.174	0.134	0.117	0.093	0.104	0.113
France	0.233	0.179	0.174	0.134	0.117	0.093	0.103	0.112
Italy	0.233	0.179	0.174	0.134	0.117	0.093	0.100	0.108
Spain	-	-	-	0.111	0.095	0.086	0.072	0.081
Poland	-	-	-	-	-	0.086	0.067	0.075
Netherlands	0.150	0.081	0.071	0.064	0.055	0.040	0.035	0.034
Greece	-	-	0.071	0.064	0.055	0.036	0.027	0.026
Czech	-	-	-	-	-	0.036	0.027	0.025
Belgium	0.150	0.081	0.071	0.064	0.055	0.036	0.027	0.025
Hungary	-	-	-	-	-	0.036	0.026	0.024
Portugal	-	-	-	0.064	0.055	0.036	0.026	0.024
Sweden	-	-	-	-	0.045	0.030	0.025	0.022

Table 5.7. (*cont.*)

$w_{n=6,9,10,12,15,25}^{QM}$	w_6^{QM}	w_9^{QM}	w_{10}^{QM}	w_{12}^{QM}	w_{15}^{QM}	w_{25}^{Ni}	w_{25}^{Cs}	w_{25}^{Cv}
Austria	-	-	-	-	0.045	0.030	0.023	0.021
Slovakia	-	-	-	-	-	0.021	0.020	0.017
Denmark	-	0.057	0.030	0.043	0.035	0.021	0.020	0.017
Finland	-	-	-	-	0.035	0.021	0.020	0.017
Ireland	-	0.057	0.030	0.043	0.035	0.021	0.018	0.015
Lithuania	-	-	-	-	-	0.021	0.017	0.014
Latvia	-	-	-	-	-	0.012	0.016	0.012
Slovenia	-	-	-	-	-	0.012	0.015	0.012
Estonia	-	-	-	-	-	0.012	0.014	0.011
Cyprus	-	-	-	-	-	0.012	0.013	0.010
Luxembourg	0	0.009	0.030	0.012	0.021	0.012	0.013	0.010
Malta	-	-	-	-	-	0.009	0.013	0.010

Application to the European Union 167

Table 5.8. *Shapley–Shubik index/population ratio for symmetric rules*

	$[\mathrm{Sh}_i(\mathcal{W})/m_i(t)]*10^9, \quad \mathcal{W} = \mathcal{W}_n^{\mathrm{SM}}$ or $\mathcal{W}_n^{\mathrm{U}}$					
	1958	1973	1981	1986	1995	2004
Germany	3.1	1.8	1.6	1.4	0.8	0.5
UK	–	2.1	1.9	1.5	1.1	0.7
France	3.7	2	1.8	1.5	1.2	0.7
Italy	3.4	2	1.8	1.5	1.1	0.7
Spain	–	–	–	2.2	1.7	0.9
Poland	–	–	–	–	–	1
Netherlands	15	8.3	7	5.7	4.3	2.5
Greece	–	–	10	8.5	6.6	3.6
Czech	–	–	–	–	–	3.8
Belgium	18	11	10	8.4	6.4	3.8
Hungary	–	–	–	–	–	3.9
Portugal	–	–	–	8.3	6.7	4
Sweden	–	–	–	–	7.6	4.5
Austria	–	–	–	–	8.3	4.9
Slovakia	–	–	–	–	–	7.4
Denmark	–	22	20	16	13	7.4
Finland	–	–	–	–	19	7.7
Ireland	–	36	29	24	13	9.9
Lithuania	–	–	–	–	–	12
Latvia	–	–	–	–	–	17
Slovenia	–	–	–	–	–	20
Estonia	–	–	–	–	–	30
Cyprus	–	–	–	–	–	55
Luxembourg	540	320	270	230	160	89
Malta	–	–	–	–	–	100

powers divided by the population for some years (1958, 1973, 1981, 1986, 1995 and 2004) for these two symmetric rules.

Note that although the population varies between enlargements and the years chosen for the calculations are those of the enlargements, qualitatively the results do not change between the mentioned dates (with the exception of German reunification, see below). As expected, it can be seen that these ratios are far from equal, and are much larger for small states than for large states. A citizen of a small state is favoured

168   *Voting and Collective Decision-Making*

Table 5.9. *Shapley–Shubik index/population ratio for the qualified majority*

	1958	1973	1981	1986	1995	Ni	Cs	Cv
					$[\mathrm{Sh}_i(W_n^{\mathrm{QM}})/m_i(t)] * 10^9$		2004	
Germany	4.3	2.9	2.8	2.2	1.4	1.1	1.9	2
UK	–	3.4	3.2	2.4	2	1.5	1.7	1.9
France	5.2	3.3	3.1	2.4	2	1.6	1.7	1.9
Italy	4.7	3.2	3.1	2.4	2	1.6	1.7	1.9
Spain	–	–	–	2.9	2.4	2	1.7	1.9
Poland	–	–	–	–	–	2.3	1.7	2
Netherlands	14	6	5	4.4	3.6	2.4	2.1	2.1
Greece	–	–	7.2	6.5	5.4	3.3	2.5	2.3
Czech	–	–	–	–	–	3.5	2.6	2.4
Belgium	17	8.3	7.4	6.4	5.3	3.5	2.6	2.4
Hungary	–	–	–	–	–	3.6	2.6	2.4
Portugal	–	–	–	6.4	5.6	3.6	2.6	2.4
Sweden	–	–	–	–	5.1	3.4	2.8	2.5
Austria	–	–	–	–	5.6	3.7	2.9	2.6
Slovakia	–	–	–	–	–	3.9	3.7	3.2
Denmark	–	11	5.9	8.3	6.8	3.9	3.7	3.2
Finland	–	–	–	–	6.9	4	3.7	3.2
Ireland	–	18	8.8	12	9.8	5.2	4.5	3.7
Lithuania	–	–	–	–	–	6.1	5	4.1
Latvia	–	–	–	–	–	5.1	6.7	5.4
Slovenia	–	–	–	–	–	6	7.6	6
Estonia	–	–	–	–	–	8.8	11	8.2
Cyprus	–	–	–	–	–	16	18	14
Luxembourg	0	27	83	32	51	26	29	22
Malta	–	–	–	–	–	22	33	24

by representation while the opposite holds for citizens from large states.

Table 5.9 gives the same ratios for the qualified majority for the same years. Table 5.9 requires the following comments. As expected, the differences under symmetric rules are much greater than under the qualified majority. Nevertheless, they are still considerable for the qualified majority. Large states still have a smaller ratio than small states. Thus, small states are relatively favoured. The premise that the

Application to the European Union 169

larger the state is, the smaller the ratio will be holds with the following exceptions: Luxemburg in the N_6 Council, Denmark in the N_{10} Council, Sweden in the N_{12} Council, and Germany in the N_{25} Council for the Constitution rule and the Convention rule.

These ratios question the system of 'clusters' (giving the same weights and thus the same bargaining power to different states). The population figures of France, Italy and the United Kingdom are similar enough for them to be allocated the same number of votes at least since 1981, but Germany's population would justify greater bargaining power, especially since reunification; (between 1989 and 1990, the year of the reunification of Germany, the ratio falls from $2.2 * 10^{-9}$ to $1.7 * 10^{-9}$). Also the Netherlands' population would justify placing it in a different cluster from Belgium (especially since 1981). The same can be said for Ireland and Denmark.

It is not meaningful to compare the variation over time of the ratio for one state (because we compare relative measures that mainly decrease when members are added, as the measures are divided by populations that increase). More interesting is the variation over time of the dispersion of the ratios. This dispersion cannot be said to decrease over time. It is also meaningful to compare the Nice rule, the Constitution rule and the Convention rule. The ratios for large states are larger with the Convention rule than with the other rules, while the ratio for small states (with the exception of Malta) are smaller with the Convention rule. This means that the dispersion of the ratio is smaller with the Convention rule than with the other rules, which in turn means that this is the best rule from this point of view. In the comparison of the Constitution rule and the Nice rule it must be noted that the differences in ratio between the large and medium states are smaller (in both relative and absolute terms) with the Constitution rule, thus making it a better candidate. But then the differences between larger and smaller states are not clearly smaller with the Constitution rule.

In short, the bargaining committee model supports the conclusion that medium and small states are over-represented compared to large states. Of the different rules that were proposed for the N_{25} Council, the Convention rule is certainly the best, in the sense that the dispersion in the ratio is the smallest. Also from this point of view, the Constitution rule can be seen to some extent as intermediate between the Nice and the Convention rules.

To conclude, it may be asked whether the over-representation of medium and small states is interpretable as sheer generosity on the part of the larger member states. Possibly not. The point of view for this assessment of such deviations is provided by a model in which the only source of asymmetry is the difference in population figures; in other words a model in which population figures are the only source of bargaining power. The (remarkably systematic: the bigger the country the further below the 'due' proportion) deviation from these proportions may be related to the fact that this is not the only source of effective bargaining power. Larger states may also have other means of increasing their effective bargaining power.

5.4 Exercises

1. Show that Luxembourg had a null seat in the N_6 Council, while Luxembourg, Ireland and Denmark had symmetric seats in the N_{10} Council.

2. Show that there is no inclusion between the set of winning configurations of Nice rule, the Constitution rule and the Convention rule.

3. Express the Nice rule, the Convention rule and the Constitution rule in terms of union and intersection of weighted majority rules.

4. Show that if n is odd, we have:

$$\alpha(W_n, p_n^*) = \frac{1}{2}\alpha(W_n, \tilde{p}_n),$$

$$\Omega_i^{i+}(W_n, p_n^*) = \frac{1}{2}\Omega_i^{i+}(W_n, \tilde{p}_n),$$

where

$$\tilde{p}_n(S) := \begin{cases} 1/x \text{ if } s > \frac{n}{2} \\ 0 \text{ otherwise,} \end{cases}$$

$$p_n^*(S) = \frac{1}{2^n}.$$

5. Show that any citizen's a priori probability of success is basically of 50% for all rules considered in the Council, irrespective of his/her nationality. Similarly any citizen's a priori integration index or

Application to the European Union 171

sovereignty index does not depend on nationality, but on the a priori ease of passing proposals. That is,

$$\Omega_k(\mathcal{W}_m^{\mathrm{EU}}, p_m^*) \simeq \frac{1}{2},$$

$$\Omega_k^{k+}(\mathcal{W}_m^{\mathrm{EU}}, p_m^*) \simeq \alpha(\mathcal{W}_n^{\mathrm{EU}}, p_n^*),$$

$$\Omega_k^{k-}(\mathcal{W}_m^{\mathrm{EU}}, p_m^*) \simeq 1 - \alpha(\mathcal{W}_n^{\mathrm{EU}}, p_n^*).$$

6. Show that

$$\frac{1}{n}\sum_{i\in N}\bar{u}_i^\lambda(\mathcal{W}_n^{\mathrm{SM}}, p_n^*) = \begin{cases} \dfrac{1}{4} + \dfrac{1}{2^{n+1}}C_{n-1}^{\frac{n-1}{2}} & \text{if n is odd} \\[2ex] \dfrac{1}{4} + \dfrac{1-\lambda}{2^{n+1}}C_n^{\frac{n}{2}} & \text{if n is even.} \end{cases}$$

$$\frac{1}{n}\sum_{i\in N}\bar{u}_i^\lambda(\mathcal{W}_n^{\mathrm{U}}, p_n^*) = \frac{1}{2} - \lambda\left(\frac{1}{2} - \frac{1}{2^n}\right).$$

Conclusions

To conclude, we briefly summarize the main conclusions and claims of the book.

1. The first requisite for a sound normative theory for the assessment and choice of (dichotomous) voting rules is a precise specification of the type of committee, council or body that makes the collective decisions under consideration. It is not possible to provide a well-founded analysis or recommendation about a vaguely specified environment, as has been the case with the traditional voting power approach.

2. In this respect we have dealt separately with two extreme clear-cut types of committee that make decisions under a yes/no voting rule as terms of reference: take-it-or-leave-it committees and bargaining committees, of which we have provided different models whose only shared ingredient is a (dichotomous) voting rule. Nevertheless, this does not exhaust all the possible environments though: other models are no doubt possible.

3. In neither type of committee is the question of 'power' or 'voting power' the first or primary issue that arises naturally, and nor can this issue be immediately addressed in a meaningful way. Each type of committee requires a different model and a different analysis, but in both cases the model proposed assumes individuals' behaviours to be consistent with the expected utility maximization model. The introduction of utilities allows (insofar as is possible) for a coherent, and unified approach to each type of committee. In particular, the normative question of the choice of voting rule for a committee of representatives of either type can be addressed by applying the egalitarian and utilitarian principles.

4. In pure take-it-or-leave-it committees behaviour follows immediately from preferences (if indifferences are discarded), so the situation is not a game situation. This means that in such a context the very notion of 'voting power' is more than dubious. In particular the notion

172

Conclusions 173

of power as the likelihood of being decisive is purely formal and devoid of any clear power-content. The notion of success or satisfaction seems in such contexts to be a sounder basis for further analysis. On this basis it is possible to introduce utilities into the model and apply the egalitarian and the utilitarian principles in order to make normative recommendations. An a priori probabilistic model of voters' behaviour or preferences leads to some recommendations that include the first and second 'square root rules' as particular cases. Nevertheless, an explicit specification of the context and a formulation of the analysis in utility terms disclose the distorting and misleading effects of presenting the first as 'equalizing voting power'. This is especially so in assessing the 'distance' of a voting rule from this 'optimum', i.e. assessing inequalities, which are magnified by the traditional approach. Apart from these differences, some other conclusions are worth remarking. First, starting with a precise specification of the environment sets limits on the scope and validity of these recommendations: they only make sense in take-it-or-leave-it voting situations, by contrast with the seemingly general-purpose recommendations of the traditional voting power approach. The limited scope of application of these recommendations may seem disappointing, given the rarity of pure take-it-or-leave-it voting situations, but it is the price that must be paid for clarifying the analysis. Second, the model discussed here is based on explicit assumptions about voters' behaviour and utilities justified for normative purposes. As a consequence, the limitations of the model can be seen clearly. As is well known, the a priori probabilistic model of behaviour (Assumption 1) is often criticized, even assuming a normative point of view. Although other models can be considered, this one seems to us to be reasonable and the simplest. Moreover, this choice has permitted us to 'embed' the traditional model within our more general model, thus showing its inconsistencies and limitations.

5. The type of situation described as a bargaining committee is much more complex than a pure take-it-or-leave-it committee. Unlike take-it-or-leave-it committees, bargaining committees represent genuine game situations, and require a game-theoretic approach. We have modelled these situations as an extension of the classical Nash bargaining model. Our model consists of a profile of expected utility preferences over the set of feasible agreements (or, in practice, the set of feasible payoff vectors associated with it à la Nash), and the voting rule that prescribes what groups of players are able to enforce agreements. The first

question that naturally arises then is what the 'value' or reasonable expectation of a player is in such an environment. The answer that we provide is also an extension of Nash bargaining theory, based on rationality requirements about a reasonable agreement in such a context. Theorem 29 provides a foundation for interpreting, in principle, most traditional power indices as candidates for measuring the 'bargaining power' that the voting rule gives to each player in a bargaining committee. The lack of compelling conditions to go further is interpretable as the degrees of freedom enclosed in our rather summary model, in other words the indeterminacy of a situation in which details not incorporated into the model are important. Non-cooperative analysis shows the importance of the bargaining protocol and its impact on the players' bargaining power. Of the power indices which are candidates to express the players' bargaining power, the Shapley–Shubik index appears associated with a very simple protocol. Finally, the question of the choice of rule in a bargaining committee of representatives is addressed and yields a new and unexpected recommendation based on the Nash bargaining solution interpreted as a compromise between egalitarianism and utilitarianism.

6. In the light of the approach presented here, power indices 'recover' their game-theoretic character. The probabilistic approach makes sense for take-or-leave-it environments, but in such contexts power as decisiveness does not make sense. It is in bargaining environments that power is relevant and decisiveness may be the source of power. It is also in this context that the (cooperative and non-cooperative) game-theoretic approach make sense.

7. Thus, it would be wrong to interpret the above summary as the result of taking the I/P-power dichotomy emphasized in [22] to its final consequences. In fact, a marginal outcome of the analysis is that it shows the lack of consistency of a distinction made at the abstract level rather than at the level of the situation considered. On the one hand, the notion of 'I-power' is revealed as a misunderstanding in a take-it-or-leave-it context (where its underlying probabilistic model makes sense), given the lack of sense of the notion of power as decisiveness in that context. On the other hand, if the resulting bargaining power in bargaining committees is interpreted as 'P-power', it turns out in general *not* to be an expected share in a fixed prize, but rather genuine bargaining power in a well-established game-theoretic sense, and it is related to decisiveness. In fact, the model presented here accounts

Conclusions 175

also for the particular preference profiles (i.e. TU-like) for which the Shapley–Shubik (and other power indices) may as well be interpreted as an expected payoff.

8. Finally, we want to stress the tentative and humble '*if … then*' character of all the results and 'recommendations' presented in the book. We have been taught humility by ten years of joint research in which we believed again and again that we had '*at last*' seen things clearly, only to later perceive further obscurities.

References

[1] Allais, M., 1953, Le comportement de l'homme rationnel devant le risque: critique des postulats et axiomes de l'école Américaine, *Econometrica* **21**, 503–46.

[2] Arrow, K., 1963, *Social Choice and Individual Values*, 2nd ed., New York, Wiley.

[3] Banks, J. S., and J. Duggan, 2000, A Bargaining Model of Collective Choice, *American Political Science Review* **94**, 73–88.

[4] Banzhaf, J. F., 1965, Weighted Voting doesn't Work: A Mathematical Analysis, *Rutgers Law Review* **19**, 317–43.

[5] Banzhaf, J. F., 1966, Multi-Member Electoral Districts: Do They Violate the One Man, One Vote Principle? *Yale Law Journal* **75**, 1309–38.

[6] Barberà, S., and M. Jackson, 2006, On the Weights of Nations: Assigning Voting Power to Heterogeneous Voters, *Journal of Political Economy*, **114**, 317–39.

[7] Baron, D. P., and J. A. Ferejohn, 1989, Bargaining in Legislatures, *American Political Science Review* **83**, 1181–1206.

[8] Barry, B., 1980, Is it Better to Be Powerful or Lucky?, Part I and Part II, *Political Studies* **28**, 183–94, 338–52.

[9] Beisbart, C., L. Bovens, and S. Hartmann, 2005, A Utilitarian Assessment of Alternative Decision Rules in the Council of Ministers, *European Union Politics* **6**, 395–418.

[10] Benoît, J-P., and L. A. Kornhauser, 2002, Game-Theoretic Analysis of Legal Rules and Institutions. In: *Handbook of Game Theory with Economic Applications*, Vol. 3, ed. Aumann R. J., and S. Hart, Amsterdam, Elsevier–North-Holland, pp. 2229–69.

[11] Bentham, J., 1789, *An Introduction to the Principles of Morals and Legislation*, London, T. Payne.

[12] Binmore, K., 1998, *Game Theory and the Social Contract II, Just Playing*. Cambridge, MA, MIT Press.

[13] Binmore, K., 2007, *Playing for Real. A Text on Game Theory*, New York, Oxford University Press.

[14] Brams, S. J., and M. Lake, 1978, Power and Satisfaction in a Representative Democracy. In: *Game Theory and Political Science,* ed. P. Ordeshook, New York University Press, pp. 529–62.

References

[15] Coleman, J. S., 1971, Control of Collectivities and the Power of a Collectivity to Act. In: *Social Choice*, ed. B. Lieberman, London, Gordon and Breach, pp. 269–300.

[16] Coleman, J. S., 1986, *Individual Interests and Collective Action: Selected Essays*, Cambridge University Press.

[17] Deegan, J., and E. W. Packel, 1978, A New Index of Power for Simple *n*-Person Games, *International Journal of Game Theory* **7**, 113–23.

[18] Dubey, P., 1975, On the Uniqueness of the Shapley Value, *International Journal of Game Theory* **4**, 131–9.

[19] Dubey, P., A. Neyman and R. J. Weber, 1981, Value Theory without Efficiency, *Mathematics of Operations Research* **6**, 122–8.

[20] Dubey, P., and L. S. Shapley, 1979, Mathematical Properties of the Banzhaf Power Index, *Mathematics of Operations Research* **4**, 99–131.

[21] Feix, M., D. Lepelley, V. Merlin, and J-L. Rouet, 2004, The Probability of Conflicts in a U.S. Presidential Type Election, *Economic Theory* **23**, 227–57.

[22] Felsenthal, D. S., and M. Machover, 1998, *The Measurement of Voting Power: Theory and Practice, Problems and Paradoxes*, London, Edward Elgar.

[23] Felsenthal, D. S., and M. Machover, 2004, Analysis of QM rules in the draft constitution for Europe proposed by the European Convention, 2003, *Social Choice and Welfare* **23**, 1–20.

[24] Felsenthal, D. S., M. Machover, and W. S. Zwicker, 1998, The Bicameral Postulates and Indices of a Priori Voting Power, *Theory and Decision* **44**, 83–116.

[25] Galloway, D., 2001, *The Treaty of Nice and Beyond: Realities and Illusions of Power in the EU*, Sheffield, Academic.

[26] Garrett, G., and G. Tsebelis, 1999, Why Resist the Temptation to Apply Power Indices to the European Union?, *Journal of Theoretical Politics* **11**, 291–308.

[27] Gibbard, A., 1973, Manipulation of Voting Schemes: A General Result, *Econometrica* **41**, 587–601.

[28] Hart, S., and A. Mas–Colell, 1996, Bargaining and Value, *Econometrica* **64**, 357–80.

[29] Hernstein, I. N., and J. Milnor, 1953, An Axiomatic Approach to Measurable Utility, *Econometrica* **21**, 291-7.

[30] Holler, M. J., and E. W. Packel, 1983, Power, Luck and the Right Index, *Journal of Economics* **43**, 21–9.

[31] Hosli, M. O., and M. Machover, 2004, The Nice Treaty and Voting Rules in the Council: A Reply to Moberg (2002), *Journal of Common Market Studies* **42**, 497–521.

[32] Kalai, E., 1977, Nonsymmetric Nash Solutions and Replications of 2-person Bargaining, *International Journal of Game Theory* **6**, 129–33.

[33] Kalai, E. and M. Smorodinsky, 1975, Other Solutions to Nash's Bargaining Problem, *Econometrica* **43**, 513–8.

[34] König, T., and T. Bräuninger, 1998, The Inclusiveness of European Decision Rules, *Journal of Theoretical Politics* **10**, 125–42.

[35] Kuhn, H. W., and S. Nasar, eds., 2002, *The Essential John Nash*, Princeton University Press.

[36] Lane, J. E., and R. Maeland, 2002, A Note on Nice, *Journal of Theoretical Politics* **14**, 123–8.

[37] Laruelle, A., R. Martínez, and F. Valenciano, 2004, On the Difficulty of Making Decisions within the EU-25, *International Journal of Organization Theory and Behaviour* **7**, 571–84.

[38] Laruelle, A., R. Martínez, and F. Valenciano, 2006, Success versus Decisiveness: Conceptual Discussion and Case Study, *Journal of Theoretical Politics* **18**, 185–205.

[39] Laruelle, A., and F. Valenciano, 2001, Shapley–Shubik and Banzhaf Indices Revisited, *Mathematics of Operations Research* **26**, 89–104.

[40] Laruelle, A., and F. Valenciano, 2002, Power Indices and the Veil of Ignorance, *International Journal of Game Theory* **31**, 331–9.

[41] Laruelle, A., and F. Valenciano, 2002, Inequality among EU Citizens in the EU's Council Decision Procedure, *European Journal of Political Economy* **18**, 475–98.

[42] Laruelle, A., and F. Valenciano, 2003, Semivalues and Voting Power, *International Game Theory Review* **5**, 41–61.

[43] Laruelle, A., and F. Valenciano, 2004, Inequality in Voting Power, *Social Choice and Welfare* **22**, 413–32.

[44] Laruelle, A., and F. Valenciano, 2004, On the Meaning of the Owen–Banzhaf Coalitional Value in Voting Situations, *Theory and Decision* **56**, 113–23. Reprinted in: *Essays on Cooperative Games. In Honor of Guillermo Owen*, ed. G. Gambarelli, Theory and Decision Library C, Vol. 36, Dordrecht, Kluwer.

[45] Laruelle, A., and F. Valenciano, 2005, Assessing Success and Secisiveness in Voting Situations, *Social Choice and Welfare* **24** 171–97.

[46] Laruelle, A., and F. Valenciano, 2005, Potential, and Power of a Collectivity to Act, *Theory and Decision* **58**, 187–94.

[47] Laruelle, A., and F. Valenciano, 2005, A Critical Reappraisal of Some Voting Power Paradoxes, *Public Choice* **125**, 17–41.

[48] Laruelle, A., and F. Valenciano, 2007, Bargaining in Committees as an Extension of Nash's Bargaining Theory, *Journal of Economic Theory* **132**, 291–305.

References

[49] Laruelle, A., and F. Valenciano, 2008, Bargaining in Committees of Representatives: the 'Neutral' Voting Rule, *Journal of Theoretical Politics* **20**, 93–106.

[50] Laruelle, A., and F. Valenciano, 2008, Cooperative Bargaining Foundations of the Shapley–Shubik Index, *Games and Economic Behavior* (forthcoming).

[51] Laruelle, A., and F. Valenciano, 2008, Non-Cooperative Foundations of Bargaining Power in Committees, *Games and Economic Behavior* **63**, 341–53.

[52] Laruelle, A., and M. Widgrén, 1998, Is the Allocation of Voting Power among the EU States Fair? *Public Choice* **94**, 317–39.

[53] Leech, D., 2002, Designing the Voting System for the EU Council of Ministers, *Public Choice* **113**, 437–64.

[54] Lehrer, E., 1988, An Axiomatization of the Banzhaf Value, *International Journal of Game Theory* **17**, 89–99.

[55] Maaser, N., and S. Napel, 2007, Equal Representation in Two-Tier Voting Systems, *Social Choice and Welfare* **28**, 401–20.

[56] Moberg, A., 2002, The Nice Treaty and Voting Rules in the Council, *Journal of Common Market Studies* **40**, 259–82.

[57] Montero, M., 2006, Noncooperative Bargaining Foundations of the Nucleolus in Majority Games, *Games and Economic Behavior* **54**, 380–97.

[58] Morriss, P., 1987, *Power: A philosophical Analysis*, Manchester University Press.

[59] Morriss, P., 2002, *Power: A philosophical Analysis*, 2nd edition, Manchester University Press.

[60] Nash, J. F., 1950, The Bargaining Problem, *Econometrica* **18**, 155–62.

[61] Nash, J. F., 1951, Non-Cooperative Games, *Annals of Mathematics* **54**, 286–95.

[62] Nash, J. F., 1953, Two-Person Cooperative Games, *Econometrica* **21**, 128–40.

[63] Nash, J. F., 1996, *Essays on Game Theory*, London, Edward Elgar.

[64] Niemi, R. G., and H. F. Weisberg, eds., 1972, *Probability Models of Collective Decision Making*, Columbus, OH, Merrill.

[65] Osborne, M. J., 2003, *An Introduction to Game Theory*, Oxford University Press.

[66] Osborne, M. J., and A. Rubinstein, 1994, *A Course in Game Theory*, Cambridge, MA, MIT Press.

[67] Owen, G., 1975, Multilinear Extensions and the Banzhaf Value, *Naval Research Logistics Quarterly* **22**, 741–50.

[68] Penrose, L. S., 1946, The Elementary Statistics of Majority Voting, *Journal of the Royal Statistical Society* **109**, 53–7.

180 References

[69] Penrose, L. S., 1952, *On the Objective Study of Crowd Behaviour*, London, Lewis.

[70] Rae, D., 1969, Decision Rules and Individual Values in Constitutional Choice, *American Political Science Review* **63**, 40–56.

[71] Rawls, A., 1972, *A Theory of Justice*, Oxford University Press.

[72] Roth, A. E., 1977, Individual Rationality and Nash's Solution to the Bargaining Problem, *Mathematics of Operations Research* **2**, 64–5.

[73] Roth, A. E., 1977, Utility Functions for Simple Games, *Journal of Economic Theory* **16**, 481–9.

[74] Roth, A. E., ed., 1988, *The Shapley Value. Essays in Honor of Lloyd S. Shapley*, Cambridge University Press.

[75] Rubinstein, A., 1982, Perfect Equilibrium in a Bargaining Model, *Econometrica* **50**, 97–109.

[76] Shapley, L. S., 1953, A Value for N-person Games, *Annals of Mathematical Studies* **28**, 307–17.

[77] Shapley, L. S., 1969, Utility Comparison and the Theory of Games. In: *La Décision: Agrégation et Dynamique des Ordres de Préférence*, Paris, CNRS, 251–63.

[78] Shapley, L. S., and M. Shubik, 1954, A Method for Evaluating the Distribution of Power in a Committee System, *American Political Science Review* **48**, 787–92.

[79] Straffin, P. D., 1977, Homogeneity, Independence and Power Indices, *Public Choice* **30**, 107–18.

[80] Straffin, P. D., 1977, Majority Rule and General Decision Rules, *Theory and Decision* **8**, 351–60.

[81] Straffin, P. D., 1982, Power Indices in Politics. In: *Political and Related Models*, ed. S. J. Brams, W. F. Lucas, and P. D. Straffin, New York, Springer, pp. 256–321.

[82] Straffin, P. D., 1988, The Shapley–Shubik and Banzhaf Power Indices as Probabilities. In: *The Shapley Value. Essays in Honor of Lloyd S. Shapley*, ed. A. E. Roth, 1988, Cambridge University Press, pp. 71–81.

[83] Straffin, P. D., M. D. Davis, and S. J. Brams, 1982, Power and Satisfaction in an Ideologically Divided Voting Body. In: *Power, Voting, and Voting Power*, ed. M. Holler, Würzburg–Wien, Physica Verlag, pp. 239–253.

[84] Taylor, M., 1969, Proof of a Theorem on Majority Rule, *Behavioral Science* **14**, 228–31.

[85] Taylor, A. D., and W. S. Zwicker, 1992, A Characterization of Weighted Voting, *Proceedings of the American Mathematical Society* **115**, 1089–94.

References 181

[86] Taylor A. D., and W. S. Zwicker, 1999, *Simple Games: Desirability Relations, Trading, Pseudoweightings*, Princeton University Press.

[87] von Neumann, J., and O. Morgenstern, 1944, *Theory of Games and Economic Behavior*, Princeton University Press.

[88] Weber, R. J., 1979, Subjectivity in the Valuation of Games. In: *Game Theory and Related Topics*, ed. O. Moeschlin, and D. Pallaschke, Amsterdam, North-Holland, pp. 129–36.

[89] Weber, R. J., 1988, Probabilistic Values for Games. In: *The Shapley Value. Essays in Honor of Lloyd S. Shapley*, ed. A. E. Roth, 1988, Cambridge University Press, pp. 101–19.

Index

a priori integration index, 145, 146, 156
a priori sovereignty index, 148, 150, 156
a priori voting behaviour, 60, 67, 71, 142
additivity, 35
Allais, M., 16, 28
anonymity, 33, 35, 110
anonymous voting behaviour, 56, 68, 139
Arrow, K., *xiii*

Banks, J. S., 128
Banzhaf index, 63, 67, 80, 83, 92, 125, 158, 159
Banzhaf, J. F., 30, 39–41, 62
Barberà, S., 96
bargaining committee, 46, 106, 107, 163
bargaining power, 113, 114, 163
bargaining problem, 31, 107
bargaining protocol, 118, 123
Baron, D. P., 128
Barry, B., 54, 55, 58, 67
battle of the sexes, 20, 22
Beisbart, C., 96
Benoît, J-P., 67, 134
Bentham, J., 71
Binmore, K., 18, 31, 113, 117
Bovens, L., 96
Bräuninger, T., 65, 67
Brams, S. J., 54, 67

Coleman indices, 63, 67
Coleman, J. S., 41, 63
combination, 2
composition of voting rules, 9, 78, 156
comprehensive, 25, 107
conditional probabilities, 58

Davis, M. D., 54, 67
decision procedure, 4
decisiveness, 54, 57, 62, 63, 67, 80, 84, 159
Deegan, J., 125
dictator seat, 7, 54
domination, 7
double weighted majority rule, 8
Dubey, P., 39, 41–43, 47, 62, 63, 67, 112, 116
Duggan, J., 128

ease of passing proposals, 57, 69, 79, 144, 145
efficiency, 32, 35, 110
egalitarianism, 71, 74, 81, 128, 157
EU Constitution rule, 140
EU Convention rule, 140
EU Nice rule, 85, 139
ex ante, 55
ex post, 54
expected utility function, 12, 74, 81, 84, 87, 159

feasibility, 110
Feix, M., 96
Felsenthal, D. S., *xii*, 44, 46, 47, 92, 141, 143
Ferejohn, J. A., 128
first square root rule, 83, 158

Galloway, D., *x*, 138, 163
game in extensive form, 22
game in strategic form, 21
Garrett, G., 97
Gibbard, A., *xiii*

Hart, S., 128
Hartman, S., 96

182

Index

Herstein, I. N., 18
Holler, M. J., 115, 125
homogeneity, 96
Hosli, M. O., 67

improper voting rule, 6, 76, 94
independence of irrelevant alternatives, 32, 111
independent voting behaviour, 56, 68
indifference, 11, 53
individual rationality, 110
intersection of voting rules, 9
invariance w.r.t. positive affine transformations, 32, 111

Jackson, M., 96

König, T., 65, 67
Kalai, E., 47, 112
Kornhauser, L. A., 67, 134
Kuhn, H. W., 31

Lake, M., 54, 67
Lane, J. E., 141
Leech, D., 64
Lehrer, E., 47
Lepelley, D., 96
losing vote configuration, 5
lottery, 12, 107
luck, 55

M-symmetric, 131
Maaser, N., 96
Machover, M., *xii*, 44, 46, 47, 67, 92, 141, 143
Maeland, R., 141
Martínez, R., 67, 142
Mas–Colell, A., 128
Merlin, V., 96
Milnor, J., 18
minimal winning vote configuration, 6
Moberg, A., 64
monotonic game, 25
Montero, M., 128
Morgenstern, O., 24, 25, 30, 31, 35
Morriss, P., 45, 55, 92

N-voting rule, 5, 107
Napel, S., 96

Nasar, S., 31
Nash bargaining solution, 33, 164
Nash equilibrium, 19
Nash, J. F., 19, 20, 31, 33, 34, 44, 47, 107, 110
negative success, 58, 73, 89, 145
Neyman, A., 43
Niemi, R. G., 48
normalization, 64
NTU games, 25, 108
null player, 35, 111
null seat, 6, 139

Osborne, M. J., 18
Owen, G., 63

Packel, E. J., 115, 125
paradox, 44, 66
Penrose index, 63
Penrose, L. S., 41, 54, 63, 67
permutation, 2
players, 10, 107
positive success, 58, 73, 89, 145
postulate, 44, 66
preferences, 11, 55, 107
prisoner's dilemma, 19, 21
probabilistic protocol, 119

q-majority rules, 8, 75
qualified majority, 138

Rae index, 62
Rae, D., 41, 48, 54, 62, 67, 75
Rawls, A., 71, 72
Roth, A. E., 35, 47
Rouet, J-L., 96
Rubinstein, A., 18, 128

second square root rule, 92
Selten, R., 10
semivalue, 43, 114, 125
Shapley, L. S., 30, 34–38, 41–43, 47, 62, 63, 67, 110, 116, 129
Shapley–Shubik index, 37, 114, 125, 163, 165
Shapley value, 36, 114
Shubik, M., 30, 37, 38, 67
simple game, 25
simple majority rule, 7, 68, 75, 138

184 Index

Smorodinski, M., 47
stationary strategy, 24, 120
stationary subgame perfect
    equilibrium, 24, 120
status quo, 31, 110, 118
Stirling's formula, 4, 79
Straffin, P. D., 48, 54, 61, 67, 96
strategy, 21
subgame perfect equilibrium, 23
success, 54, 57, 62, 65, 67, 69, 73, 74,
    80, 149, 152
superadditive game, 25
support of the lottery, 12
symmetric bargaining problem, 32
symmetric gain-loss, 112, 116
symmetric seats, 7, 139
symmetric voting rule, 7, 74, 115

T-oligarchy, 7
T-unanimity rule, 7
take-it-or-leave-it committee, 46, 52,
    68, 142
Taylor, A. D., 8
Taylor, M., 75
transfer, 42, 112, 116
Tsebelis, G., 97

TU games, 24
TU-like preferences, 108
two-stage indirect voting procedure, 9,
    78, 81, 87

unanimity rule, 7, 68, 75, 109, 138
union of voting rules, 9
utilitarianism, 71, 74, 87, 128, 159
utility function, 11, 71, 156

veil of ignorance, 61, 72
veto seat, 6, 144
vNM preferences, 13, 76, 107, 109
von Neumann, J., 24, 25, 30, 31, 35
vote configuration, 5
voting behaviours, 56, 143
voting situation, 57

Weber, R. J., 43, 48
weighted majority rule, 8, 91, 94, 138
Weisberg, H. F., 48
Widgrén, M., 145
winning vote configuration, 5

Zwicker, W. S., 8, 46

For EU product safety concerns, contact us at Calle de José Abascal, 56–1°,
28003 Madrid, Spain or eugpsr@cambridge.org.

www.ingramcontent.com/pod-product-compliance
Ingram Content Group UK Ltd.
Pitfield, Milton Keynes, MK11 3LW, UK
UKHW020400060825
461487UK00008B/733